Plants and Diet in Greece from Neolithic to Classic Periods

The archaeobotanical remains

Fragkiska Megaloudi

BAR International Series 1516

2006

Published in 2016 by
BAR Publishing, Oxford

BAR International Series 1516

Plants and Diet in Greece from Neolithic to Classic Periods

ISBN 978 1 84171 949 8

BAR Publishing is the trading name of British Archaeological Reports (Oxford) Ltd.
British Archaeological Reports was first incorporated in 1974 to publish the BAR
Series, International and British. In 1992 Hadrian Books Ltd became part of the BAR
group. This volume was originally published by Archaeopress in conjunction with
British Archaeological Reports (Oxford) Ltd / Hadrian Books Ltd, the Series principal
publisher, in 2006. This present volume is published by BAR Publishing, 2016.

Printed in England

BAR
PUBLISHING

BAR titles are available from:

BAR Publishing
122 Banbury Rd, Oxford, OX2 7BP, UK
EMAIL   info@barpublishing.com
PHONE   +44 (0)1865 310431
FAX   +44 (0)1865 316916
www.barpublishing.com

CONTENTS

LIST OF FIGURES

LIST OF TABLES

PREFACE

Environmental Archaeology has been in Greece generally underestimated. Through the most comprehensive and compelling means possible this work gives an opportunity to learn about ancient plants and diet in the Greek peninsula during a period spanning from the 7th millennium BC to the end of 4th century BC. This book provides a research tool that allows one to examine the role of plant foods in the Aegean region diachronically.

The appearance of *Plants and Diet in Greece from Neolithic to Classic Periods: The archaeobotanical remains* marks the culmination of 5 years of effort and collaboration with many researchers and disciplines. From start to finish Fragkiska Megaloudi has been taught and guided by experts in Greece and abroad in order to obtain the acquisition of the expertise on the field of Archaeobotany. She studied in Greece and in France and the staff of each of the Institutions contributed substantially to the PhD thesis, which has been completed and reshaped to this book. Fragkiska Megaloudi undertook a difficult task as no book of this scope has ever been published before and these periods were not sufficiently covered by the existing bibliography.

Knowing Fragkiska from the beginning of her university studies I was happy to tutor her, see and evaluate the progress and the fruit of her efforts. It has been rewording working with her and I am proud to see one of my students becoming a promising researcher today.

Lilian Karali
Professor of Environmental Archaeology
University of Athens

ACKNOWLEDGEMENTS

This book is predominantly based on my Ph.D research, submitted at the Ecole des Hautes Etudes en Sciences Sociales (Paris, France) in september 2004. A project of this kind would have never been possible without the financial help of the State Scholarship Foundation of Greece (I.K.Y.) that awarded me a 3 year scholarship. Research grants were also provided by the French School at Athens (Ecole Francaise d'Athenes) and by the Ministry of Research in France, which allowed me to conduct research as a visiting fellow at Boston University (Archaeology Department), USA. Additional funding (for archaeobotanical analysis) was provided by the Centre d'Anthropologie (CNRS UMR 8555) in Toulouse, France.

The present work was accomplished while I was the Environmental Research Fellow (2005-2006) at the Wiener Laboratory of the American School of Classical Studies at Athens. I deeply thank the director of Wiener Laboratory, Dr. Sherry Fox, for creating such a stimulating and scientific work environment. I am grateful for the liberty that I had to combine my own research for this book together with the research project at the Wiener Laboratory.

I wish to express my gratitude to Professor Lilian Karali who has introduced me to the magical world of Environmental Archaeology twelve years ago. I deeply thank her for her support, during difficult moments when my confidence was runing low and for her friendship. This book owes a great deal to her.

I am grateful to Dr. Helmut Kroll for sharing his great knowledge in archaeobotany with me and for his instructions in the identification methods of archaeobotany during my stay as a visiting fellow at his Laboratory in the Institute of Pre- and Proto-history at Kiel University (Germany).

I deeply thank Professor Jean Guilaine for help in every aspect of work involved in my Ph.D research and for his continuous support every time I solicited him. I would like to thank Dr. Philippe Marinval, researcher at the CNRS, for his help during my stay at the Centre d'Anthropologie in Toulouse (France).

This research would never have been possible without the positive response of the Ephorates of Antiquities undertaken by the directors of the excavations who kindly allowed me to study archaeobotanical remains from a number of sites. I am particularly grateful to Dr. Stratis Papadopoulos for the sites of Limenaria and Aghios Ioannis Loukas and to the late Dr. Marina Sgourou for the material from the Necropolis of Limenas. Many thanks go to Professor Adamantios Sampson for granting me material from the Sarakenos Cave and from the settlement of Ftelia on Mykonos.

I would like to thank Professor Julie Hansen for exhanging views and information about archaeobotanical material during my stay at the Archaeology Department as a Visiting fellow to Boston University (U.S.A).

I also thank Professor Ioannis Liritzis and all my colleagues at the Department of Mediterranean Studies of the University of the Aegean for their support, during the last two years that I have been teaching Environmental Archaeology at the Department.

I would like to deeply thank all my colleagues and friends at the Wiener Laboratory: Thanos Webb, Elissavet Hitsiou, Paraskevi Tritsaroli, Evi Margariti, Niels Andreasen, Dimitris Kontogiorgos who, despite their own work, had always the time to respond to my questions and share their knowledge with me.

Special thanks go to my friends, Manoli Stafanakis, lecturer of Classical Archaeology at the University of the Aegean, and Pelagia Romnaki, tour guide, for their constant support and help.

This book has been accomplished thanks to Aleksandar Medovic's involvement. His help during my time in Kiel and in Toulouse has enabled me to publish this book today. I will never have enough words to express my gratitude and my regrets for the things that I feel I owed him and never returned.

Mostly and above all I want to thank my family: my parents Nikos and Eleni, my sister Stephania and my dear nephew Nikos. This work is dedicated to them as an expression of my love.

CHAPTER 1

INTRODUCTION

Over the past twenty-five years numerous studies have appeared, particularly in Europe, regarding the production and consumption of food in prehistoric and historic Greece. The ancient Greek diet is no longer studied solely in connection with the Greek symposia described by Plato and Xenophon; modern scholarship includes studies of the production and processing of various foods. In addition, the cultural significance of various foods and diets both in prehistory and in antiquity has recently been addressed by Vaughan and Coulson (1999) and by Wilkins et al. (1995).

In Greece, information on food plants has been recovered mainly through archaeobotanical studies. This monograph aims to provide a synthesis of those results and to integrate new, unpublished data. My principal goal is to present the first diachronic study of the use of vegetal species in the Aegean region in the period spanning the millennia between the Early Neolithic (ca. 7000 B.C.) and Classical times (4th century B.C.). This chronological range is vast, but it provides the necessary framework for a diachronic approach to the history and evolution of food plants in prehistoric and historic Aegean communities. For this study I have compiled the archaeobotanical data from 79 Greek sites published between 1879 and 2003. I integrally conducted and published (or have in press) the archaeobotanical analysis of 9 of these settlements. Concerning the published data compiled here, it is important to note that this monograph takes into account only those sites that were published at the time of writing; thus, the review proposed here is not exhaustive. The data compiled here can shed light on several aspects of ancient food and diet, including the geographical and chronological distribution of cereals and legumes, the beginnings of arboriculture in Greece, and the use and symbolic meaning of plants in ancient times.

The geographical focus of this study is the eastern part of Greece. According to geographical and cultural criteria (see, e.g., Treuil 1983) this area is traditionally called the Aegean and comprises the following (from north to south): the shores of Macedonia and Thrace, the northern Aegean islands, Thessaly, Central Greece, Attica, the Peloponnese, the Cyclades, the southern Aegean islands, and Crete (*Figure 1.1*). I have excluded the archaeobotanical material from the western part of Greece because very few sites in the region have been investigated for macrobotanical remains: Mesopotamon in Epirus (Dennel 1974); the northern part of Epirus, today belonging to Albania (e.g., Konispol Cave, Hansen 1999); and Maliq (Xhuvel and Schultze-Motel 1995).

The first chapter of this book provides a brief description of the cultural phases considered in this work, as well as of the climate and vegetation of the area under study. In the second chapter I define the terminology used in this text and review the history of archaeobotanical studies in Greece. *Chapter 3* deals with the methodological problems related to the preservation of plant remains, sampling and recovery techniques, and sources of information. In *Chapter 4* I present the sites considered in this study, describe the data analysis conducted, and comment briefly on the identification problems associated with some of the species identified in my samples. *Chapter 5* surveys the history of the principal cultivated or gathered plants in the Aegean regions, a history that can be derived from the archaeobotanical analysis of the sites presented in this book. The sixth chapter synthesizes the archaeobotanical data (fruits and seeds) for the period from the Early Neolithic to the fourth century B.C. in Greece.

A. Chronology

All dates given in this text are expressed in true calendar years. It is important to note that absolute dates for the Neolithic and Bronze Ages in the Aegean are not yet reliably established, and thus one finds different sets of dates applied to the same phase or period. The major debate that has been raging since 1987 (Betancourt 1987; Betancourt and Michael 1987; Aitken et al. 1988) over the absolute date of the volcanic explosion of the island of Thera (modern Santorini) early in the Late Bronze Age has thrown into a state of flux all other dates in the first two-thirds of the second millennium B.C. (Manning 1995; Betancourt 1998). The chronology of Neolithic and Bronze Age Macedonia, Thrace, Thessaly, and Epirus has been reviewed by Andreou et al. (1996), who proposed a new set of dates for these regions based on the archaeological surveys conducted in mainland Greece (including Thessaly) during the previous two decades. Johnson (1999) has recently reviewed the problem of the transition from Final Neolithic to Early Bronze Age. For the most recent surveys of absolute and relative chronology in the Aegean, see Manning (1995), The Absolute Chronology of the Aegean Early Bronze Age: Archaeology, Radiocarbon, and History.

The chronology of the historic (Archaic and Classical) periods used in this text is based on the regional surveys conducted in southern Greece in the Argolid and Pylos projects (van Andel and Runnels 1987; Jameson et al. 1994).

The following table summarizes the major chronological periods covered in this book:

<u>Neolithic Period</u>
- Aceramic Neolithic (7000/6500 B.C.)
- Early Neolithic (6700/6500–5800/5600 B.C.)
- Middle Neolithic (5800/5600–5400/5300 B.C.)
- Late Neolithic (5400/5300–4700/4500 B.C.)
- Final Neolithic (4700/4500–3300/3100 B.C.)

<u>Bronze Age</u>
- Early Bronze Age (3300/3100–2300/2200 B.C.)
- Middle Bronze Age (2300/2200–1700/1500 B.C.)
- Late Bronze Age (1700/1500–1125/1100 B.C.)

<u>Submycenaean to Geometric Peirods</u>

- Submycenaean : 1100–1050 B.C.)
- Protogeometric (1050–900 B.C.)
- Geometric (900–700 B.C.)

<u>Archaic Period</u>
- 8th century B.C.–end 6th century B.C.

<u>Classical Period</u>
- 480–323 B.C.

B. The natural environment

This section provides a brief description of the natural environment (i.e., climate and vegetation) in the Aegean region.

Climate

> *The Greeks occupy a middle position [between hot and cold climates] and correspondingly enjoy both energy and intelligence...for this reason they retain their freedom and have the best of political institutions.* Aristotle, Politics 1.1252a (trans. H.Racham)

Greece is situated at the most southeastern part of Europe, located between the 34° and 42° parallel N, with a meridional extent from 19° to 28° E, and borders the Aegean, Ionian, and east Mediterranean Seas. The climate in Greece is typically Mediterranean, with mild and rainy winters, relatively warm and dry summers, and, generally, extended periods of sunshine throughout most of the year. Greece's mountains, including the great chains along its central part, influence the air masses that come from the moisture sources of the central Mediterranean Sea. As a result, a variety of climate subtypes, always within the Mediterranean climate frame, are observed in the different regions of the country.

Two main climatological seasons can be distinguished in Greece: a cold and rainy period that extends from October until the end of March, and a warm and dry season lasting from April through September. The coldest months are January and February, with a mean minimum temperature of 5–10°C near the coasts and 0–5 °C over the mainland. Below-freezing temperatures and snow occur only in the mountains. The cold weather of January and the first half of February is often interrupted by sunny days—"halcyon days," as they have been known since ancient times..

During the warm and dry period the weather is usually stable, the sky is clear, the sun is bright, and there is almost no rainfall. However, infrequent and brief intervals of heavy rain or thunderstorms sometimes occur, chiefly over mainland areas. The warmest weather occurs during the last ten days of July and the first ten days of August, when the mean maximum temperature lies between 29° and 35°C. During the warm period, fresh sea breezes, known to the ancients as the "Etesians," blow in the coastal areas of the country, mainly in the Aegean.

Detailed information on Greek meteorology and climatology is available on the web sites of the Hellenic National Meteorological Service (*http://www.emy.gr*) and the National Observatory of Athens (*http://www.noa.gr* or *http://www.meteo.gr*).

Landscape and modern vegetation

Greece has one of the highest levels of flora biodiversity in Europe. Strid and Tan (1992) recorded 4900 to 5500 plant species belonging to Greek flora. Three-fourths of Greece is mountainous and 85% of the Greek landscape is either bare or covered with thorny, woody shrubs, leaving only a scant 15% to forest belts (Sfikas 1978). Only about a fifth of the land in Greece is suitable for farming (Sfikas 1978), and much of that land either has poor soil or is too dry for crops to be grown without irrigation. Fertile soil is often lost to erosion caused by the runoff of winter rains from the mountains.

Mediterranean ecosystem

The Mediterranean ecosystem is dominated by evergreen trees, which can grow during the wetter but well-illuminated winter, and can also resist dry conditions during summer (Smith 1992). Under natural climatic conditions, evergreen forests composed mainly of the (ever) green oak *Quercus ilex* and the parasol pine *Pinus pinea* develop; there is some variation, however, according to local conditions (Polunin and Huxley 1974). The downy-leafed, deciduous oak *Quercus pubescens* may also be present, and certainly would be increasingly important inland.

This ecosystem is very fragile, and in modern times most of the original Mediterranean woodland has been eradicated by humans, who have cleared it of timber and turned the land over to agricultural use. The origins of steppelike formations in former woodland areas can be traced to various causes: grazing by domesticated animals, which prevents tree regeneration; fires, whether accidentally or deliberately set; and heavy autumn rainfalls that wash away much of the soil once it is left uncovered by trees. The process of forest degradation can be summarized as follows:

Evergreen forests → scrubland vegetation → discontinuous shrub cover → steppelike formations.

The scrubland vegetation of the Mediterranean region (maquis) is composed primarily of leathery, broad-leafed evergreen shrubs or of small trees that can reach 2 meters high. Maquis occurs primarily on the lower slopes of mountains between 100 to 500 meters and includes a variety of plant species. The characteristic shrub of this group is the kerm oak *Quercus coccifera*, a spiny-leafed evergreen that forms low mounds or, in sheltered conditions, larger bushes. Other characteristic plants of "high" maquis vegetation are the strawberry tree *Arbutus unedo*, the evergreen pistachio *Pistacia lentiscus*, the (ever)green oak *Quercus ilex*, the locust bean *Ceratonia silica*, the oleaster *Olea europaea var. oleaster,* and the myrtle *Myrtus communis*. In bushy and rocky places, as well as in woodland margins, the evergreen shrub species of Cistus sp.. dominate (Polunin and Huxley 1974).

The garrigue (Gk. phryganes) covers the degraded areas and is composed of a discontinuous cover of shrubs. The garrigue elements are hardy, and therefore more resistant to the stress caused by human activities and the local climate. The shrubs are spinous, aromatic, and small, ranging from 15 cm to 1 m in height (Polunin and Huxley 1974). The common species in the Greek borderlands include aromatic plants (e.g., thyme *Thymus capitatus,* sages *Salvia* sp., oregano *Origanum* sp.), perfumed species (such as lavender *Lavandula stoecha*), and ornamental bulbs (e.g., asphodel *Asphodelus microcarpus*, red squil *Urginea maritima*, and feather hyancinth *Muscari comosum*).

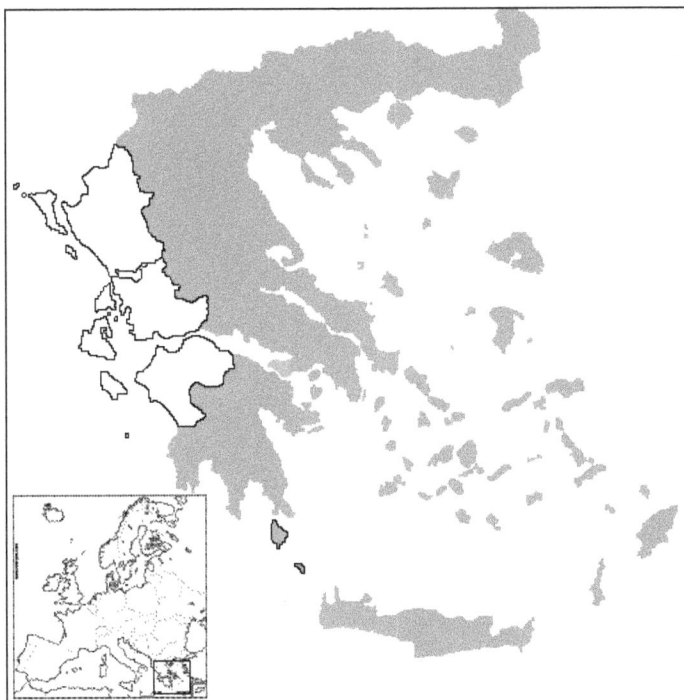

Figure 1.1 : Map of Greece showing the region under study (in grey)

CHAPTER 2

TERMINOLOGY

A. Definitions

Archaeobotany is the study of macrobotanical remains (seeds and fruits) that have been preserved in archaeological sediments. Because one also regularly encounters terms such as palaeobotany and palaeoethnobotany, it is worthwhile to say a few words about this related terminology. A useful source on this topic is D. Pearsall's *Palaeoethnobotany: A Handbook of Procedures* (1989), which analyzes the terms that have been used in the English-speaking literature to define the study of botanical remains. J. W. Harshberger introduced the term ethnobotany in 1895 to describe the use of plants by the aboriginal people of Australia. Palaeoethnobotany, a term introduced in 1959, is a special branch of ethnobotany that studies the human-plant relation through the archaeological botanical remains (Pearsall 1989). J. Renfrew (1973), defines palaeoethnobotany as the study of the remains of plants cultivated or utilized by man in ancient times, which have survived in archaeological contexts. R. Ford (1979) defines palaeoethnobotany as the interpretation of human-plant interactions, in any way that plants were used.

In southwest Europe (France, Spain, and Italy) the term "carpology" (Fr. *carpologie*) is widely used to describe the study of macrobotanical remains. This term, derived from the Greek word *karpos* (fruit), was first introduced in the 1980s by the French researchers P. Marinval and M.-P. Ruas (Karali et al. 2001; Marinval 1999).

In this book, I have used the term archaeobotany, to refer specifically to the macrobotanical remains (seeds and fruits) retrieved from the archaeological excavations.

B. Aims

The collection of macrobotanical remains from archaeological contexts has as its goal the reconstruction of ancient plant-human interactions and their changes over time. The major research themes are the recovery and identification of plant remains, the use of wild plants, the origins of agriculture, the beginnings of cultivation, and the spread of cultivated plants.

C. Applications of the discipline

Study of macrobotanical remains can provide insight into the following aspects of ancient life:

- diet and food preparation (through identification of the vegetal ingredients)
- farming and gathering practices
- craft uses of plants (fibers for textiles, gourds for net floats, reeds for mats or house construction, basketry, etc.)
- uses of plants for fuels
- uses of plants for medicinal purposes
- seasonality of an inhabited site (i.e., whether it was occupied year-round, or only during certain seasons)
- role of plants in the social life (e.g., ritual meals, funeral or sacrificial vegetal offerings)

D. Brief history of the discipline in Greece

It was not until the end of the 1970s that the study of botanical macro-remains became a systematic part of archaeological research in Greece (*Figure. 2.2*). The earliest recorded find of fossilized botanical remains, however, goes back to 1878, when M. Kalokairinos discovered carbonized beans and peas in pithoi from the Bronze Age palace at Knossos (Evans 1900–1901). A year later, in 1879, M. Fouqué reported the presence of barley and peas at the Bronze Age sites of Thera and Therasia in the Cyclades (Fouqué 1879). The first professional botanist to examine archaeobotanical material in Greece was L. Whittmack, who was asked by H. Schliemann to identify the grape seeds discovered at Tiryns (Schliemann 1885) and went on to identify macrobotanical remains from the sites of Sesklo, Dimini, Marmariani (Tsountas 1908), and Orchomenos (Bulle 1909). P. Newberry studied remains of wheat and peas found in the Late Bronze Age site of Palaikastro, on Crete (Bosanquet 1901). Vegetal remains (acorns, vetch, wheat, and lentils) from the site of Vardarophtsa in Macedonia were identified by C. Martin, director of the Natural History Museum of South Kensington (Heurtley and Hutchinson 1926; Heurtley 1939). In the 1930s F. Netolitsky identified legumes, figs, and olives from the sites of Kephalonia, Knossos and Phaistos (Netolitsky 1934). The first synopsis of archaeobotanical and archaeozoological studies in the Aegean from the beginning of the twentieth century to 1936 was published by K.F. Vickery in his work *Food in Early Greece* (1936); in the same year W. Lamb reported the presence of macrobotanical remains (including a desiccated apple) from the Late Bronze Age levels of Thermi on the island of Lesbos (Lamb 1936).

In the late 1950s, so-called New Archaeology led researchers away from artifacts and toward the study of people's behavior and the interaction between humans and their environment. This movement had a positive effect on the advancement of botanical studies; the new approach contributed to the application of new methods for the recovery of archaeological material (such as water-separation methods) and to the introduction of

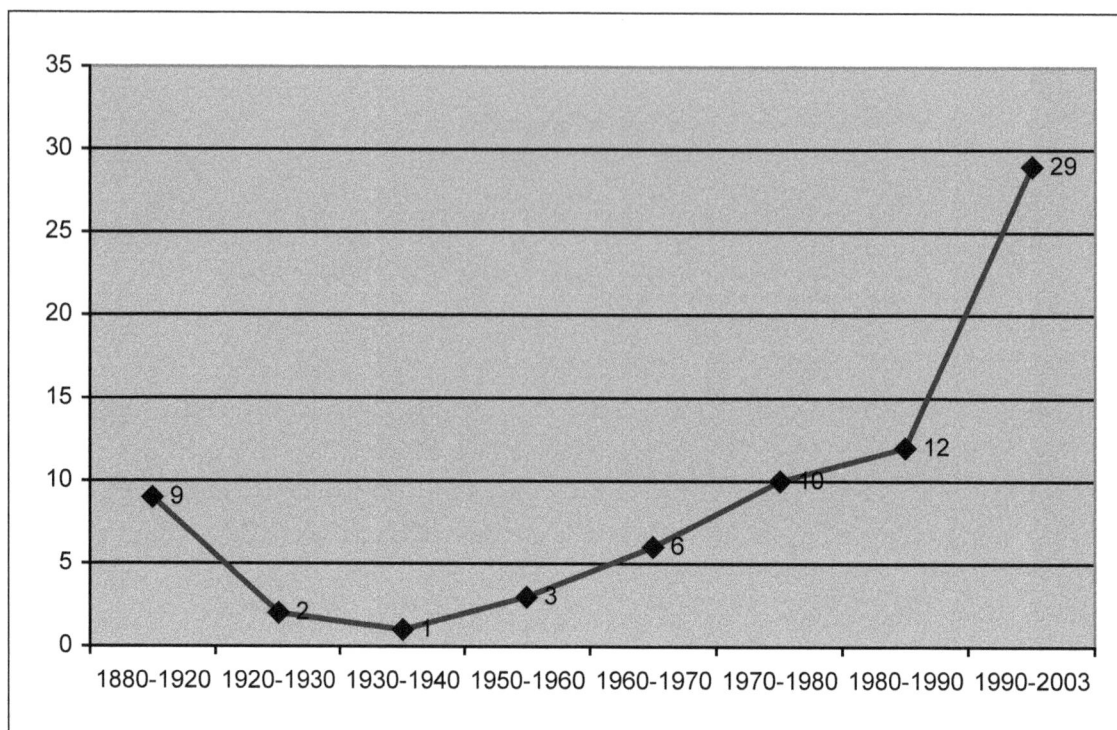

Figure 2.2: Number of archaeobotanical studies conducted in Greece between 1880 and 2003

environmental studies in the excavations. Earlier findings of botanical material in Greece had been limited to chance finds or large caches of carbonized material found in vessels or in heaps on floor surfaces. Excavators did not apply any technique for the collection of bio-archaeological material, and much information was lost as a result. From 1961 on, however, M. Hopf conducted several specifically archaeobotanical studies in Greece, identifying macrobotanical remains from the sites of Lerna in the Argolid, Argissa Magoula in Thessaly, and the agora at Athens (Hopf 1961, 1962a,1962b, 1971). J. Renfrew's work on palaeobotany in Greece (which is described in more detail below) spanned almost three decades and focused on various sites in Thessaly (Renfrew 1966, 1989), the Cyclades (Renfrew 1968, 1977), Macedonia (Renfrew 1969, 1997; Renfrew et al. 1986), and Crete (Renfrew 1972).

The changes brought by New Archaeology—an awareness both of the potential significance of botanical material and of the need for effective recovery methods—led to important findings of macrobotanical remains in Greece. The first deliberate attempts to use a recovery method for the collection of carbonized bio-archaeological material from archaeological contexts were made by Renfrew, at the site of Saliagos near Antiparos in the Cyclades (Renfrew 1968). Her method consisted of sieving excavated material in a bucket of water and stirring carefully in order to allow the organic material to float to the surface. The less dense organic material (light fraction) such as charred seeds, wood, and bone floated to the surface, while the inorganic material (heavy fraction) sank to the bottom. Renfrew continued

these flotation experiments at the Late Neolithic sites of Kephala on Kea (Coleman 1977) and Sitagroi in Thrace (Renfrew et al., 1986), as well as at Franchthi Cave in 1968 (Renfrew 1973). A few years later, in 1971, the first flotation machine was used in Greece at Franchthi Cave (Diamant 1979; Hansen 1985, 1991); it was an adaptation of the flotation machine used by D.H. French for the Asvan project in Eastern Turkey (French 1971 ; Diamant 1979). A complete description of the recovery system set up at Franchthi appears in Hansen (1991).

Our understanding of Aegean prehistory was greatly advanced by the excavation of Franchthi Cave in the early 1970s, thanks in part to the large body of archaeobotanical data recovered there, which offered a view of human-plant exploitation in southeastern Greece from the end of the Upper Paleolithic to the Neolithic period (Hansen 1978, 1980, 1991, 1992; Hansen and Renfrew 1978). Around the same time, W. van Zeist identified the plant remains from the Early Neolithic site of Nea Nikomedeia in Macedonia (van Zeist and Bottema 1971).

From the end of the 1970s onward, archaeobotany in Greece developed considerably. The recovery and study of macrobotanical remains became an integrated part of large-scale archaeological projects such as that at Kastanas (Kroll 1982, 1983) and Assiros Toumba (Jones 1979; Jones et al. 1986; Wardle 1989), both in Macedonia.[1] R.N.L.B. Hubbard (1979) conducted a preliminary study of the botanical remains from Servia in

---

[1]   E. Margariti studied part of the botanical remains from Assiros Toumba (Room 24; Margariti 1998).

Macedonia, work that was continued by R.A. Housley (1981). M. Follieri identified plant remains from the sites of Aghia Triada, Chania, and Festos in Crete (Follieri 1979, 1982; Follieri and Coccolini 1979). A. Sarpaki, who identified the plant material from the Late Bronze Age site of Akrotiri (Sarpaki 1987), was one of the first Greek archaeobotanists to work in his home country. A complete review of published archaeobotanical studies conducted at Greek archaeological sites through the end of the 1980s can be found in Kroll (1991).

During the last two decades, various archaeobotanists have conducted studies in Greece. M. Mangaffa identified plant material from the Late Neolithic/Early Bronze Age site of Dikili Tash (Mangaffa 1990); her archaeobotanical work was interrupted by her premature death. Plant remains from the Late Neolithic levels of Dikili Tash were also studied by I. Cerceau, by V. Matterne, and by S. Valamoti (Cerceau 1992; Matterne 1993; Valamoti 2004). Valamoti is mainly engaged in studies on

plant remains discovered in prehistoric sites located in the regions of Macedonia and Thrace in northern Greece (Valamoti 2004). K. Flint-Hamilton identified the botanical remains from the Zeus Cave on the island of Naxos in the Cyclades (Flint-Hamilton 1994), and D. Kučan (1995) studied a large quantity and variety of plant remains that were found in waterlogged deposits of the seventh-century B.C. Samian Heraion.

In other European countries, such as the Netherlands (Bakels 1991, 1997), Great Britain (Jessen and Helbaek 1944; Greig 1991), Switzerland and Germany (Körber-Grohne 1987; Knörzer 1991), and France (Marinval 1988; 2001; Matterne 2000), archaeobotanical studies are more abundant, as archaeobotany became an integrated part of archaeological research much earlier than in Greece. Archaeobotanical studies in Greece, however, are now in full expansion, and increasing numbers of young researchers are conducting work on organized archaeobotanical projects at several archaeological sites.

7

CHAPTER 3

THE ARCHAEOBOTANICAL EVIDENCE

A. Preservation

Botanical macro-remains in archaeological contexts can survive only under special preservation conditions, which depend on both environmental factors and human activity. Remains can be preserved in the following ways:

- charring (by deliberate or accidental exposure to fire)
- waterlogging
- mineralization
- desiccation
- metal-oxide preservation
- imprinting (e.g., in pottery)

Plant remains may also be found in preserved human faeces (coprolite), which often contains numerous identifiable plant fragments and pollen grains (Arobba and Muriado 2001). Coprolite examination is well developed in environmental archaeology in the United States, where it has been used in cave archaeology as well as in pueblos (Pearsall 1989). In Europe, this type of examination is found chiefly in the west and north, where it is used for pollen analysis (Poland: Kowalski et al. 1976; the Netherlands and France: Vermeeren and Kuijper 1996; Germany: Maier 1995; and Italy: Arobba et al. 1999, Arobba and Muriado 2001).

The types of preservation of macrobotanical remains in archaeological excavations have been thoroughly analyzed by scholars since the early 1970s (cf. Renfrew 1973; Pearsall 1989; Zohary and Hopf 2000). There is also an important number of influential papers dealing with preservation types and the representation of plant remains in archaeological contexts (cf. Dennell 1976; Green 1979; Hillman 1981, 1984; Boardman and Jones 1990; Hubbard and Al Azm 1990; Körber-Grohne 1991; Sarpaki 1992, 1999; Bouby 2000; Gustafson 2000; Jacomet et al. 2002).

Macrobotanical remains retrieved from archaeological contexts are a precious source of information on various aspects of ancient life, but problems of taphonomy and recovery bias must be overcome for researchers to provide a realistic basis on which to rest their interpretations. Taphonomic processes are linked with the dispersal and preservation of plant remains: not all plants remains are equally well preserved, and there is a whole range of plant species that is not recoverable. Waterlogging and charring, in particular, limit the range of species represented. At Aegean sites, where nearly all of the botanical remains have been preserved through carbonization, it is common to find only species that are likely to have been exposed to fire in some way

(Dennell 1976; Hillman 1981; Sarpaki 1992). Cereals, for example, are often parched at some stage of their processing, and this increases their chances of preservation in archaeological contexts. On the other hand, vegetables and other plant parts such as leaves, roots, and tubers, are highly perishable and are unlikely to be preserved through carbonization. This accident of preservation can lead to the underrepresentation of several species in the archaeobotanical record.

Another bias stems from the variability of effectiveness in the retrieval of seeds, especially when froth flotation machines are used. Several scholars have noted differences in the ranges of species preserved, due to crop processing or to taphonomic factors (Green 1975; Jones 1981; Wilson 1984). Some species, such as cereals, seem to be retrieved more efficiently by excavators, giving the false impression that cereal species were as dominant in ancient times as they are in the recovered samples.

The attitude of the excavator and the type of site excavated constitute another type of recovery bias. Consider, for example, the paucity of archaeobotanical data from protohistoric and historic sites. It is not possible to detect plant remains in archaeological contexts without systematic sampling and good methods of retrieval; many excavators, however, especially in classical archaeology, do not collect soil samples—assuming, wrongly, that all the information the site can yield will come in the form of stone architecture, or of various artifacts. In addition, there is a tendency for archaeologists working in historical periods, for which texts survive, to assume that written sources will provide the information they need. This viewpoint has led to a real neglect of archaeobotanical recovery from sites from the Late Bronze Age onwards. Literary evidence is a precious source of information, but it can be misleading—to give just one example from archaeobotany, the translation of terms relating to crops is highly problematic. While written sources do contain interesting data on the history of crop plants and agricultural techniques, they are best used in combination with archaeobotanical data. The biases described here are unfortunate, because plant remains, charcoal, and charred seeds and fruits are present and awaiting study in virtually every stratigraphical layer of an archaeologically investigated site. The study of these remains is usually conducted at prehistoric sites, but classical archaeology still lags behind.

B. Sampling strategies

Sampling strategy is a critical question in archaeobotany, as its choice influences the degree of reliability in the archaeobotanical record. Sampling methods involve the selection of contexts, the distribution of samples in the excavated area, and the sample volume. The choice of sampling strategy depends on various factors: the type of site excavated, the type of plant preservation, the available technical equipment, the time schedule of the specialist, and the procurement and reservation of the necessary funds for environmental studies. These factors may vary from one archaeological site to another, but they should be always taken into consideration before applying a sampling method. Sampling strategies have received much attention in the scholarly literature and several models have been proposed. The following sources combine to give a complete discussion of sampling strategies: Buxó 1993, 1997; Jones 1991; Pearsall 1989; van der Veen and Fieller 1982; and van der Veen 1984, 1985.

The level of interpretation of archaeological plant remains depends on the sampling method used, and the archaeobotanist should collect as much information as possible. Still, some bias will always exist in the samples because it is not always possible, for practical reasons, to process the total volume of sediment from an archaeological site. A good alternative is to take large samples from the contexts that are most likely to present archaeobotanical material. Macrobotanical remains are frequently preserved in hearths, on floors around hearths, in pits, or in storage contexts, and so in such areas an extensive sampling should be performed at all levels. Sampling should not be limited to these contexts, however; some samples might be taken in areas outside these structures to ensure comparability of all contexts. In the Late Neolithic layers of Sarakenos Cave, for example, a mass of carbonized cereals was uncovered in hearths. Some comparative samples were taken outside these structures (Megaloudi in press), but no plant remains were recovered and there was no need for further sampling. At the Late Neolithic site of Ftelia (Mykonos), the majority of botanical remains was recovered from the hearths and floors (Megaloudi and Marinval 2002), but samples were also taken outside these hearths in order to view the deposition of remains throughout the site. While concentrations of legumes had been found in the hearths and on floors, the samples taken outside the hearths, in open areas, revealed remains of barley and wheat, species that had not yet been identified at Ftelia.

There is no "standard" amount of sediment that should be processed, but large samples are of course preferable, since they can maximize the amount of botanical material recovered. A large number of seeds of a given species can help to elucidate some critical questions regarding the status of that species—such as whether it is wild or domesticated. Grape seeds, for example, present different morphological features when domesticated, but the variation within a wild population can overlap that of a domesticated one. In such a case, a large sample of seeds help to determine whether the seeds in question are from a wild or a domesticated

variety. In addition to that, large samples ensure the representation of "secondary" plants that may be present in small amounts, such as weeds in a harvested crop. Their presence might help to determine the type of soil that the crop was grown in, or the type of harvesting method.

The sample size can vary from one liter to 100% of the sediment excavated, depending on the contexts and the questions that need to be answered. It is best to establish a standard-size sample, though, because it facilitates the comparison of remains recovered from several contexts. A good standard size would be from 10 to 12 liters, an amount that corresponds to the volume of the type of bucket commonly used in excavations.

The quantity of sediment sampled should be always recorded, so that one can determine the density of plant remains per liter of sediment, and thus can measure the intensity of activity in different areas through time. At the Sarakenos Cave, for example, where the total weight of carbonized plant material per liter of sediment was determined for each sample (Megaloudi, in press), these measures helped to outline the intensity of occupation at the site over its history.

C. Recovery methods

There are many different types of recovery systems, and complete summaries of these methods have been assembled (cf. Jarman et al. 1972; Renfrew 1973a; Wagner 1988; Pearsall 1989; Buxó 1989, 1997; Alonso 1997; Karali et al. 2001). All methods are based on the principle that carbonized material, such as charcoal and carbonized seeds, has a lower specific gravity than water, and thus floats into water.

The choice of a recovery method is an important one, as it has a major impact on the interpretation of the macrobotanical remains uncovered in archaeological contexts. Some factors may dictate a particular choice: the sample volume (large amounts of soil are usually processed with the aid of a flotation machine, while a few small samples can simply be floated in a bucket), the availability of water, and the type of sediment to be processed.

In general, there are two main methods of flotation. In the first method the sediment is dumped into a bucket of water, agitated slightly by hand, and the floating remains are poured off through fine mesh sieves (2–0.25 mm) (*Figures 3.3* and *3.4*). The heavy fraction that stays on the bottom may be washed through a fine screen in order to recover any organic material that did not float. Although washing of heavy fraction is often neglected, mostly because of the time it requires, it is a very important step. Mineralized seeds, nutshells (e.g., almonds or walnuts), and legumes such as broad bean and grass pea, generally do not float and must be recovered in the heavy fraction.

Figure 3.3. : Water- sieving at Ftelia (Mykonos)

Figure 3.4 : Water-sieving at the sanctuary of Artemis of Hyampolis (Kalapodi)

In the case of large-scale sampling with a great number of soil samples, a flotation system is recommended (*Figure 3.5*). These devices come in several types but generally involve a mechanized system that pumps water into a tank. The machines are very useful for treating large quantities of soil rapidly, but they do have some disadvantages. Their size and weight make them difficult to move, and thus they tend to be available only for large-scale excavation programs. Moreover, flotation machines are not suited for all kinds of samples. When the carbonized material is too fragile, for example, a mechanized system should not be used, as it might destroy important anatomical characters of the species and thus make identification difficult or impossible.

Figure 3.5 : Flotation machine at Limenaria

The greatest disadvantage of flotation machines is that they require a certain quantity of water, and this can make their use problematic in areas—like Greece—where fresh water is not abundant. It is possible, however, to use salt water for sieving. Experiments conducted with salt and fresh water in Culebra Bay in Costa Rica have shown that salt does not destroy plant remains (Lange and Carty 1975). On the contrary, salt water can be a better flotation material and can result in better recovery. In Greece, salt water was used to recover plant material at the Neolithic site of Ftelia on Mykonos, where fresh water is in short supply (Megaloudi and Marinval 2002; Karali et al. 2001). When salt water is used, plant remains should then be rinsed with fresh water; otherwise, the salt will crystallize once the remains dry out, breaking up the carbonized material (Wagner 1988). Because rapid drying in the sun can damage carbonized material, flotation samples of charred remains should be placed on paper towels and left to dry slowly indoors.

It is essential that the archaeobotanist adequately record and label all samples, keeping a complete record of the samples' location, their relation to their archaeological contexts, the quantity of sediment floated from each stratigraphic unit, and the type of sample. This record keeping enables the archaeobotanist to interpret the material and to determine the density of remains from one area to the next. A recording sheet should be created and completed each time a sample is taken.

Long-term storage of plant remains should be avoided, and samples must be kept in a rigid container to prevent crushing. Film canisters, jars, plastic boxes, or cigarette boxes are ideal and easy to procure. Carbon samples that have been designated for dating purposes should be put in a glass or metal container, or wrapped in aluminum foil, before being stored.

The plant remains are then examined, identified, and analyzed in the laboratory under a binocular microscope, with the aid of a comparative plant collection and atlases. Recently, several complementary tests have become available for the analysis of plant species, especially in the identification of the wild progenitors of cultivated crops. Extraction of plant DNA, for example, provides a good new source of information on ancient techniques of plant domestication, food residues on pottery, and plant-derived products such as dyes and fibers used in artifact production.

D. Sources of information

Publications concerning Greek flora span the period from 1753 to the 1990s and number almost ten thousand (Strid 1996). For the most complete modern reference to the flora of the Greek landscape, the reader is referred to the two volumes of *Flora Hellenica* (Phitos et al. 1997, 2002). The volumes of *Flora Europaea* provide a partial treatment of Greek vegetation but do not include the Aegean islands, for which one must consult P.H. Davis' multivolume work (1965–1986) *Flora of Turkey and the East Aegean Islands*. Information specific to high-altitude species (1400 m and above) can be found in the two volumes of *Mountain Flora of Greece* (Strid 1986; Strid and Tan 1991).

CHAPTER 4

THE SITES UNDER STUDY

This mongraph reviews archaeobotanical studies conducted in the Aegean region between 1879 and 2003, and provides data from 79 sites. These sites present 123 archaeological levels, ranging from the Early Neolithic to the Classical period.[1] For 70 of the 79 sites I have consulted publications that reported plant remains; the remaining 9 represent my original work, and thus are presented in greater detail.

The sites are separated into two groups. Group 1 deals with sites on which I have done the original study, and which have not been previously published. Group 2 includes sites that that have been studied and published by various specialists. Because of their prior publication they are presented very briefly in this monograph.

GROUP 1

1. Limenaria

The prehistoric settlement of Limenaria is situated on the south edge of the island of Thasos, in the modern village Limenaria. The site has been excavated since 1993 by the Archaeological Unit of Kavala, as part of a rescue excavation program. Prehistoric occupation at the site spans the Early/Middle Neolithic, the Late Neolithic, and the Early Bronze Age (Papadopoulos and Malamidou 2002; Malamidou and Papadopoulos 1997). Limenaria represents the most ancient habitation known on Thasos, with the earliest layer dated by calibrated C-14 to the middle of the 6th millennium B.C. The Neolithic community settled at the southwest end of a Middle or Upper Pleistocene terrace that was 2–3 m lower than at present (Papadopoulos and Malamidou 2002). The choice of the site seems to have been based on its location adjacent to areas of different types of terrain, with soils that are easy to cultivate. In the southern part of the valley there is permanent groundwater that the prehistoric community exploited by digging a well (Papadopoulos and Malamidou 2002).

Excavation of the Middle Neolithic occupations uncovered a peripheral zone with open-air hearths, benches, storages pits, and refuse pits on the outer perimeter (*Figure 4.6*). Bronze Age levels at Limenaria belong to later phases of the Early Bronze Age, and little is known for the occupation at the settlement during this period. The earlier of the two habitation phases uncovered includes a floor of pebbles, sherds, and compacted earth; a refuse pit; a hearth; and a clay bench. The later phase includes a wide, slightly curving wall and a stone-paved area containing a large number of erected stones. This may have been an open space but it is difficult to interpret its exact use.

Since 2000 I have carried out archaeobotanical investigation of the site, studying several samples from the Middle Neolithic and Early Bronze Age levels that correspond to various habitation phases. The archaeobotanical material has been fully studied and is presented in this volume. Preliminary reports of the results are in press (Megaloudi in press)

2. Aghios Ioannis Loukas

The natural bay of Aghios Ioannis Loukas is situated in the southeastern area of Thasos, an island in the northern part of the Aegean sea, approximately 3 kilometers north of Alyki (*Figure 4.7*). In 1909 J. Baker-Penoyre located the remains of two towers on the hills that form the natural limits of the bay (Thasos *JHS* 29, 1909, 235). In 1930 A. Bon pointed out the isolation of the site ("Les ruines antiques dans l'île de Thasos et en particulier les tours helleniques," *BCH* 54, 1930, 162). In 1983 a small excavation undertaken by the Archaeological Unit of Kavala at the eastern edge of the bay brought to light building remains of the late Roman Period (*AΔ* 38, 1983, 1989, 316). In 1998 a second excavation project of the Archaeological Unit of Kavala in the west bay uncovered a large olive workshop dated to the second half of the 6th century A.D. (Papadopoulos 2000).

A prehistoric settlement consisting of structures made of perishable material was also discovered north of the Roman remains (*Figure 4.8*). Hearths with clay or pebbled floors on slabs, stone built benches, trash pits, and clay/beaten earth floors were also found (Papadopoulos et al. 2002). Numerous hearths were gathered in an area of approximately 20 square meters. They are not all contemporary, and the larger one seems to have served in household activities: a bench, mortars and pestles, cooking vessels, and spindles were found around it. These remains point to the existence of an outdoor space where a group of women were engaged in cooking and weaving. The site must have been settled because it offered a rich pasture land and possibilities of olive cultivation, fishing, and hunting, but the duration of the settlement was brief. The site is dated to the Final Neolithic, and according to calibrated C-14 dates its occupation spanned the period from 3600 to 3000 B.C. (Papadopoulos et al. 2002).

---

[1] Two sites dating to the Hellenistic period—the site of Ossa, from the second phase of the Hellenistic period, and the city of Messene, from the end of the 2nd century B.C.—have not been included in this study, as the limited number of Hellenistic contexts (2) do not allow us to draw conclusions about plant species at that time.

Figure 4.6 : The Prehistoric settlement of Limenaria (Thasos)

Figure 4.7 : Bay of Aghios Ioannis Loukas (Thasos)

Figure 4.8 : The Prehistoric settlement of Aghios Ioannis

I undertook extensive archaeobotanical research at Aghios Ioannis Loukas from 2001 to 2005. In addition to the the 2001 samples, I studied others from previous excavation campaigns (1998–2000). The first results have been published (Papadopoulos et al. 2002), while the material collected in the 2005 campaign still awaits publication.

3. Necropolis of Limenas (a. Soultos; b. Chryssogelos)

The necropolis of Limenas, at the north edge of the island of Thasos, once covered an extensive area that is now occupied by the modern town of Limenas. The archaeological investigation of the site started in the 1970s as a part of a rescue excavation program of the Archaeological Unit of Kavala (*AΔ* 29 1973–1974 B2, 788; 30, 1975 B, 278; 37, 1982 [1989] B2, 316–322). The largest portion of the ancient necropolis, which was discovered on two separate farms (Soultos and Chryssogelos), revealed significant archaeobotanical remains.

The farm of Soultos (*Figure 4.9*) revealed 54 graves covering an area of 15 square meters. A burnt deposit (*pyra* B) was discovered among the graves, but it was impossible to relate it to a tomb. The deposit was associated with a cooking pottery assemblage (*kuathia* and *lopadia*) dated to the end of the 4th century B.C. The charred plant remains consisted of fragments of walnuts (*Juglans regia*), an olive pip (*Olea europea* var. *sativa*), a grain of *Malva sp.* and two leguminous seeds. A large number of charred pieces of wheat bread were also identified in the sample.

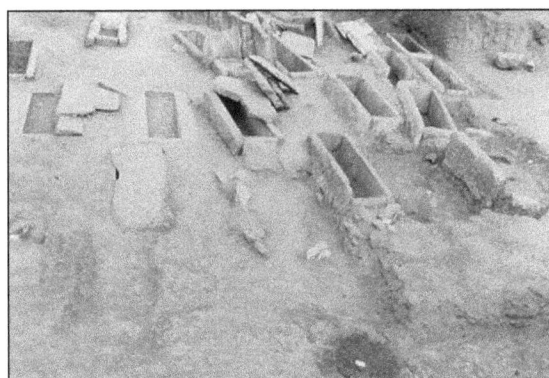

Figure 4.9: The necropolis of Limenas (Thasos) : Soultos cemetery

Excavation of the farm of Chryssogelos (*Figure 4.10*), located 1.5 kilometers west of the modern port of Thasos, yielded 17 graves. A burnt deposit was related to Grave 12, the burial of a young child. The charred plant assemblage was associated with burnt cooking pots, a silver bag, and numerous small statues that allowed the finds to be dated to the second half of the 4th century B.C. The plant remains were particularly interesting. They consisted of 55 garlic cloves (*Allium sativum)*, 22 grape pips (*Vitis vinifera),* 3 pomegranate seeds (*Punica*

granatum) and a single grain of bread wheat (*Triticum aestivum*). Small fragments of charred bread remains were also uncovered in the assemblage.

The material was fully studied and has been published (Megaloudi 2004; Megaloudi in preparation).

Figure 4.10: The necropolis of Limenas (Thasos) : Chrysogelos cemetery

4. Sarakenos Cave

Sarakenos Cave is located at the higher levels of the former lake of Kopais in the region of Boeotia, in central Greece (*Figure 4.11*). The cave of Sarakenos is the largest karstic formation in the area, today found much higher than the level of the plain and the road. The cave has a large entrance, which offers good light in the chamber and an excellent view to what was once the lake. Like other sites in the area, the cave was used as a sheep-pen in the recent past, hence large amounts of dung cover its floor.

Figure 4.11: Sarakenos Cave (Boiotia) : General view (entrance and Kopais basin)

The area had three lakes—Kopais, Hyliki, and Paralimni—and much marshland. The Kopais basin was a shallow, seasonal lake until the late 19th century A.D., when it was permanently drained and converted into the well-irrigated plain that is now one of central Greece's most fertile agricultural areas. Inscriptional evidence tells us that drainage programs were undertaken in the Kopais in Classical Greek and Roman times as well. The modern drainage of the Kopais has also revealed that the basin was drained in late Mycenaean times (14th century B.C.), a project that is believed to have been carried out by the Minyes people of Orchomenos (Iakovides 1989).

Excavation in the Sarakenos Cave began in the early 1970s under the direction of T. Spyropoulos, and had yielded finds of different chronological periods; the publication of this material, however, was never realized. Since 1994, A. Sampson of Aegean University has directed important excavation work. An assemblage of excellent stratigraphical data inside the cave has offered a succession of distinct cultural phases, from the level of the modern floor down to the natural bedrock of the cave. These phases date from the Middle Paleolithic to the Middle Helladic, when the cave was abandoned for reasons yet unknown (Sampson 2000). The period of most intensive occupation was the Late Neolithic (4th millennium B.C.): an extended floor with holes for piles may indicate that partitions were built inside the cave to accommodate diverse functions, and large quantities of carbonized seeds testify to the cultivation of cereals in the Kopais region. Pollen analysis from all the excavation strata has shown a specific succession, from the frigid Paleolithic flora, to the hot flora of the beginning of the Holocene, and arriving at the cultivated species of the Late Neolithic.

The vast majority of the Sarakenos Cave material studied comprises the samples collected between 1998 and 2001. The bulk of this material was recovered from Squares 8, 9, 10, and 11 (Trench A) and in all cases was associated with hearth-type structures and cooking pottery fragments. All the samples are dated to the last phase of Late Neolithic IIb (ca. 3800–3300 B.C.). The archaeobotanical remains from the site have been fully studied (Megaloudi, in press).

5. Ftelia

The Neolithic settlement of Ftelia is situated in the innermost part of the large Panormos Gulf, in the northern part of the island of Mykonos (*Figure 4.12*). The site may have been associated with the death of Aias, son of Oileus and leader of the 40-ship Locrian contingent at Troy (Hom. *Od.* 4. 499–511). Ftelia is contemporaneous with the Neolithic settlement on the islet of Saliagos near Antiparos, and with Kephala on Kea island.

The systematic radiocarbon dating of samples originating from consecutive archaeological layers showed that Ftelia was occupied during the Late Neolithic period for about six centuries (ca. 5050–4460 B.C.).

The broad sandy beach, oriented to north, is interrupted by a low elevation of sandstone. It was upon this rock that the Neolithic settlement was laid out, with man-made deposits covering the majority of it. This sandstone was quarried during the Hellenistic period, and the building material of various monuments on Delos is known to have originated in Ftelia. Traces of ancient quarrying activities, which destroyed a part of the settlement, are still visible along the western side of the hill.

In the Late Neolithic the coastline must have extended some 100 meters to the north, assuming that the level of the Aegean has risen approximately 1 meter each millennium (Sampson 2002). The valley of Ftelia would originally have been larger and the settlement would have been located in its center. To the south and west of the hill extends a level tract of land that would have been cultivated, since water supplies are sufficient and the soil is fertile.

Systematic excavations of Ftelia, begun in 1995 under the direction of A. Sampson of Aegean University, have continued through the summer of 2005. The archaeological investigation revealed the architectural remains of a large prehistoric settlement (*Figure 4.13*). The settlement's thick deposits of soil, measuring 1.60 to 2.30m, have rescued four phases of construction, of which the earliest is the best preserved. The excavation revealed a building of the megaron type, as well as an apsidal building and two circular structures that were possibly used as granaries. Inside the buildings, pottery fragments as well as intact vases were found, exhibiting a notable variety in shapes and in the quality of surface treatment. In addition, there was a remarkable abundance of obsidian implements; among these, numbers of arrowheads and spearheads of excellent workmanship furnish evidence of a particular specialization in hunting. The relatively small quantity of shells and fishbones shows that the Neolithic inhabitants of Ftelia were mainly concerned with land cultivation, animal husbandry, and hunting, and less with fishing.

Figure 4.12 : Bay of Panormos at Ftelia (Mykonos)

Figure 4.13 : The Prehistoric settlement of Ftelia

The samples studied were collected during 2000–2001 and originated from Trenches A3, A4, A5, A7, B3, and B4. The archaeobotanical material was fully published (Megaloudi and Marinval 2002).

6. Ipsili

The Geometric site of Ipsili is located in the modern village of the same name, on Andros island in the Cyclades. Ipsili is in the area of Aprovatou, midway up the west coast of the island and 15 kilometers from the site of Zagora. Ipsili was excavated by C. Televantou of the Archaeological Unit of Cyclades in 1981.

The village was built on a large, rocky hill with a fortified acropolis on its peak. In the center of the acropolis, a large 6th-century B.C. temple, probably dedicated to Demeter and Persephone, was found to have been built on the ruins of a Geometric temple. Excavations in the area of the acropolis revealed architectural remains of the Protogeometric, Geometric, and Archaic periods, as well as some structures dated after the Hellenistic period. It seems that although the village was largely abandoned in the late 8th century B.C., life in certain areas of the acropolis continued (Televantou 1998).

The archaeobotanical material comes from the acropolis of Ipsili; the remains were collected from two receptacles dating to the 7th century B.C. The material consisted of 20 olive pips (Olea europaea). (Figure 4.14).

Figure 4.14: Olive remains from the archaic settlement of Ipsili (Andros)

AUTHOR'S NOTE

The botanical remains of the sites discussed in this book are grouped in *Tables 5.6* to *5.14*. It is important to note that not all botanical remains are presented in absolute numbers. In most cases I had access only in reports and preliminary publications that did not give detailed numbers of the plant remains (the reader is referred to the publication of each site). Where I did not have absolute numbers I only mention that the species is present. It is also important to note that the compilation tables include only the primary edible plants and they are not exhaustive.

The database includes results of the preliminary analysis of two sites that are no longer studied by the author: Dimini in Thessaly (Mycenaean, 15th–12th centuries B.C.) and Kouphovouno in the southeast Peloponnese (Middle Helladic levels).

The samples collected by archaeologists at Dimini came from the occupation levels of the palace and were sieved in September 2000 by the author. A total of 500 liters of material was processed with the aid of a flotation machine. The samples contained pips attributed to *Malus/Pyrus* sp. The study of the archaeobotanical material is now in the hands of S. Valamoti.

The excavation of Kouphovouno, located 5 kilometers from the city of Sparta, is a joint venture of the École Française d'Athènes and the British School of Archaeology at Athens. During the excavation campaign of July 2001, samples were collected from Sectors B, C, and D. A total of 800 liters was treated with a flotation machine built for that purpose on the site. The samples contained 7 olive nuts (*Olea* sp.), 2 barley seeds (*Hordeum vulgare*), 2 seeds of emmer wheat (*Triticum dicoccon*), 1 pip of vine (*Vitis sylvestris*) and grains of *Sherardia arvensis* and *Convolvulus arvensis*. The archaeobotanical study is being continued by A. Bogaard.

GROUP 2

1. Makri

The tell of Makri is situated in meridional Thrace, approximately 10 kilometers west of Alexandroupolis, and 500 meters south of the modern village of Makri. Two Neolithic cultural periods have been identified at the site: Makri I, which ended around 5500 B.C., and Makri II, which continued after this date and constitutes the main cultural period of the settlement (Efstratiou et al. 1998). The archaeobotanical samples have been attributed to the habitation phases of Makri II and have been studied and published by S. Valamoti (Efstratiou et al. 1998; Valamoti 2004).

2. Nea Nikomedeia

The Neolithic site of Nea Nikomedeia is situated in northern Greece, on the southwest edge of the plain of Macedon, 60 kilometers west of Thessalonica. The site was excavated in 1961 and 1963 under the direction of R. Rodden of the University of California at Berkeley. It is a low settlement mound with Early and Late Neolithic levels of occupation. The archaeobotanical material was recovered from the Early Neolithic levels (ca. 5470 B.C.) and was studied and published by W. Van Zeist and S. Bottema (1971).

3. Dikili Tash

Dikili Tash is situated in eastern Macedonia, approximately 17 kilometers outside the city of Kavala.

The site has been excavated since 1961 by both the École Française d'Athènes and the Archaeological Unit of Eastern Macedonia. Prehistoric occupation at the site spans the Late/Final Neolithic, the Early Bronze Age, and the Late Bronze Age (Treuil 1992).

Four samples from the silo dated to the last phase of Middle Neolithic were studied by I. Cerceau (1985 [1992]), while samples dated to Late/Final Neolithic were studied by M. Mangaffa (1990) and V. Matterne (1993). Archaeobotanical samples retrieved in 1989, 1993, and 1994 and dated to Final Neolithic and Early Bronze Age were studied and published by S. Valamoti (2004).

4. Dimitra

The prehistoric settlement of Dimitra is situated in northern Greece, in the plain of Serres, about 15 kilometers from the modern town of Amphipolis. The site consists of a 9.2-meter-high tell that was first excavated by D. Theocharis in 1961. A second archaeological campaign took place from 1978 to 1980 under the direction of D. Grammenos. The archaeobotanical study concerns two cultural phases: Late Neolithic levels (the samples from which were studied and published by J. Renfrew [1997]) and a Late Bronze Age wall (studied by C. Foster [1997]).

6. Sitagroi

The prehistoric village of Sitagroi is situated in northern Greece, on the northwest edge of the plain of Drama, on the banks of the river Angitis. The site presents five occupation phases, spanning from Middle Neolithic (5500–5200 B.C.) to Early Bronze Age (2700–2200 B.C.). The archaeobotanical material of the settlement has been studied by J. Renfrew, with its first publication coming in 1986 (Renfrew et al. 1986) and the final publication in 2003 (Renfrew 2003).

7. Aghios Mamas

Aghios Mamas is situated in the region of Chalkidike, in northern Greece, midway between the Kassandra and Sithonia peninsulas. The Bronze Age settlement of Aghios Mamas, a toumba (tell), was first located by Heurtley (1939). New excavations were undertaken in the 1990s by J. Aslanis of the Archaeological Museum of Thessalonica and B. Hansel of the Free University of Berlin. The archaeobotanical material comes from the Middle Bronze Age buildings at the site and was fully studied and published by H. Kroll (2003).

8. Assiros Toumba

Assiros Toumba is situated in central Macedonia, near the modern village of Assiros. The site, consisting of a toumba 14 kilometers high, presents evidence of continuous occupation from 1800 B.C. (Middle Bronze Age) to the end of the 8th century B.C. The devastating fire that overwhelmed the site around 1300 B.C. preserved details of the storage containers in the granaries—large baskets, pithoi, and clay bins—as well as hundreds of kilograms of charred seeds of wheat, barley, and other crops. The archaeobotanical material has been studied by G. Jones (Jones 1979, Jones et al. 1986, Wardle 1989); E Margariti studied the samples from Room 24 (Margariti 1998).

9. Kastanas

Kastanas is situated in Macedonia, on the banks of the river Axios (Vardar), on the road between Thessalonica and the Yugoslavian border. The site consists of a tell (toumba) 13 meters high and 120 meters long. The site presents nine periods of occupation (K I to K IX) covering a period from the Early Bronze Age to the classical period. The excavation of Kastanas was a joint program of the Archaeological Unit of Central Macedonia and the Free University of Berlin. The archaeobotanical material was fully studied and published by H. Kroll (1983).

10. Achilleion

The prehistoric settlement of Achilleion is situated in the fertile plain of Thessaly on the banks of the Peneios River, a short distance from the city of Pharsala. The settlement presents levels of occupation dated between 6400 and 5600 B.C. (Gimbutas 1989). The archaeobotanical samples were collected during the excavations of 1961, 1973, and 1974; the material was studied and published by J. Renfrew (1989).

11. Argissa Magoula

The settlement of Argissa Magoula is situated in the plain of Thessaly, on the river Peneios. The site consists of a tell (magoula) with occupation levels spanning from Pre-Pottery Neolithic to the Middle Bronze Age. The site was investigated in the 1960s under the direction of V. Milojcic (1962) and its archaeobotanical material (Pre-Pottery Neolithic, Early Neolithic, Early and Middle Bronze Age) was fully studied and published by M. Hopf (1962).

12. Prodromos

The modern village of Prodromos is situated 4 kilometers east of the city of Karditsa, in the fertile region of Thessaly. Rescue excavations were carried out between 1970 and 1972 under the direction of G. Chourmouziades at three locations: Prodromos 1 and 2 (occupied through the Early Neolithic until the transition to the Middle Neolithic) and Prodromos 3. The bulk of the archaeobotanical material comes from Prodromos 2 and was studied by G. Jones (Halstead and Jones 1980).

13. Platia Magoula Zarkou

The prehistoric mound (magoula) of Platia Magoula Zarkou, in the plain of Thessaly, was excavated from 1974 to 1989 under the direction of K. Gallis of the Archaeological Unit of Larissa. Occupation of the site spanned the period from the Early Neolithic to the Middle Helladic. Five archaeobotanical samples of charred remains collected from an occupation level were studied by G. Jones (Jones and Halstead 1993) and four samples (Early and Middle Bronze age) were studied by H. Kroll (Becker 1991).

14. Neolithic Dimini

The Neolithic settlement of Dimini is situated about 5 kilometers northwest of the city of Volos in Thessaly. The site was excavated at the beginning of the twentieth century by P. Tsountas (1901–1903) and a new excavation program was carried out in 1977 under the direction of G. Chourmouziades. Archaeobotanical samples dated to the Late Neolithic period were studied and published by H. Kroll (1979). C. Tsountas (1908) and A. J. B. Wace and H. Thompson (1912) also reported the presence of cereals and fruits in the LN levels.

15. Prehistoric sites in Thessaly

During the summer of 1965 J. Renfrew studied archaeobotanical samples that were excavated by Theocharis at sites belonging to Aceramic Neolithic, Early Neolithic, Late Neolithic, and Late Bronze Age Thessaly: Achilleion (Aceramic and Early Neolithic), Ghediki (Aceramic Neolithic), Sesklo (Aceramic, Early and Late Neolithic), Soufli (Early Neolithic), and Pyrasos (Late Neolithic). Renfrew also studied 11 samples from Late Bronze Age Iolkos and a sample of 40 figs from Late Neolithic Rachmani excavated in 1910 by A. J. B. Wace. A report on these finds, as well as a record of finds from older excavations, was published by J. Renfrew (1966).

16. Otzaki, Arapi Magoula, Pefkakia (Thessaly)

H. Kroll (1983) reports the presence of archaeobotanical material in the Early Neolithic (Proto-Sesklo culture) and the Middle Neolithic (Sesklo culture) levels of Otzaki, in the Late Neolithic levels (Dimini culture) of Arapi Magoula, and in the Late Neolithic levels (Dimini culture) of Pefkakia, with some samples from Pefkakia belonging to the Early and Middle Bronze Age.

17. Thermi

Thermi is situated on the east coast of the island of Lesbos in the northeastern Aegean Sea. The prehistoric settlement is divided into five occupation levels (Thermi I–V) from the Neolithic period to Early Bronze Age II. The archaeobotanical samples belong to Late Neolithic levels (5300–5000 B.C.) and were studied by S. Valamoti (1992). W. Lamb reports the discovery of seeds and fruits in the Late Bronze Age levels revealed during the first excavation campaign of 1929–1931 (Lamb 1936).

18. The fort at Phylla Vrachos

The ancient fort at Phylia in central Euboea is situated on a hill called Vrachos, 3.5 kilometers from the prehistoric settlement at Lefkandi and halfway between Chalkis and Eretria (Coulton et al. 2002). The main occupation phase at Phylia is related to the defeat of Chalkis by the Athenians in 507 B.C.; the fort itself was destroyed during the Persian invasion of 490 B.C. The archaeological investigation of the site took place a century ago and the area was resurveyed in 1994 by the Archaeological Unit of Chalkis and the British School of Archaeology at Athens. A. Sarpaki conducted the archaeobotanical study of the site, but the remains are limited to a vine pip and two unidentifiable seeds (Coulton et al. 2002).

19. Skoteini Tharounia

Skoteini Cave is situated in the southwest of the island of Euboea, in the area of Tharounia. The site was excavated from 1986 to 1991 under the direction of A. Sampson (1993); the excavations revealed occupation levels from the Late Neolithic to the Early Bronze Age (5800–3300 B.C.). The archaeobotanical samples were studied and published by M. Mangaffa (1993).

20. Gla

The Late Bronze Age (Late Helladic IIIB2) fortress of Gla is situated in central Greece in the region of Boeotia. During the excavations in the southern enclosure ("Agora"), S. Iakovides uncovered a building complex ("H") that has been identified as a storage area. The excavator collected small samples of charred grains from a series of locations in the houses; these were studied and published by G. Jones (1995).

21. Toumba Balomenou

The settlement of Toumba Balomenou, in the region of Chaeronia (Boeotia) consists of a mound, or toumba, situated on the north bank of the Kifisos river. G. Sotiriades undertook the first investigation of the site between 1902 and 1910. A new excavation campaign took place in 1986 and in 1989 under the direction of H. Tzavella-Evjen of the University of Colorado at Boulder. The site presents occupation levels belonging to the Early Neolithic until the Late Bronze Age (1700 B.C.) The archaeobotanical samples, which belong to the Early and Middle Neolithic periods, were studied and published by A. Sarpaki (1995).

22. Thebes

Excavations of 1981 in the town center of Thebes (Boeotia) uncovered a destruction level dated to Late Helladic I (Late Bronze Age). The episode included a polychrome-style krater containing charred pulse remains. This material was studied by G. Jones (Jones and Halstead 1993).

23. Saliagos

Saliagos is an islet situated between the islands of Paros and Antiparos in the Cyclades. During the excavations at Saliagos (1964–1965) fossilized grains and grain impressions were discovered in mud brick that was perhaps used in the construction of the houses. The occupation level at Saliagos is dated to Final Neolithic (4500–3500 B.C.) The material was studied and published by J. Renfrew (1968).

24. Kephala

The Late Neolithic site of Kephala on the island of Kea was excavated in the 1960s by J. L. Caskey of the University of Cincinnati. The archaeobotanical samples came from "Area K," where grains were probably stacked in large vessels that were later broken. The material was studied by J. Renfrew (Renfrew 1977).

25. Akrotiri

Archaeological investigation of the prehistoric town of Akrotiri on the island of Thera in the Cyclades began in 1967 under the direction of S. Marinatos. Since 1974 C. Doumas has carried out the archaeological research and the restoration program on the site. The archaeobotanical study at Akrotiri is focused on one building at the settlement, the West House, which is the most completely excavated house at the site (Sarpaki 1987).

26. Agora, Athens

The archaeobotanical evidence from the Athenian Agora is limited, consisting of a few physical remains and imprints preserved in pottery. These finds belong to the Neolithic, Middle Helladic, Mycenaean (Late Bronze Age), Geometric, and Byzantine periods. The material was studied by M. Hopf and was published in 1971 (Immerwahr 1971).

27. Franchthi Cave

Franchthi Cave is situated at the southern edge of the Argolid (Peloponnese). The site was excavated from 1967 to 1979 under the direction of T. W. Jacobsen of the University of Indiana. The cave presents several cultural phases, with the oldest dated to Upper Paleolithic (25,000 B.P.) and the earliest to Late Neolithic (5000 B.P.). The archaeobotanical material has been studied and published by J. Hansen (Hansen 1991).

28. The citadel of Midea

The Mycenaean citadel of Midea is located in the eastern part of the Argive plain and is built on a hill 270 meters above sea level, southwest of the cemetery of Dendra (Walberg 1998). An Aceramic Neolithic settlement was also discovered in the Dendra cemetery that was inhabited in the Early and Middle Helladic periods. The citadel was destroyed in the Late Helladic IIIB period and it is generally thought that it was not resettled thereafter. A few Protogeometric and Geometric vases have also been found in the cemetery. Archaeobotanical samples were analyzed by T. C. Shay and J. Shay (Shay et al. 1998). Most of the samples came from destruction debris or floor deposits and date to the Late Bronze Age (ca. 1300–1100 B.C.), but Roman contexts were also represented.

29. Tirynth

Tirynth is situated in the gulf of Argos, a few kilometers from the town of Nauplio in the Peloponnese. The site was first occupied in the Neolithic (5000 B.C.) but flourished during the Bronze Age. Tirynth was discovered by H. Schliemann in 1876 and the archaeological investigation of the site is mainly carried out by the German Archaeological Institute at Athens. The archaeobotanical samples, which come from several locations within the palace, belong to the Early and Late Bronze Age and to the Submycenaean period. The material was studied and published by H. Kroll (1982, 1984).

30. Nichoria

The village of Nichoria is situated in Messenia in the southwest Peloponnese, about 2.5 kilometers from the Messenian Gulf. The site was excavated jointly by the University of Minnesota and the Archaeological Unit of Olympia from 1969 to 1973. During the excavation seasons of 1971–1973 palaeobotanical samples (charcoal and seeds) were collected directly from the excavation trenches belonging to seven major periods: Middle Helladic (MBA), Late Helladic II and III, Dark Ages I and II, and the 4th century B.C. The material was published by J. M. Shay and C. T. Shay (1978).

31. Lerna

The fortified site of Lerna is situated on the west coast of the Argolid Gulf (Peloponnese), not far from the marshland of the lake of Lerna. The site was excavated from 1952 to 1958 by the American School of Classical Studies at Athens. The archaeobotanical samples from Lerna date to the Late Neolithic and Early and Middle Bronze Age, with one sample belonging to the 4th century B.C. The material was studied by M. Hopf (1962, 1964).

32. Kalythies Cave, Rhodes

Kalythies Cave is situated in the northeastern part of the island of Rhodes, in the region of Kalythies, and was excavated in 1979 and 1980 under the direction of A. D. Sampson. The archaeobotanical material consists of 20 identifiable impressions found in the Late Neolithic pottery and 6 samples of carbonized material. The material, studied by G. Jones (plant impressions) and by A. Sarpaki (physical remains), is published in Sampson 1987.

33. Debla

The site of Debla is situated in western Crete, on top of the hill of Debla in the White Mountains. This small settlement, excavated in 1971, is dated to Early Minoan period (mid-3rd millennium B.C.). In the central building 13 vessels were discovered containing impressions of cereals and some olives. The material from Debla was published by J. R. A. Greig and P. Warren (1974).

34. The Minoan Unexplored Mansion at Knossos (Crete)

The Unexplored Mansion at Knossos was discovered by A. Evans in 1908 during the excavation of the Little Palace, but the site remained unexplored until 1967. The excavations at the mansion were completed in three campaigns (1967, 1972, and 1977) by the British School of Archaeology at Athens. The Unexplored Mansion is a large Late Minoan building (LM IA); after a fire around 1425 B.C., the mansion was abandoned in LM IIIB. Storeroom P, which was destroyed in Late Minoan II, contained numerous deposits of carbonized fruits and seeds that were studied and published by G. Jones (1984).

35. Myrtos (Crete)

The Early Minoan II settlement of Myrtos, on the southern coast of Crete, was built on the top and upper slopes of the highest of four oval-shaped knolls that rise above the southern end of Fournou Korifi ridge, 3.5 kilometers from the modern village of Myrtos. The settlement, excavated by the British School of Archaeology at Athens, was founded in 2600/2500 B.C and its final destruction was no later than 2150 B.C. The archaeobotanical material from the site consists of grape pips discovered in Rooms 80 and 90, one olive stone from Area 2, and barley impressions in mud plaster. The material was studied by J. Renfrew (1972).

36. Aghia Triada

Aghia Triada, situated on the southern coast of Crete in the fertile Messara Plain, was excavated by the Italian School of Archaeology at Athens. The site is dated to the second Palace Period (1600–1400 B.C.) and the archaeobotanical material was discovered within four vessels dated to the first half of 15th century B.C. (Early Minoan I). The material was studied by M. Follieri (1979).

37. Chania

Chania is situated in the western coast of Crete. Two

samples were stored at the Archaeological Museum of Chania. The first comes from a rural house situated in the region of Amigdalokefali-Sternes; the second, from the property of Manoussogianakis "Kastelli," in the historical center of Chania. Both are dated to Late Minoan III B. The samples were studied and published by M. Follieri (1982).

38. Chamalevri-Tzambakas House

Chamalevri is a village on the coast of Crete, 10 kilometers east of Rethymno. The site was an important Minoan settlement (MM I, ca. 2160–1900 B.C.). The archaeobotanical material, which comes from Tzambakas House, was studied by A. Sarpaki and a preliminary report has been published in the National Archaeological Museum exhibition publication *Minoans and Mycenaeans: Flavours of Their Time* (1999).

39. Iolkos

The town of Iolkos is situated on the gulf of Magnesia, about 15 kilometers from the city of Volos in Thessaly. Excavations conducted at Iolkos in 1979 by G. Chourmouziades revealed a burnt destruction episode associated with a Geometric floor. In 1981 excavations at a second location some 200 meters away uncovered a burnt destruction episode on a Protogeometric floor. The archaeobotanical samples from both destruction levels were studied and published by G. Jones (Jones 1982).

40. Kalapodi (Sanctuary of Artemis and Apollo at Hyambolis)

Kalapodi, a sanctuary of Artemis and Apollo, is located in the region of Lokrida in central Greece, about 10 kilometers from the city of Atalanti. The sanctuary presents a long sequence of cultural phases from Mycenaean times to the 4th century B.C. The site was excavated between 1973 and 1982 under the direction of R. Felsch. In 2004 a new excavation program at the sanctuary was begun by the German Institute of Archaeology under the direction of W. Nemeier. The archaeobotanical material from the first archaeological campaign has been fully studied and published by H. Kroll (1993). In 2005 new samples were taken, and the archaeobotanical investigation is being continued by the author.

41. Delphi, "L'aire du pilier des Rhodiens"

The area called "Pilier des Rhodiens" is located next to the temple of Apollo at Delphi, in central Greece. New stratigraphic excavation and restoration work was conducted at this area by the École Française d'Athènes from 1990 to 1992. The archaeobotanical study of this area covers a long chronological sequence from the Mycenaean period (13th century B.C.) to the 6th century B.C. The work was conducted by P. Marinval and is in press (Luce et al., forthcoming).

42. Heraion, Samos

At the Samian Heraion a large quantity and variety of plant remains were found in waterlogged deposits of the 7th century B.C. The sanctuary, situated on the island of Samos in the southeast Aegean, was investigated archaeobotanically from 1984 to 1991 and the majority of the samples came from the southern edge of the sanctuary. The noncarbonized remains were fully studied and published by D. Kucan (1995).

43. The Sanctuary of Demeter and Kore at Corinth

The sanctuary of Demeter and Kore at Corinth (Peloponnese) covers roughly 770 square meters on the north slope of Acrocorinth and its use extended from the Late Helladic IIIC to the end of the 4th century B.C. The sanctuary was excavated by the American School of Classical Studies at Athens between 1961 and 1973. In 1994 a small excavation program investigated two small areas that typify the dining establishments in the sanctuary. During that session archaeobotanical samples were taken and studied by J. Hansen (Bookidis et al. 1999; Hansen et al. 1995).

Reports

In this section I have grouped the sites for which I did not have access to the final publication. In these cases information was provided by secondary sources, by the preliminary reports, or by the researcher who carried out the archaeobotanical study.

Photoleivos toumba
Photoleivos toumba in Macedonia consists of a tell situated near the village of Sitagroi. The site was excavated in two seasons (1968–1969). Information on the Photoleivos archaeobotanical material, the bulk of which dates to the Middle and Late Neolithic periods, can be found in Renfrew 1969 and Logothetis 1970.

Iria and Synoro
Both sites are situated in the Argolid plain in the northeast Peloponnese and were excavated in 1939. The archaeobotanical material was studied by U. Willerding. The samples from Iria were dated to Late Bronze Age, while the Synoro material, limited to three vine impressions, was dated to the Early Bronze Age (Willerding 1973).

Giannitsa B
The site, situated in central Macedonia, belongs to the Early Neolithic period. The archaeobotanical samples derive from habitation levels and have been studied by S. Valamoti (Valamoti 1995, 2001).

Archondiko
Archondiko is a Late Bronze Age settlement in Macedonia (ca. 2100–1900 B.C.). The archaeobotanical study of this site was conducted by S. Valamoti

(Valamoti 1997, 2001). The samples that represent burnt occupation levels revealed the presence of the "new" glume wheat *Triticum timopheevi* (see Jones et al. 2000).

Stavroupoli
Stavroupoli is a Late Neolithic site not far from the city of Thessalonica in northern Greece. Archaeobotanical research at the site was carried out from 1995 to 1998 and was published by E. Margariti (2002a).

Krania
The archaeobotanical remains from the Geometric site of Krania located in the area of Platamonas (Pieria, Macedonia) were studied and published E. Margariti (2002b). The remains come from broken receptacles that were stored in a circular structure destroyed by fire.

Miscellaneous Finds

The sites in this section were used in my database but their archaeobotanical material was only briefly reported in the excavation reports. For further information I refer the reader to the supplemental publications listed below.

Olynthos (central Macedonia): Figs, millet, and wheat were reported from a Late Neolithic level (Mylonas 1929; Vickery 1936; Renfrew 1973a).

Eutresis (Boeotia): Wheat was reported from the Early Bronze Age levels (Goldman 1931; Mylonas 1959).

Orchomenos (Boeotia): Barley, emmer wheat, bitter vetch, broad bean and oat was reported from Middle Bronze Age levels (Vickery 1936).

*Marmariani (Thessaly)***:** Emmer wheat and millet were reported at this Late Bronze Age site (Tsountas 1908; Wace and Thompson 1912; Vickery 1936).

Citadel of Mycenae: H. Schliemann reported the presence of wheat and barley in the Late Bronze Age levels (Schliemann 1880).

*Balos and Therasia (Cyclades)***:** Pulses and barley were reported by F. Fouqué in the Late Bronze Age levels (Fouqué 1879; Vickery 1936).

Palaikastro (Crete): Wheat and pulses from the Late Bronze Age levels (Bosanquet 1901; Vickery 1936).

Knossos (Crete): Broad beans and field peas (Evans 1900–1901).

Nirou Chani (Crete): Field peas (Evans 1900–1901; Vickery 1936).

*Gournia (Crete)***:** Field peas were reported from the Middle Bronze Age levels and lentils from the Late Bronze Age levels (Renfrew 1969; Hawes 1909).

Kamares Cave (Crete): Wheat was reported from the Middle Bronze Age level (Dawkins and Laistner 1912).

Lebena (Crete): Vessels containing olive nuts were reported from funeral contexts dated to Early Bronze Age (Alexiou 1958, 1960).

Mallia (Crete): Wheat and lentils were reported in Late Bronze Age levels (Chapoutier and Charbonneaux 1928).

Vathypetro (Crete): Vine was reported from the Late Bronze Age levels (*Praktika* 1949, 1950, 1951, 1952).

A. Data analysis

I have carried out data analysis based on the frequency of species in the archaeological sites considered in this work, in order to examine the plant species diachronically (from the Early Neolithic to the Classical periods). In addition, I wish to explore the distribution of plant species geographically (northern/southern Greece), the sampling and recovery methods used, and the archaeological contexts of the samples.

I have defined 123 archaeological levels as units belonging to a site and to a chronological period. Among the 79 sites considered here, 54 sites had one chronological level, 14 sites had two, 5 sites had three, 4 sites had four, and 2 sites had five. For the geographical analysis I have subdivided Greece into 12 regions, following the administrative division (*Figure 4.15*). Epirus and the Ionian islands were excluded, as no archaeobotanical study of this area was considered in our data. The recuperation and recovery techniques used at each site were defined, and the archaeological context of each site was also explored, allowing me to define 13 contexts of plant remains.

The first stages of the data analysis, done in Excel, involved the evaluation of sample composition for each sample or for different periods. Presence analysis was conducted to explore the frequency of plant species diachronically and geographically. Presence analysis does not consider the total counts of species, and thus can give a better impression of how common a species is within the set samples than seed numbers can (Hubbard 1980). Statistical methods were not used to calculate diversity for the different periods and region because of taphonomic and sampling problems. As a result only the presence or absence of plant species within each period and in each region was compared, in order to give an impression of the spectra of cultivated plants. I considered only species that were recorded more than twice, making a total of 165 plant species. Spatial analysis of the plant remains was conducted to investigate the distribution of individual plant remains in the northern and southern parts of the country and the relation between them. "Northern Greece" in this study comprises Thrace, Macedonia, Thessaly, central Greece (up to Boeotia), and the north Aegean islands; "southern Greece" includes Attica, the Peloponnese, the south Aegean islands, and Crete.

In addition, I have used data analysis (specifically, the STATA package) to describe the distribution of the recovery techniques and recuperation methods used at the various sites, as well as the archaeological contexts that have yielded plant remains. The results of this analysis are presented below.

B. Preservation modes

Four types of preservation have been observed for archaeobotanical material in Greece: carbonization (charring), mineralization, preservation through waterlogging, and preservation in impressions (*Figure 4.16*).

Charred remains represent the majority, occurring in 119 of the 123 levels under study (and 74% of the sites)—not a surprising statistic, since the climatic conditions of the Aegean favor this type of preservation.

Mineralized remains (seeds) are recorded in just 19 of the 123 levels (and 12% of the sites). Large quantities of mineralized fig pips were recovered from the Mycenaean and Archaic levels at Delphi (Luce et al., forthcoming), as well as from the Middle Neolithic levels of Limenaria on Thasos island (Megaloudi, forthcoming). In the latter case, the fig pips were dispersed in all occupation levels but were rarely found associated with the carbonized remains of the fruit (pips). The number of fruits consumed at Limenaria seems to have been significant, but it is difficult to calculate the original number since noncarbonized remains of fig occur very rarely in archaeological deposits (see *Chapter 3 Section A*).

Mineralized plant remains were also found in a sewer pit at the West House of Akrotiri at Thera (Sarpaki 1987). Mineralized seeds were recovered from Franchthi Cave in the Peloponnese (Hansen, 1991), in the same deposits in which carbonized remains of the same species were found. One possible explanation is that some of the seeds are not in situ, perhaps having been exposed to mineralizing conditions in a different deposit and being displaced by anthropogenic, biogenic, or geogenic processes.

Preservation through waterlogging is rare in Greek archaeology. Waterlogged plant remains are found in places where the water table has remained high enough to inhibit destruction by decay-causing organisms, and such environments are not common in the dry Aegean region. Only five archaeological levels have yielded waterlogged remains (corresponding to 3% of the total number). At the Sanctuary of Hera on Samos (7th century B.C.), the waterlogged deposits of the sanctuary allowed the recovery of a wide range of plant species that could not have survived otherwise (Kučan 1995).

Figure 4.15: Administration Map of Greece (source: Ministry of Foreign Affairs)

Preservation mode	Number	Percentage
■ Carbonisation	119	74%
■ Mineralization	19	12%
■ Waterlogging	5	3%
■ Imprinting	17	11%
Total	160	100%

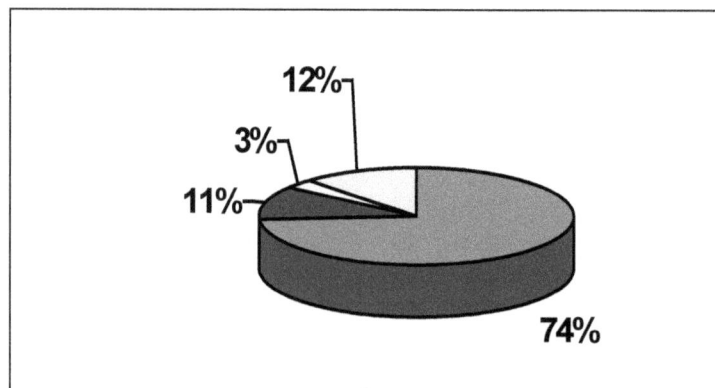

Figure 4.16: Graphic showing the preservation modes in Greece (in percentages)

Impressions of basketry in clay objects are commonly found in the Aegean, especially at Neolithic sites (Cerceau 1983). Plant impressions in pottery and in timber are found relatively often in Greece. In the 1950s Zervos (1957) reported the discovery of ceramics with plant impressions that were identified as laurel (*Laurus nobilis*) and vine (*Vitis vinifera*).

At the sites included in my database, plant impressions have been recorded in 17 contexts (11%). At Myrtos (Crete), barley remains (*Hordeum vulgare*) are identified in mud plaster (Racham 1972). The Late Neolithic pottery of Kalythies Cave at Rhodes has yielded 20 imprints of barley (*Hordeum* sp.), einkorn (*Triticum monococcum),* emmer wheat *(Triticum dicoccon),* bread wheat/club wheat *(Triticum aestivum/durum)* and bitter vetch (*Vicia ervilia*) (Halstead and Jones 1987). Imprints of einkorn were discovered in several potsherds dated to Late Neolithic IIb at the Sarakenos Cave in Boeotia (Megaloudi in press) while at Ftelia (Mykonos) imprints of red pea or grass pea (*Lathyrus* sp.*)* and barley *(Hordeum vulgare)* were identified in potsherds dated to the Final Neolithic (Megaloudi and Marinval 2002). Naked barley (*Hordeum vulgare nudum),* bitter vetch (*Vicia ervilia*), grass pea (*Lathyrus* sp.) and garden pea (*Pisum* sp.) were among the plant species identified in the Neolithic pottery of the Athenian Agora (Hopf 1971). In the Mycenaean pottery of the same site imprints of naked barley and leaves of vine were identified (Hopf 1971).

C. Geographical distribution of sites

Figure 4.17a illustrates the location of the sites where archaeobotanical analysis has been performed. A significant proportion of the sites (44%) is divided between Thessaly (28%) and central Greece (16%). This is not surprising if we consider that the fertile alluvial soils of the Thessalian plain were occupied from the Aceramic period, and that settlement density and size are significantly higher there. The Peloponnese is also relatively well documented in terms of archaeobotanical studies, with a total of 20 sites (18%).

The available macrofossil evidence from Macedonia is very poor: only 11 levels are represented there, corresponding to 10% of the total number of sites. Charred plant remains are almost unrepresented in Thrace, with only one site having produced archaeobotanical evidence.

D. Chronological distribution

Figure 4.18 illustrates the chronological distribution of the archaeobotanical studies in Greece.

Prehistoric sites represent the vast majority, with a total of 81%, while the protohistoric and historic periods represent only 19%. Within these chronological periods the number of sites is not equal, as all subperiods do not have the same number of archaeobotanical sites.

Forty percent (40%) of the total number of archaeobotanical studies belong to Neolithic period and 41% to the Bronze Age. Within these periods, Late/Final Neolithic and Late Bronze Age are the best documented, with a total of 21% each (26 studies for each period). Thus there is a coherence in the archaeobotanical data from Neolithic and Bronze Age Greece.

The predominance of prehistoric archaeobotanical studies reflects the large number of excavated sites that predate protohistoric and historic periods. In addition, the majority of researchers working on Neolithic and Bronze Age sites emphasize the socioeconomic organization of past societies and the way in which people interacted with their natural and social environment. Agriculture has received particular attention as its development was a critical turning point in the development of human society (Harlan 1995; Harris and Hillman 1989). The Neolithic period was a time of innovation and of the appearance of a new range of species, and it was at that time that human societies shifted to an economy of production. These Neolithic farming communities paved the way for the emergence of civilization in the Bronze Age, when the economy of production was well established and further developed.

When the discussion turns to archaeobotanical evidence from protohistoric and historic periods, however, evidence is scarce. Protogeometric and Geometric sites that were studied archaeobotanically represent only 5% and 3% respectively; in the Archaic period the percentage is limited to 4%, and in the Classical, 5%. The majority of archaeobotanical studies conducted so far in Greece are from archaeological sites that predate the historical period by at least several hundred years. Even today, when the importance of bioarchaeological remains is widely recognized, many excavators do not apply any techniques for the collection of such remains—relying solely on literary evidence, architecture, or artifacts. Such sources, however, rarely contain the type of information we need to understand the dynamics of farming economies, diet, and the cultural significance of various foods.

A special aspect of plant remains is their use as ritual plants in the composition of sacrificial or funeral offerings. Information regarding burnt sacrificial offerings comes from written texts (including inscriptions) and from iconographical evidence from vase paintings and votive reliefs. Little is known, however, concerning the composition of such offerings in the Archaic and Classical periods, as the most detailed information from those periods concerns animal sacrifices. The only way to determine the composition of plant offerings is to collect macroremains. At times this can provide new and unexpected information: for example, the archaeobotanical analysis of funeral offerings from the necropolis of Limenas and of sacrificial offerings from Messene shows that in the composition of such offerings there are no "ritual plants" per se, but the range of species presented in such contexts consists of plants used in the daily diet (Megaloudi 2005c).

Region	Percentage
▪ Thrace	1%
▪ Eastern Macedonia	5%
Central Macedonia	3%
Western Macedonia	2%
▪ Thessaly	28%
▪ Central Greece	16%
▪ Attica	4%
Peloponnesus	18%
▪ Creta	12%
▪ North-eastern Aegean islands	4%
▪ Cyclades	5%
South-western Aegean islands	2%
Total	100%

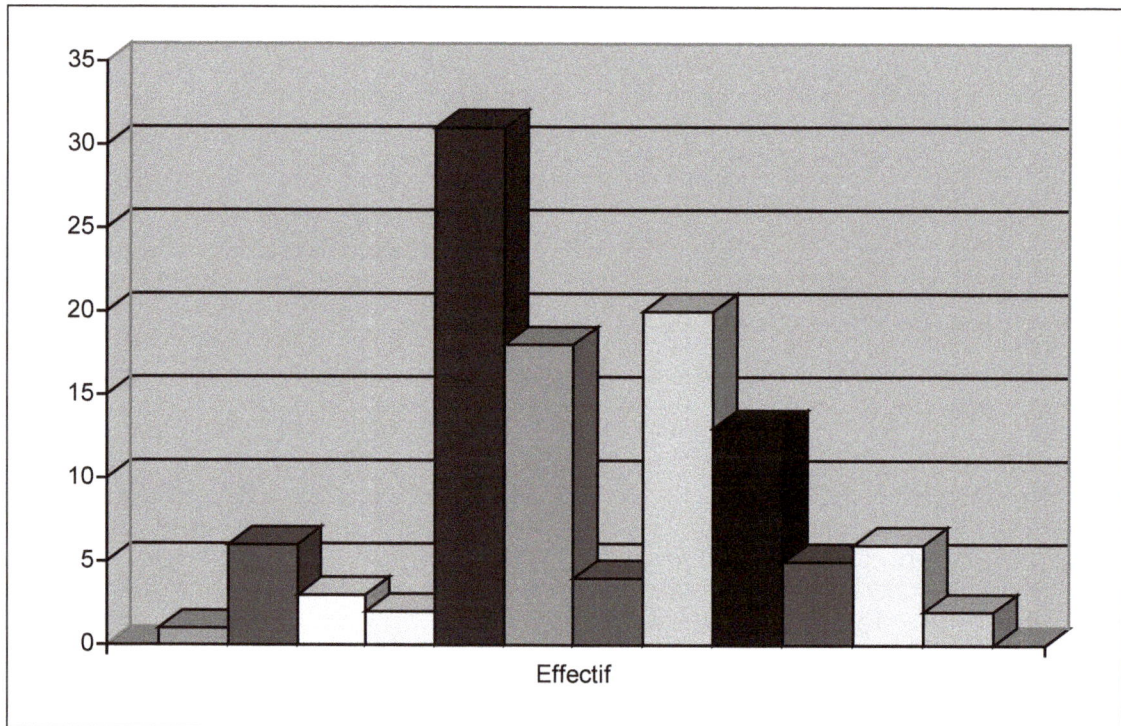

Figure 4.17a : Geographical distribution of Aegean sites with plant remains

26

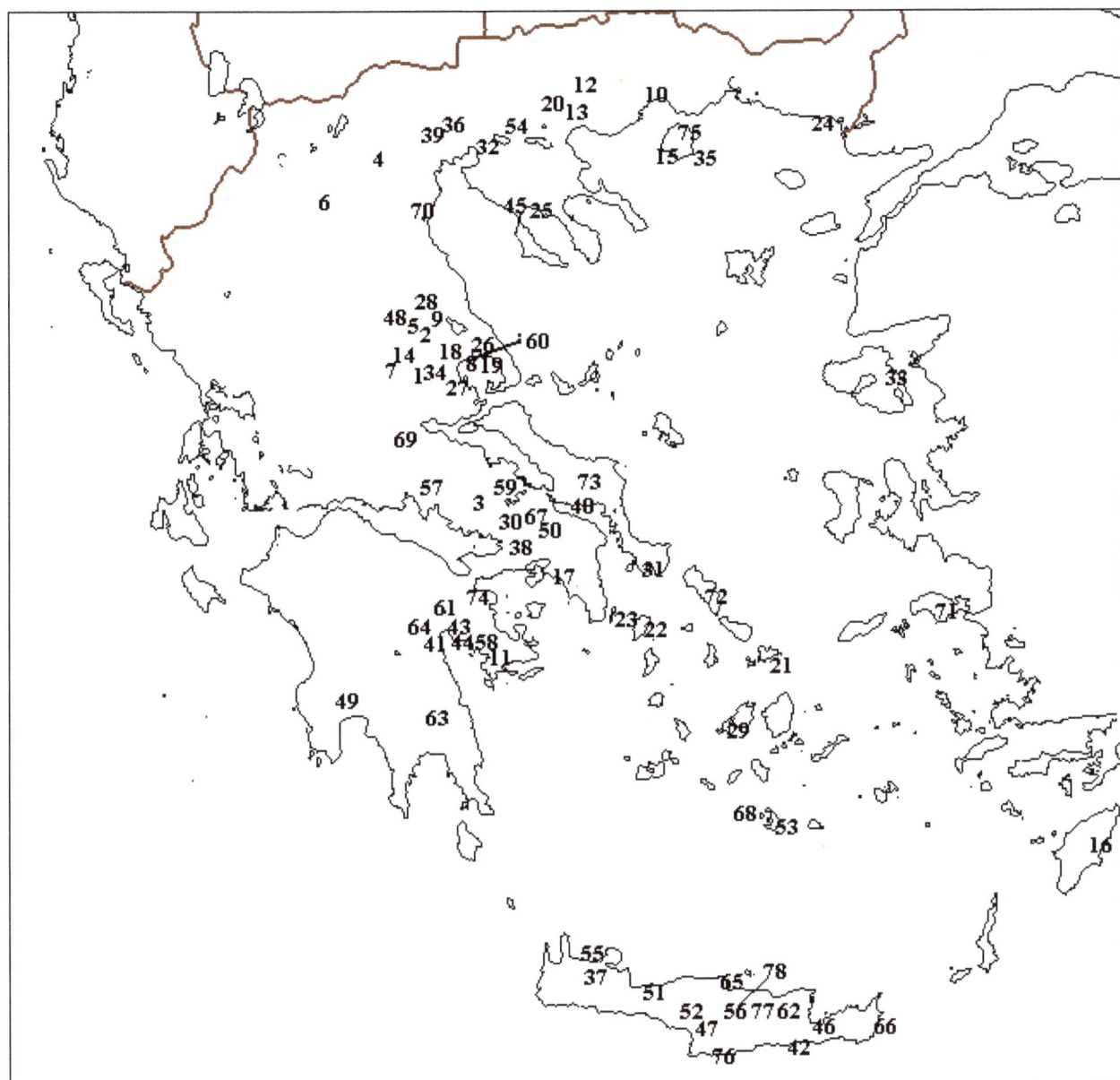

1. Achilleion EN
2. Argissa Magoula AN/EN, EBA, MBA
3. Balomenos EN, MN
4. Giannitsa b EN
5. Otzaki Magoula EN, MN
6. Nea Nikomedeia EN
7. Prodromos EN
8. Sesklo AN, EN, MN, LN
9. Soufli Magoula AN/EN
10. Dikili Tash MN, LN
11. Francthi Cave UP, M, EN, MN, LN/FN
12. Photoleivos MN, LN
13. Sitagroi MN, LN, EBA
14. Zarkos MN, LN, EBA, MBA
15. Limenaria MN, LN, EBA
16. Aghios Georgios (Kalythies) LN
17. Agora Athens LN, MBA, LBA, G, B
18. Arapi Magoula LN
19. Dimini LN

20. Dimitra LN, LBA
21. Ftelia LN/FN
22. Kephala LN
23. Kephala FN
24. Makri LN
25. Olynthus LN
26. Pefkakia LN
27. Pyrassos LN
28. Rachmani LN
29. Saliagos LN
30. Sarakenos Cave LN
31. Skoteini Cave (Tharounia) LN, EBA
32. Stavroupoli LN
33. Thermi LN, LBA
34. Visvikis LN
35. Aghios Ioannis LN/FN
36. Archondiko LBA
37. Debla EBA
38. Eutresis EBA

39. Kastanas EBA, LBA, PG, G, A/C
40. Lefkandi LBA
41. Lerna LN, EBA, MBA, C
42. Myrtos EBA
43. Synoro EBA
44. Tirynth EBA. LBA, SM
45. Aghios Mamas MBA
46. Gournia MBA, LBA
47. Kamares Cave MBA
48. Marmariani LBA
49. Nichoria MBA, LBA, PG, C
50. Orchomenos MBA
51. Chamalevri (Rethymno) MBA
52. Aghia Triada LBA
53. Akrotiri LBA
54. Assiros LBA
55. Chania LBA
56 Knossos (unexplored mansion) LBA
57. Delphi LBA, PG/G, A/C
58. Midea LBA

59. Gla LBA
60. Iolkos LBA, PG, G
61. Iria LBA
62. Malia LBA
63. Kouphovouno MBA
64. Mycenae LBA
65. Nirou Chani LBA
66. Palaikastron MBA, LBA
67. Thebes LBA
68. Balos and Therasia LBA
69. Kalapodi LBA, PG, G, A/C
70. Krania G
71. Heraion A
72. Ipsili A
73. Phylla Vrachos A
74.Corinth C
75. Limenas C
76. Lebena EBA
77. Vathypetro LBA
78. Knossos EN, MBA

Table 4.17b: Main Aegean Sites with plant remains and the cultural periods represented. Abb. UP: Upper Palaeolithic, M: Mesolithic, AN: Aceramic Neolithic, EN: Early Neolithic, MN: Middle Neolithic, LN/FN: Late Neolithic, Final Neolithic, EBA: Early Bronze Age, MBA: Middle Bronze Age, LBA: Late Bronze Age, SM: Submycenaean, PG: Proto-Geometric, G: Geometric, A: Archaic, C: Classic, H: Hellenistic, R: Roman, B: Byzantine

E. Archaeological contexts (*Figure 4.19*)

The analysis of the archaeological contexts that have yielded plant remains revealed that 36% of those correspond to occupation levels. The majority of these contexts are burnt habitation layers (18% of the total). Macrobotanical remains are found in hearths (7 % of the total), receptacles (5%), granaries (2%) and storage pits (1%); 2% of the remains were associated with structures related to cooking (such as ovens). Macrobotanical remains recorded in funeral or sacrificial contexts represent 7% of the total number of contexts.

F. Recovery techniques

All samples from Limenaria, Aghios Ioannis Loukas, the necropolis of Limenas, Ftelia, Sarakenos Cave, and Ipsili were processed by the author. Processing at Limenaria, Sarakenos Cave, and Aghios Ioannis Loukas was carried out using a variant of the Ankara Machine (French 1971), while manual flotation was used at the necropolis of Limenas, Ftelia, and Ipsili. Floated material was collected with a set of two sieves with apertures of 1mm and 0.5 mm. Both coarse flot (retained by the 1mm sieve) and fine flot (retained by the 0.5 mm sieve), as well as the heavy residue that did not float, were retained for study at the laboratory.

Analysis of the recovery techniques used at the sites concerned in this work revealed that in 53% of the cases no sophisticated recovery technique was used, but the plant remains were collected from the exposed surface when observed with the naked eye. Manual flotation was used at 36% of the sites and a flotation machine was used at 11% (*Figure 4.20*).

G. Identification

Identification of the plant species from Limenaria, Aghios Ioannis Loukas, the necropolis of Limenas, Ftelia, Sarakenos Cave, and Ipsili was carried out by the author with the help of reference material, identification keys, and the relevant literature (Schoch et al. 1988; Berggren 1969, 1981; Beijerinck 1976).

Einkorn (*Triticum monococcum* L.) and emmer wheat (*Triticum dicoccum* Schubl.)

Both einkorn and emmer wheat are represented in our samples by grain, glume bases, and spikelet forks (*Figures 4.21* and *4.22*).

Einkorn grains are elongated and thin. The ventral and dorsal sides are longitudinally curved, and the grains are pointed at both ends. The ventral furrow is narrow and the dorsal side has a sharp ridge. Einkorn spikelet forks are smaller and narrower than those of emmer, and the secondary scar is wider in relation to the total of the spikelet fork. Emmer grains had a typical narrow shape, with the maximum lateral height closely behind the embryo and a flat ventral side. The width of the fork in emmer spikelet forks is greater than in einkorn, the secondary scar is smaller, and the glume base is larger.

Cultural Period	Cultural components	percentage
Aceramic Neolithic	5	4%
Early Neolithic	9	7%
Middle Neolithic	10	8%
Late/Final Neolithic	26	21%
Early Bronze Age	14	12%
Middle Bronze Age	10	8%
Late Bronze Age	26	21%
Proto-Geometric	6	5%
Geometric	4	3%
Archaïc	5	4%
Clasic	6	5%
Hellenistic	2	2%
Total	123	100%

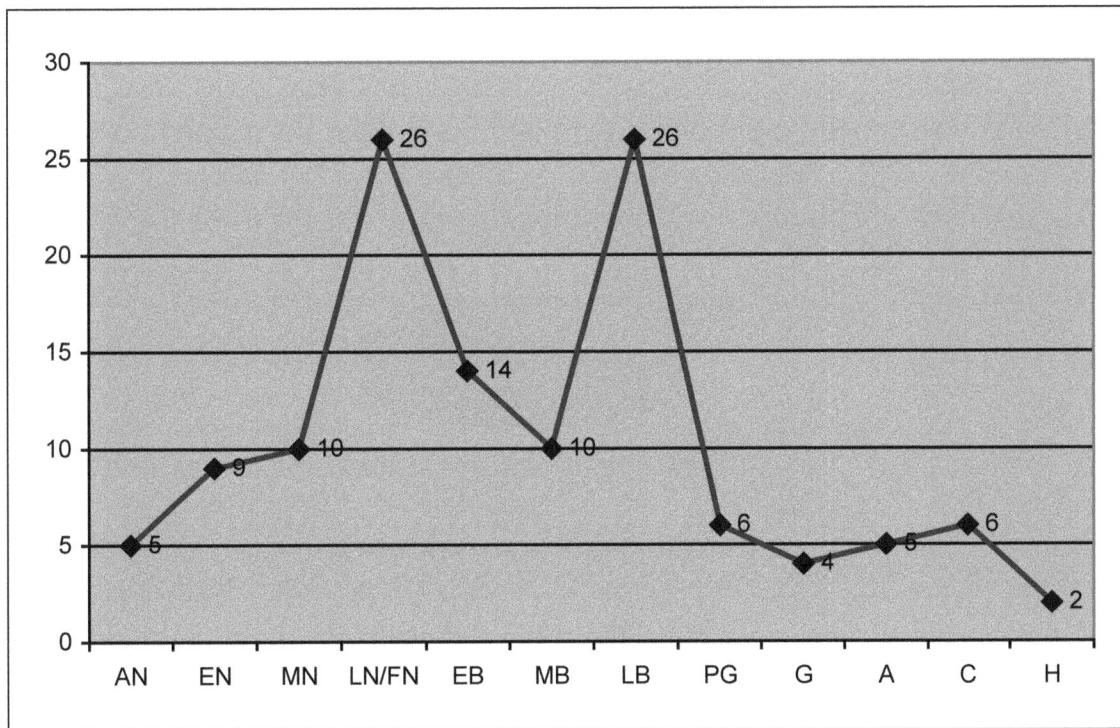

Figure 4.18: Number of cultural components with plant remains. Total sites=79, Total Components=123. (the sites of Chamalevri-Rethymno (Middle Minoan), Midea at Nemea (Late Bronze) and Plylla Vrachos (Late Archaic) are not included here)

Context	Number	Percentage
Silo	1	1%
Rural Sanctuary	10	6%
Occupation level	58	36%
Cave	6	4%
Well/Pit	10	6%
Hearths	11	7%
Destruction layer	29	18%
Wall	5	3%
Potery	9	5%
Kiln	2	2%
Urban Sanctuary	1	1%
Grenary	2	2%
Not specified	16	10%
Total	160	100%

Figure 4.19: Numbers and percentages of archaeological contexts

Technique	Number	Percentage
☐ Water-sieving	44	36%
◾ Flotation machine	14	11%
◼ Naked eye	65	53%
Total	123	100%

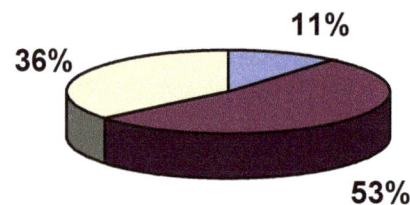

Figure 4.20: Graphic showing in percentages the recovery techniques of macro-botanical remains

Two-grained einkorn was not observed in our samples, although grains from two-grained spikelets are similar to those of emmer and distinguishing the species can be problematic. Caryopses from two-seeded einkorn are broader than they are thick (Hansen 1991, p. 85) and the T/B index is between 1 and 1.79 with a medium of 1.32 (Renfrew 1973a, p. 48).

Oat (*Avena* sp.)
Only caryopses of the oats have been preserved in our samples.

Identification among the *Avena* species (*Avena fatua, Avena sterilis Avena sativa)* is possible only when glumes and spikelets are preserved. The manner in which the spikelets separate from the plant in maturity is the identifying characteristic of the species (Thomas and Jones 1976: p. 2, cited in Hansen 1991, p. 83). Common oat caryopses are narrow-ellipsoid with a somewhat marked longitudinal furrow on the ventral side.

Grass pea (*Lathyrus sativus* L./*Lathyrus cicera* L.)
Lathyrus seeds are of rectangular shape, with a protruding embryo in the lateral view and triangular shape of the proximal face. Identification between *Lathyrus cicera* and *Lathyrus sativus* is not always possible (Kroll 1979), but biometric criteria, such as the length of the seed, can be used to identify the species. *Lathyrus cicera* length ranges between 2.5 and 4 mm, and *Lathyrus sativus* between 4 and 7 mm (Marinval 1986b, Zohary and Hopf 2000, Buxó 1997).

In our samples, 6000 seeds of grass pea discovered at the Neolithic site of Ftelia are attributed to *Lathyrus cicera* (*Figure 4.23*) (Megaloudi and Marinval 2002; Megaloudi et al. 2003). In order to identify the species, 560 seeds were measured. Their length was between 3.8 and 4.1 mm (*Table 4.1*). Only 90 seeds were slightly larger than 4 mm, but these could be seeds from the top of the tegument.

Figure 4.21 : Einkorn remains from Sarakenos cave

Figure 4.22: Einkorn spikelets from Sarakenos cave

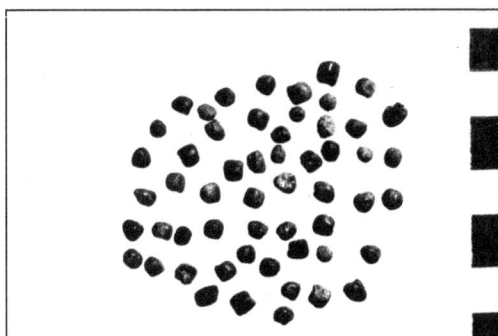

Figure 4.23: Remains of Lathyrus cicera from Ftelia (Mykonos)

Grape (*Vitis vinifera* L./ *Vitis vinifera* L. ssp. *sylvestris* [CC Gmelin] Hegi.)

Wild grape pips (*Vitis vinifera* L. ssp. *sylvestris*) are small, globular to heart-shaped, and have a short stalk; grape pips of the domesticated variety (*Vitis vinifera*) are larger and more ovate, with a longer stalk (Stummer 1911; Smith and Jones 1990). In order to distinguish the two subspecies, archaeobotanists use the breadth-to-length indices (Stummer indices): B/L indices of 0.44 to 0.53 characterize domesticated vine while and indices between 0.76 and 0.83 indicate the wild variety. Charring has a major impact on the shape and of seeds, however, and pips of the domesticated vine might, if their ratios were altered by charring, present measures of the wild variety (Schliemann 1953; Logothetis

1970; Kroll 1983; Smith and Jones 1990). The ratio of stalk length to total seed length has been proposed as a better distinguishing criterion of the two subspecies (Smith and Jones 1990). In 1996, M. Mangaffa and Kotsakis proposed four formulae for the distinction of wild and cultivated vine pips. The formulae, based on the vine-pip measurements carried out on modern domesticated and wild populations, proposed to measure the length of the stalk, the placement of chalaza length, and the indices length of stalk to length and placement of chalaza to length.

Grape pips occur in our samples from the necropolis of Limenas, dating to the 4th century B.C. The low number of these finds (10 whole pips and 12 fragmented), and the absence of chalaza on the preserved pips, meant that the Mangaffa and Kotsakis method could not be applied (*Figure 4.24*). The preservation of part of the pericarp, which was visible as an amorphous black mass surrounding the seed, indicates that whole fruits were burnt. Charring experiments carried out with grape vines show differential carbonization of fresh and dried fruit (Margariti and Jones, in press). While dried raisins shrivel up and swell after being charred, it is fresh grapes react differently. The soft and juicy parts of the fruit boil away, leaving a black mass surrounding the seed.

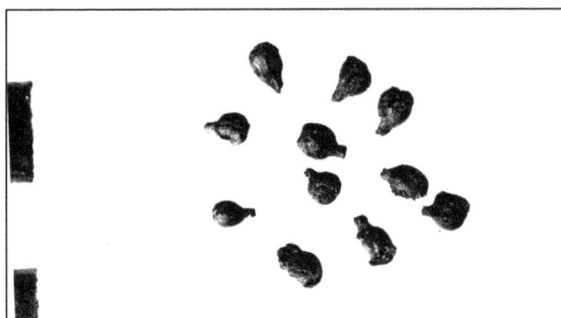

Figure 4.24: Grape remains from the Necropolis of Thasos

Garlic (*Allium sativum* L.)

Garlic cloves are recognized by their curved angular shape, with obliquely set blunt points at both ends. They were discovered related to a funeral burnt offering (*pyra*) at the necropolis of Limenas (4th century B.C.). Measurements of the cloves showed that they are 15 to 19 mm in length (*Table 4.2*) which indicates the cultivated species *Allium sativum* L. This is the first documented archaeobotanical evidence of the presence of this species in Greece (*Figure 4.25*).

Walnut (*Juglans regia* L.)

Walnuts are thick oval nuts with a point. The shells' halves have a broad margin and an irregular surface with deep grooves and a pitted inner side. Walnut remains—consisting of a large fragment of shell presenting the characteristic surface of the stone and part of the broad margin—were discovered at a 4th century grave at the necropolis of Limenas.

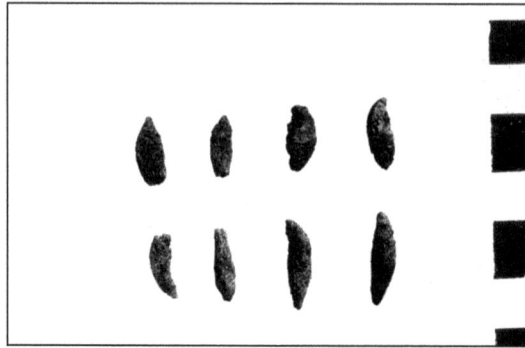

Figure 4.25: Garlic remains from the Necropolis of Thasos

Square 12, layer 5	Length	Breathd	Thickness	L/B	B/T
Average N=228	3.9	3.5	3.4	1.14	1.02
Stand. Dev.	0.57	0.49	0.52	0.22	0.17
Minimum	2.5	2.1	2	0.65	0.56
Maximum	5.6	4.7	4.6	2.2	1.8
Square 12, layer 6	**Length**	**Breathd**	**Thickness**	**L/B**	**B/T**
Average N=23	3.84	3.41	3.45	1.13	0.98
Stand. Dev.	0.37	0.42	0.34	0.08	0.07
Minimum	2.9	2.7	2.5	1.02	0.85
Maximum	4.4	4.2	4	1.3	1.11
Square 12-16, layer 5	**Length**	**Breathd**	**Thickness**	**L/B**	**B/T**
Average N=57	4.12	3.69	3.77	1.11	0.98
Stand. Dev.	0.39	0.4	0.33	0.09	0.08
Minimum	3.5	2.9	3.3	0.9	0.8
Maximum	5.2	4.6	4.6	1.12	1.1
Square 16, layer 5	**Length**	**Breathd**	**Thickness**	**L/B**	**B/T**
Average N=72	3.82	3.4	3.4	1.12	0.98
Stand. Dev.	0.33	0.3	0.26	0.09	0.08
Minimum	3	2.7	2.8	0.94	0.79
Maximum	4.6	4.1	4	1.39	1.17
Square 16, layer 6	**Length**	**Breathd**	**Thickness**	**L/B**	**B/T**
Average N=34	3.84	3.4	3.5	1.13	0.97
Stand. Dev.	0.42	0.45	0.39	0.09	0.08
Minimum	3	2.5	2.7	0.95	0.87
Maximum	4.5	4.4	4	1.33	1.16
Square 11, layer 6	**Length**	**Breathd**	**Thickness**	**L/B**	**B/T**
Average N=12	3.62	3.2	3.3	1.12	0.97
Stand. Dev.	0.46	0.52	0.44	0.08	0.07
Minimum	2.9	2.6	2.8	1.02	0.89
Maximum	4.3	4.1	4	1.25	1.09

Table 4.1: Measurements of Lathyrus cicera (Ftelia, Mykonos)

	Length	Breathd
Minimum	14.7	4.5
Average N=8	16.5	5.0
Maximum	18.9	5.9

Table 4.2: Measurements Allium sativum

CHAPTER 5

THE HISTORY OF WILD AND CULTIVATED PLANTS

This chapter presents the main plant species that emerge from the archaeobotanical analysis of the sites mentioned in *Chapter 4*. This list is not an exhaustive, but it contains those species that, according to the archaeobotanical record, seem to have played an important role in the Greek diet throughout prehistoric and historic times. I have adduced literary evidence about various species, when it is available. It is important to note that the written sources used in this chapter include a much wider range of plant species, but in this work are used only in relation to the species described, and not for a general discussion of food plants in Greece in antiquity.

A. Cereals

"Cereals" in this book refers to wheat, barley, rye, oat, and rice. Wheat and barley seem to be the traditional staples in Greece from Neolithic times onward, and are found at nearly all prehistoric and historic sites. Rye, oat, and rice are included in this section as they are recorded in the archaeobotanical record, but they seem to be either weeds of cultivation (rye, oat) or intrusive (rice).

Emmer wheat (*Triticum dicoccum* Schübl.)

Hulled emmer wheat is a low-yielding, tall (2 m) cultivated tetraploid wheat. Together with einkorn, it was among the Neolithic founder species; it appeared at the earliest farming sites and spread west as far as northern Europe and east to India and beyond. Today emmer is on the verge of extinction, its cultivation restricted to remote mountainous areas scattered across Europe, southwest Asia, India, and Ethiopia (Zohary and Hopf 2000).

Emmer wheat was collected from the wild long before its domestication. It seems that the species is related to a wild wheat native to the Near East *Triticum dicoccoides* (Korn) Aarons that its distribution is limited to the "arc" of the Near East (Zohary and Hopf 2000). *Triticum dicoccum* may be cultivated in either winter or spring (Brinkkemper 1993), but in central Europe it is considered a spring crop as the young plant cannot tolerate frost (Körber-Grohne 1987).

Emmer wheat was the most common constituent of the crop assemblage that started agriculture in the Aegean region around the 7th millennium B.C. However, a glume identified as belonging to *Triticum dicoccum* is reported from the Upper Paleolithic levels of Theopetra Cave (Larissa) in Greece (Mangaffa 2000).

Emmer wheat is the main species of Pre-Pottery Neolithic sites in Thessaly (Renfrew 1966, 1969, 1973b, 1989) and

is very well represented in Early Neolithic levels of Nea Nikomedeia (van Zeist and Bottema 1971) and Prodromos (Halstead and Jones 1980). The species continued in wide use at least until the beginnings of the Iron Age.

Most authorities have considered emmer to be the main cereal for the whole of Greece throughout the Neolithic and Bronze Age (Zohary and Hopf 2000; Renfrew 1973, 1979; Hansen 1988, 2000) or have seen emmer and einkorn as being of equal importance (Hubbard 1975). The archaeobotanical evidence from Kastanas and Assiros Toumba in Macedonia, however, suggests that in the Late Bronze Age einkorn predominated over emmer (Kroll 1983; Jones 1979, Jones et al. 1986; Wardle 1989). This is not the case in Dimitra (Renfrew 1997) and Mandalo (Valamoti 2004), where emmer dominates in the samples. In the southern part of Greece, the archaeobotanical finds from the last phase of Late Bronze Age at Tirynth (Kroll 1982) and from the Late Minoan Unexplored Mansion at Knossos in Crete (Jones 1984b) indicate that, at least at those sites, emmer was the dominant cereal, followed by hulled barley. This seems also to have been the case in Early/Middle Bronze Age Lerna (Hopf 1961, 1962a).

According to the archaeobotanical finds, emmer was a rare commodity at most sites in northern Greece. While the species is found in much smaller quantities than einkorn, emmer is always present in the samples, and very well represented from Early Neolithic times. On the contrary, in southern Greece, emmer largely dominates and in some cases is the only cereal represented in the samples (see *Tables 5.3* and *5.4*).

The archaeobotanical evidence from Protogeometric and Geometric levels at Iolkos in Thessaly (Jones 1982) suggests that six rowed barley (*Hordeum vulgare*) underwent considerable development at that time and predominated over emmer. The decline of emmer in relation to barley and bread wheat is also confirmed by the archaeobotanical record of historic periods: *Triticum dicoccum* is reported only in small quantities from the 8th /6th century B.C levels at Delphi (Luce et al. forthcoming), and from the 4th century B.C. levels at the sanctuary of Artemis at Kalapodi (Kroll 1993) and at Kastanas (Kroll 1983).

In Classical Greece, emmer was identified under the names *zeia* (ζεία) and *olira* (όλυρα) (Amouretti 1986). Classical literary sources denigrate emmer as a food for humans: Pliny indicates that it was not important in Greece, and Artemidoros regarded the appearance of *zeia* in a dream as a sign of poverty (Sallares 1991, p. 365). Despite the testimnoia of Pliny and Artemidorus on emmer wheat, *chondros* (χόνδρος), however, a kind of bulgur made from emmer, was a very popular food staple in antiquity (Ath. *Deipn.* 108f–116a). *Chondros* is probably the *alica* of the Romans (Tromaras 1988), and was also consumed in Byzantine times (Koukoules 1952). It was probably similar to the bulgar of modern times, a cereal product widely used in the Mediterranean and the Middle East as a side dish (Abdalla 1990). Bulgur was common in modern Greece until a generation ago, and it is still very popular among the Greeks from the Black Sea area and the Caucasus Mountains.

Einkorn wheat (*Triticum monococcum* L.)
Einkorn wheat (*Triticum monoccocum*) is a hulled wheat with delicate ears and spikelets. Most cultivated einkorn varieties produce one grain per spikelet, but varieties with two grains also exist. It is a small (70 cm maximum height), relatively low-yielding plant. While it produces bread of poor rising quality, the plant was useful because it can survive on poor soils without manure (Körber-Grohne 1987).

Einkorn was one of the principal crops in the Neolithic food production of the Near East, and, together with emmer and barley, it played a major role in the early spread of Neolithic agriculture. *Triticum monococcum* today is a relic crop, sporadically grown in Western Turkey, the Balkan countries, Germany, Switzerland, Spain, and in the Caucasus (Zohary and Hopf 2000). The ancestor of the species seems to be a weedy wheat that spreads over Western Asia and penetrates into the southern Balkans and is referred to as "wild einkorn" or *Triticum boeticum*. Wild einkorn has been identified in Greece, but this find is limited to a single grain discovered at the Mesolithic levels of Theopetra Cave in Thessaly (Mangaffa 2000).

Einkorn is thought to have been the main cereal of northern Greece, at least for the Late Bronze Age (Hansen 1988). Archaeobotanical evidence from the sites of Kastanas and Assiros Toumba indicates that einkorn, followed by millet and bitter vetch, were the main components of the Late Bronze Age agriculture (Kroll 1979, 1983 ; Jones 1979; Jones et al. 1986; Wardle 1989). Further south, in the region of Boeotia, einkorn is probably the only cereal identified at Gla (Jones 1995). In southern Greece, as stated above, emmer wheat seems to have been the main cereal, according to the finds at Tirynth (Kroll 1982) and Lerna (Hopf 1961, 1962a).

The archaeobotanical evidence from sites dated prior to the Late Bronze Age, however, suggests that the dominance of einkorn in northern Greece was not limited to the Late Bronze Age. *Triticcum monococcum* predominates in the samples from that region at least from Middle Neolithic times: einkorn is the main cereal in the Middle and Late Neolithic samples from Sitagroi in Macedonia (Renfrew 1969, 1973a, 1973b: Renfrew et al.

1986) and in the Middle Neolithic samples from Limenaria (Megaloudi forthcoming). In the Late Neolithic samples of Makriyalos I and II (last quarter of the 6th millennium B.C. and second quarter of the 5th millennium B.C.), Arkadikos, Dikili Tash, and Makri, einkorn predominates by far, suggesting, according to Valamoti (2004, p.114) "a regional pattern throughout the Neolithic and Bronze Age of northern Greece." This pattern seems to exist in the region of Boeotia, in the area of Kopais: large einkorn concentrations were discovered in the Late Neolithic levels of the Sarakenos Cave (Megaloudi in press) and in the Early/Middle Neolithic levels of Balomenos Toumba (Sarpaki 1995). In Thessaly, einkorn predominates in the samples of Zarkos (Jones and Halstead 1993; Becker 1991), while it is very well represented in Arapi and Pefkakia (Kroll 1983).

The predominance of einkorn over emmer in northern Greece is also observed at Balkan sites dated to the 5th and 4th millennia B.C., such as Selevac and Gomolava in Serbia (McLaren and Hubbard 1990; van Zeist 1978) and Gulmenitsa in Bulgaria (McLaren and Hubbard 1990), as well as at 6th millennium sites of northern and southeastern Europe (Kroll 1991). The same predominance of einkorn has also been noted for Neolithic Cyprus (Miller 1991).

Several economic, cultural, and environmental factors have been considered to explain the predominance of einkorn over other wheats (van Zeist 1981; Miller 1991; Dennell 1985; Barker 1985). For some sites, such as Kastanas and Assiros Toumba, the predominance of einkorn is attributed to the hardiness of the species, its capacity for long-term storage (Halstead 1994), and the demands of a growing population, and the need for surplus to be exchanged for Mycenaean pottery (Kroll 1983).

The evidence for the predominance of einkorn over wheat, however, looks somewhat different when we consider the frequency of the species. *Tables 5.3* and *5.4* present the results of the data analysis carried out on all finds of emmer and einkorn for all sites mentioned in this study. The finds were analyzed geographically and chronologically in order to examine the presence of both species in northern and southern Greece. These results indicate that, in terms of frequency of occurrence, both species were present in northern Greece in the same percentage from Early Neolithic to Early Bronze. In terms of the number of individual finds, einkorn predominates by far over emmer. In southern Greece, however, emmer predominates over einkorn both in frequency and in the number of individual finds. This discrepancy in the representation of the species— depending on whether we examine the number of individual finds or the presence/absence of the species— could be attributed to the limited scale of sampling and the limited publication of results from prehistoric sites. Valamoti (2004) argues that cultural factors underlie the preference for einkorn and that Neolithic farmers, at least at some sites, made a choice to cultivate this hardy species.

In Classical times einkorn was identified under the name of *tifi* (τίφη) (Theophr. *Hist. pl.* 8.9.2). Like emmer, einkorn was gradually replaced by hulled barley and bread wheat in subsequent periods.

Free-threshing wheat (*Triticum aestivum/durum* L.)
Free-threshing wheat appears to be part of the Neolithic crop list for Greece (Renfrew 1973), but the species is not common in the Neolithic archaeobotanical assemblages: its presence is reported from Early Neolithic Otzaki and Sesklo (Kroll 1983), but it was only in the Late Neolithic that the presence of free-threshing wheat started to become more common (*Table 5.5*). There is evidence that free-threshing wheat was grown at Late Neolithic Makri and, to a lesser extent, at Arkadikos, as a crop in its own right (Valamoti 2004). The species is also reported at Late Neolithic Dimitra (Renfrew 1997), Thessaly (Renfrew 1966), Skoteini Cave at Tharounia (Mangaffa 1993), and the Aegean islands (Thermi on Lesbos and Kalythies Cave on Rhodes: see Valamoti 1992; Halstead and Jones 1987). According to Valamoti (2004, p. 114) the limited representation of free-threshing wheat in the Neolithic archaeobotanical assemblages reflects the choice of the Neolithic farmers to cultivate this crop on a very limited scale; they would have preferred glume wheats that are more resistant to insect or fungi attack.

From the Late Bronze age onward the species was even more common. At Assiros Toumba (1350 B.C.) free-threshing wheat was cultivated as a crop, as is evidenced by its predominance in some samples (Jones et al. 1986). Free-threshing wheats are also reported from the Unexplored Mansion at Knossos (Jones 1984b), from Aghia Triada in Crete (Follieri 1979), and from the Late Bronze Age levels at Kalapodi (Kroll 1993) and at Delphi (Luce et al., forthcoming). Free-threshing wheat seems to have been common in the historical periods as well. The species is reported from the Geometric deposits of Iolkos (Jones 1982), Delphi (Luce et al., forthcoming), and Kastanas (Kroll 1983). At Kalapodi free-threshing wheat is very well represented, and even replaces other wheats as the main crop besides barley (Kroll 1993). The increasing popularity of the species could indicate culinary innovation, or the existence of varieties that were better adapted to local conditions. Free-threshing wheat is also reported from deposits at Delphi dating to the 8th and 7th centuries B.C. (Luce et al., forthcoming), from the 5th-century B.C. sanctuary of Demeter and Kore at Corinth (Bookidis et al. 1999), from the sanctuary of Hera on Samos, where a single grain was identified (Kucan 1995), and from Limenas on Thasos, in deposits of the 4th century B.C. (Megaloudi 2004).

In the Classical period free-threshing wheat was probably called *pyros*. Durum wheat was sometimes called *pyros*, but it seems that this could be distinguished as *semidalis;* for an analysis of the origin and spread of classical naked

wheats the reader is referred to Sallares 1991, pp. 309–361). Flour made of durum wheat was probably also called *semidalis*, while the flour of *pyros* was called *aleuros* (Hom. *Od.* 20.109; Dalby 1996). A. Dalby (1996, p. 240, n. 224) argues that *pyros* cannot be bread wheat, since *pyros* was well known in Greece "from the time of the earliest literature while archaeobotany suggests that bread wheat will have been almost or entirely unknown there at that time." Dalby prefers the term *silignion*, used in Theophrastus (*Hist. pl.* 8.4.3) and in Galen (*On the property of foods* 1.2.5), to designate bread wheat.

Until very recently it was not possible to distinguish between archaeobotanical remains of tetraploid and hexaploid naked grains, and the earliest remains of the species must be attributed to tetraploid durum-like forms and not hexaploid bread wheat (Zohary and Hopf 2000, p.50). In recent years it has been pointed out that the structure of rachis fragments could be used as distinguishing traits between tetraploid and hexaploid naked grains (Jacomet 1987; Hillman et al. 1996; Maier 1996). Zohary and Hopf (2000, p.34) give a set of five morphological traits (lower part of the glumes, shape of the rachis node and internode, structure of the edge of the internode, and the transverse section through the internode) that seem to be diagnostically reliable for such an identification. Hexaploid bread wheat derives from an hybridization between a wild grass (*Aegilops squarrosa*) and a cultivated tetraploid wheat (*Triticum turgidum*) that must have come into existence outside the "fertile crescent," probably between 6000 and 5000 B.C. (van Zeist 1976; Zohary and Hopf 2000). Naked wheat is reported from Greek Late Neolithic sites, where in some cases it was cultivated as a crop (see above). Zohary and Hopf (2000, p.57) argue that from the 5th millennium B.C., the increasingly common finds of free-threshing wheat in the archaeological assemblages could represent not only tetraploid forms, but hexaploid cultivars as well. Consequently, free-threshing bread wheat could have been known to Greek Late Neolithic farmers and it could have been mentioned in early literature. Theophrastus (*Hist. pl.* 8.4.2–3) groups together all the naked wheats into a single *genos* ("kind") but his allusion to *polla gene* ("many kinds") indicates that the different varieties of free-threshing wheat were known to ancient authors. Correlation between the botanical scientific names of the species and those mentioned in written sources, however, is very difficult, if not impossible (see also Kroll 2000).

Although wheat is often mentioned in written sources, is not easy to locate the regions where it was cultivated, as *sitos* (σίτος), the word that appears most frequently, could indicate wheat and/or barley (Amouretti 1986). The word *artos* (άρτος) is used to describe a wheat loaf-type bread made of wheat flour. Ancient sources indicate the existence of various kinds of flour; both white and brown bread were known, and the latter was considered to have better digestive qualities (Amouretti 1986).

Species	AN	EN	MN	LN/FN	EBA	MBA	LBA	PG	G	A	C
N of components	5	9	9	19	8	4	10	4	3	3	3
Hordeum vulgare	60	55.6	66.7	79	75	75	50	100	100	100	67
Hordeum vulg.nudum	20	33.3	22.2	21	0	0	10	25	0	0	0
Hordeum distichum	40	0	0	5.3	0	0	0	0	0	0	0
Panicum miliaceum	20	11.1	22.2	10.5	12.5	0	40	50	33.3	33.3	33.3
Secale cereale	0	0	0	5.3	0	0	10	50	0	0	0
Triticum aestivum	0	33.3	11.1	42.1	50	25	40	75	100	66.7	66.7
Triticum dicoccum	100	77.8	88.9	73.7	75	75	60	75	100	66.7	66.7
Triticum monococcum	60	77.8	88.9	73.7	75	50	50	75	66.7	66.7	33.3
Triticum spelta	0	0	0	10.5	37.5	0	20	50	33.3	0	0

Table 5.3: Percentage of Appearances of Cereal species per component (northern Greece)

AN: Aceramic Neolithic, EN: Early Neolithic, MN: Middle Neolithic, LN/FN: Late Neolithic, Final Neolithic, EBA: Early Bronze Age, MBA: Middle Bronze Age, LBA: Late Bronze Age, PG: Proto-Geometric, G: Geometric, A: Archaic, C: Classic

Species	AN	EN	MN	LN/FN	EBA	MBA	LBA	PG	G	A	C
N of components	0	0	1	7	6	6	7	2	1	2	3
Hordeum vulgare	0	0	0	57.1	50	33.3	25	0	0	50	33
Hordeum vulg.nudum	0	0	0	42.3	16.7	50	6.2	0	0	0	0
Hordeum distichum	0	0	100	14.1	0	0	2	12.5	0	0	33.3
Panicum miliaceum	0	0	0	0	0	0	6.2	0	0	0	0
Secale cereale	0	0	0	0	0	0	0	0	0	0	0
Triticum aestivum	0	0	0	14.2	0	0	12.5	0	0	50	33.3
Triticum dicoccum	0	0	0	42.9	50	33.3	25	0	0	50	0
Triticum monococcum	0	0	0	28.6	16.7	0	18.8	0	0	0	0
Triticum spelta	0	0	0	0	0	0	6.2	0	0	0	0

Table 5.4: Percentage of Appearances of Cereal species per component (southern Greece)

AN: Aceramic Neolithic, EN: Early Neolithic, MN: Middle Neolithic, LN/FN: Late Neolithic, Final Neolithic, EBA: Early Bronze Age, MBA: Middle Bronze Age, LBA: Late Bronze Age, PG: Proto-Geometric, G: Geometric, A: Archaic, C: Classic

Species	AN	EN	MN	LN/FN	EBA	MBA	LBA	PG	G	A	C
N of components	5	9	10	26	14	10	26	6	4	5	6
Hordeum vulgare	60	56	60	73	64	50	35	67	75	80	50
Hordeum vulg.nudum	20	33	20	27	7	30	8	17	0	0	0
Hordeum distichum	40	0	10	8	0	0	0	0	0	0	0
Hordeum dist.nudum	20	0	0	0	0	0	0	0	0	0	0
Panicum miliaceum	20	11	20	8	7	0	19	33	25	20	17
Secale cereale	0	0	0	4	0	0	4	33	0	0	0
Setaria italica	0	0	0	0	7	0	4	17	0	0	0
Triitcum aestivum	0	33	10	35	29	10	23	50	75	60	50
Triticum dicoccum	100	78	80	65	64	50	38	50	75	60	33
Triticum monococcum	60	78	80	62	50	20	31	50	50	40	17
Triticum spelta	0	0	0	8	21	0	12	33	25	0	0

Table 5.5: Percentage of Appearances of Cereal species per component (total)

AN: Aceramic Neolithic, EN: Early Neolithic, MN: Middle Neolithic, LN/FN: Late Neolithic, Final Neolithic, EBA: Early Bronze Age, MBA: Middle Bronze Age, LBA: Late Bronze Age, PG: Proto-Geometric, G: Geometric, A: Archaic, C: Classic

Spelt wheat (*Triticum spelta* L.)

Spelt wheat is a hulled wheat that grows in the plateau of Iran, Armenia, and Turkmenistan (Körber-Grohne 1987). The species is today a relic crop; spelt wheat was abandoned mainly because farmers found other wheats easier to grow. Spelt's grain has a close-fitting husk that makes it harder to thresh, and its very long straw means that summer winds can blow the plants down (Körber-Grohne 1987). The species is now returning as a crop, and small quantities of spelt are grown in northern Spain and southern Germany. Because spelt wheat is very rich in gluten it is prized by bakers.

Triticum spelta seeds present morphological similarities with those of *Triticum dicoccum*; in archaeological remains spelt wheat can be distinguished by the upper rachis segment and the characteristic structure of the glumes.

Spelt wheat was already grown in the Caspian belt by the 5th millennium B.C. and the species must have reached Europe during the 4th millennium B.C., as it is reported from the settlement of Sakharova in Moldavia (Janushevich 1984, cited in Zohary and Hopf 2000).

In Greece spelt wheat appears to have been a later arrival. The species is reported from the Late Neolithic levels of the Macedonian sites Dikili Tash (Matterne 1993) and Stavroupoli (Margariti 2002a). Spelt wheat seems to have become an established crop during the Bronze Age: it is reported from the Early Bronze Age levels of Skoteini Cave in Euboea (Mangaffa 1993) and of Archondiko in Macedonia (Valamoti 1997). It is also reported from Middle Bronze Age Argissa (Hopf 1962b; Kroll 1981, 1983), while at Assiros Toumba spelt wheat was found mixed with emmer and probably represented maslin crops (Jones 1979; Jones et al. 1986; Wardle 1989). Small quantities of spelt wheat were also found at Kastanas in levels dated to the end of the Bronze Age (Kroll 1983), and from the Geometric levels of Iolkos (Jones 1982) and Kalapodi (Kroll 1993). It seems that spelt wheat was introduced in Greece from the northern Balkans and Central Europe—where it occurs at an earlier date than in Greece (Zohary and Hopf 2000)—but the archaeobotanical evidence indicates that it was probably cultivated as a secondary crop.

Timopheev's wheat (*Triticum timopheevi* Zhuk.)

Triticum timopheevi is a tetraploid species that comprises both cultivated and wild forms. The species derives from a group of brittle wild forms from Central Asia, known as *Triticum timopheevi* ssp. *araraticum* (Zohary and Hopf 2000). In the archaeobotanical assemblages the species appears rarely, and it was first identified at Bronze Age Feudvar in the region of Vojvodina in Serbia (Kroll, in preparation).

Cultivated timopheev is hulled, and its close morphological similarities to cultivated emmer and einkorn makes its identification difficult. In a recent publication (Jones et al. 2000) it was argued that the morphology of the glume bases and the spikelet forks can be used to distinguish the "new" species from emmer and einkorn.

Glume bases and spikelets forks identified as belonging to *Triticum timopheevi* are reported from Late Neolithic Makri, Arkadikos, Makrigialos, and from Late Bronze Age Assiros (Valamoti 2004; Jones 1979; Jones et al. 1986; Wardle 1989). The identification of these finds is based on the calculation of diploid and tetraploid spikelets separately on the basis of grains and glume bases from Assiros (Jones et al. 2000). The authors argue that some of the grain identified as emmer or einkorn in archaeobotanical assemblages could have originated from the new wheat. A large-scale reexamination of emmer or einkorn remains from archaeobotanical assemblages, however, has not been attempted.

The status of timopheev wheat in Neolithic and Bronze Age agriculture is not yet clearly understood and the evidence is still scant. It is very likely that the role of the species will be much better understood in a few years.

Barley (*Hordeum* sp.)

Barley (*Hordeum* sp.) was, along with wheat, one of the main cereals of Neolithic food production. The wild ancestor of cultivated barley is well established: a wild and weedy barley form, *Hordeum vulgare* ssp. *spontaneum*, that is spread over the eastern Mediterranean basin and the western Asiatic countries (Zohary and Hopf 2000). Barley is a very resistant species that can tolerate poor and dry soils, as well as some salinity, and this made the species well adapted to the climatic conditions of the Aegean.

Domesticated barley can be divided into two principal types:

- Six-rowed forms (*Hordeum vulgare hexastichum*), in which the three spikelets in each triplet bear seed and are usually all awned. Each ear has six rows of fertile spikelets. Six-row barley is a winter crop and is mainly used in human diet or as a fodder.

- Two-rowed forms (*Hordeum distichum*), in which only the median spikelet in each triplet is fertile and usually has a prominent awn. Each ear has only two rows of fertile spikelet. Two-rowed barley is usually cultivated as a spring crop and is the preferred species for brewing beer.

Wild and cultivated barley have hulled grains but naked varieties are also known.

Cultivated barley, which emerged in Greece during the 6th millennium B.C., is represented by both two-rowed and six-rowed forms and also by naked grains. Wild barley (*Hordeum vulgare* ssp. *spontaneum*) is identified in the Mesolithic levels at Franchthi Cave (Hansen 1991).

37

Naked six-rowed barley (*Hordeum vulgare nudum*) is present in Aceramic and Early Neolithic levels at Argissa and Otzaki (Renfrew 1966; Kroll 1983), but always in small quantities. The species is also reported from Middle Neolithic Limenaria (Megaloudi, forthcoming) and Argissa (Hopf 1962b; Kroll 1981, 1983), as well as in Early, Middle and Late Bronze Age levels at Lerna (Hopf 1961, 1962a) Argissa (Hopf 1962b), Athenian Agora (Hopf 1971), and Delphi (Luce et al., forthcoming). Finds of six-rowed naked barley are not reported from the historical periods.

Two-rowed barley occurs in Aceramic Neolithic levels at Ghediki and Sesklo (Renfrew 1966), from the Early Neolithic levels at Soufli (Renfrew 1966), from the Middle and Late Neolithic levels of Franchthi Cave (Hansen 1991), and from Late Neolithic sites in Macedonia (Valamoti 2004) and Saliagos (Renfrew 1968).

Six-rowed barley is a common find in Greece throughout the Neolithic period and, as *Table 5.5* show, it seems to have replaced two-rowed barley by the beginning of the Bronze Age. It seems that Neolithic farmers had the choice between the two barley varieties; six-rowed barley was probably favored because it can produce three times as much grain as two-rowed barley.

In Classical times barley, identified as *krithi* (κριθή), was the typical food of Sparta and was also widely cultivated in Attica (Sallares 1991; Amouretti 1986). M.-C. Amouretti (1986) notes that barley played a very important role in human food consumption in Classical Greece; even when Aristophanes seems to denigrate barley, he is referring to Spartiates that were eating only barley, and not to the species (Amouretti 1986). Barley was eaten in the form of *alphita* (άλφιτα) and *maza* (μάζα). *Alphita* was a porridge made of roasted ground barley that Pliny describes as a typical Greek recipe (*HN* 18.72). According to Aristophanes, a wealthy household is one with plenty of *alphita* (*Pl.* 805). In *Lysistrata* (561–564) Aristophanes makes a joke about a phylarch, one of the ten commanders of the Athenian tribal cavalry, who buys *alphita* from an old woman in the market and then eats it out of his bronze helmet.

The most common food in Classical Greece seems to have been *maza*, a mash made of barley and wheat. *Maza* was made of *alphita* and water, sometimes with the addition of honey and milk (Amouretti 1986). This porridge was very common in Athens, at least until the end of the 4th century B.C. (Amouretti 1986). There are several references to *maza* in the comedies of Aristophanes indicating that it symbolized, together with bread, "the human food" (*Peace* 662–664). In the cities people seem to have abandoned other barley preparations in the favor of *maza* (Amouretti 1986, p. 125).

Xenophon refers to the making of *maza* and he considers this porridge as one of the pleasures of man (*Oec.* 10.10, *Cyr.* 1.12). On the other hand, barley bread was

designated for slaves, while grains of fresh barley were considered food for peasants (Amouretti 1986). The armies of Classical Greece ate *alphita,* while for Roman soldiers barley was a punishment (Galen *On the Properties of Foods* 1.11.2).

Barley was thought to have healing properties, and barley gruel, mainly *ptisane* (φθισανή), was recommended by Hippocrates against acute diseases (*Du rég.* 42.3, *Des mal. aig.* 3.17).

Barley Beer
Although barley beer was known in Greece, written sources show that it was considered an inferior, barbaric beverage. The earliest reference to beer comes from Archilochus (7th century B.C.), who speaks of Phrygians or Thracians drinking beer during feasts (reported in Ath. *Deipn.* 10.447a–c). Herodotus comments that the Egyptians use a drink made from barley in place of wine (2.77). Hecataeus of Miletus (6th or early 7th century B.C.) and Hellanicus of Lesbos (5th century B.C.) associate Thracians, especially Paeonians, with beer (Ath. *Deipn.* 10.447a–c). Sophocles comments in *Triptolemus* that drinking inland beer was not pleasant, while in Aeschylus' *Lycurgus*, a character gets drunk on strong beer and becomes boisterous (Curtis 2001, p. 294). The intoxicating power of beer was noticed by Aristotle, who comments that those drinking too much beer always fall over backwards (Curtis 2001, p. 294). H. Martlew suggests that barley beer could have been produced in the Early Minoan (ca. 2200 B.C.) settlement of Myrtos Koryphe in southern Crete (Tzedakis and Martlew 1999, p. 159). Chemical analysis of two pithoi that contained wine indicates that barley and/or a barley product was added to the receptacles. The mere presence of a barley product is not a strong argument for beer making, however, and the evidence is not conclusive. Literary evidence clearly suggests that for the Greeks drinking alcoholic beverages meant drinking wine.

Millets (*Panicum miliaceum* L., *Setaria italica* L.)
Broomcorn millet (*Panicum miliaceum*) and foxtail millet (*Setaria italica*), hardy dehusked cereals that can tolerate intense heat, poor soils, and severe droughts, are grown today in eastern and central Asia, India, the Middle East, and North Africa (Zohary and Hopf 2000). Both species are used boiled and cooked, like rice, or ground for the preparation of porridges. In some countries millets are used in beer brewing (such as for the millet beer of sub-Saharan Africa).

The wild ancestor of *Panicum miliaceum* is not fully established, and the species is related to weedy forms of this millet that are widespread in central Asia, from the Caspian basin to Mongolia (Zohary and Hopf 2000). Foxtail millet (*Setaria italica*) shows close morphological affinities to the wild weed *Setaria viridis* that spread across Eurasia (Zohary and Hopf 2000).

Site	Nea Nikomedia	Achileion	Argissa	Prodromos	Soufli	Sesklo	Otzaki	Balomenos	Giannitsa B
Reference	van Zeist and Bottema 1971	Renfrew 1989	Hopf 1962	Jones and Halstead 1980	Renfrew 1966	Renfrew 1966	Kroll 1983	Sarpaki 1995	Valamoti 1995
Horeum vulgare			x	17		x	x		x
Horeum vulgare nudum	2167		x				x		
Hordeum distichum					10				
Hordeum distichum nudum									
Hordeum sp.		26		12				38	
Panicum miliaceum			x						
Secale cereale									
Triticum aestivum/durum						x	x		x
Triticum dicoccum	2859	47		826	20	x	x		x
Triticum monococcum	274	16		285	4	x	x	450	x
Triticum spelta									
Triticum sp.								51	
Cicer arietinum							1		
Lathyrus cicera								2	
Lathyrus sativus				200					
Lathyrus cicera/sativus								50	
Leguminosae	3						x	64	
Lens culinaris	5431	12		13			x	212	x
Lens esculenta					3				
Pisum sativum	48							21	
Pisum sp.				281	8	x			
Vicia ervilia	37					x	x	2	
Vicia faba									
Linum usitatissimum							x		
Ficus carica						x	x	318	
Amygdalus communis						x			
Cornus mas	3			14					x
Corylus avellana									
Crataegus sp									
Malus sp.									
Olea oleaster									
Olea sp.						x			
Pistacia atlantica									
Pistacia sp.		5							
Pistacia terebinthus								38 (94)	
Pistacia vera									x
Portulaca oleracea						x	x		
Prunus spinosa	1								
Quercus	10	5	x	47		x			
Rubus sp								166	
Sambucus ebulus									
Sambucus sp.									x
Vitis sp.								20	
Vitis sylvestris		1				x		10	x
Astragalus sp.									
Avena sp.		6				x		40	
Boraginaceae									
Bromus cf secalinus						x			
Chenopodiaceae						x	x	1	
Fumaria sp.							x		
Galium aparine								4	
Galium sp.								3	x
Galium spurium						x			
Graminae						x	x	x	
Lolium sp.								5	x
Lolium temulentum								7	x
Plantaginaceae						x	x		
Polygonaceae						x	x	x	x
Rumex sp.								17	x
Stellaria sp.									
Teucrium sp									x

imp = impression, x = present

Table 5.6: Plant remains from Early Neolithic deposits

x=present

( ) mineralised seeds

Site	Dikili Tash	Sitagroi	Achilleion	Sesklo	Otzaki	Zarkos	Balomenos	Francthi	Photoleivos	Limenaria
		Renfrew *et al*				Jones and Halstead				
Reference	Materne 1993	1986	Renfrew 1989	Renfrew 1966	Kroll 1983	1993	Sarpaki 1995	Hansen 1991	Renfrew 1973	Megaloudi in press
Hordeum vulgare		x		x	x	5			x	34
Hordeum vulgare nudum										6
Hordeum distichum								x		
Hordeum distichum nudum										
Hordeum sp.			2				7			1
Panicum miliaceum					x					x
Secale cereale										
Triticum aestivum/durum										2
Triticum dicoccum		x	9	x	x	1			x	5
Triticum monococcum		x	7	x	x	13	338		x	25
Triticum spelta										
Triticum sp.							20			4
Lathyrus cicera								x		7 (1)
Lathyrus sativus										
Lathyrus cicera/sativus							5			
Leguminosae					x		6			11
Lens culinaris	x	x		x	x	1	37	x	x	2
Pisum sativum		x					1			
Pisum sp.			2		x					
Vicia ervilia		x			x	1300	2		x	
Linum usitatissimum				x						
Ficus carica				x	x		89			24 (58)
Cornus mas		x								
Juniperus spp										1
Malus sp.			1							
Pistacia sp.		x	2					x		
Pistacia terebinthus							14			82
Quercus		x	29							
Rubus sp							36			
Vitis sp.										1 (1)
Vitis sylvestris		x			x				x	3
Avena sp.		x	6	x	x		30			
Bromus spp.										1
Chenopodium album										21
Chenopodiaceae							1			11
Fumaria sp.					x					
Fumaria officinalis										1 (1)
Galium sp.								x		
Galium aparine										1
Graminae							8			
Lithospermum arvense			1595	x	x					2
Lolium temulentum					x	1	2			
Medicago sp.					x					
Plantaginaceae				x	x					
Polygonaceae				x	x					2
Polygonum aviculare										5
Rumex spp										2

Table 5.7: Plant remains from Middle Neolithic Deposits

Site	Makri	Dikili Tash	Olynthus	Dimitra	Sitagroi	Zarkos
Reference	Efstratiou *et al* 1998	Materne 1993	Mylonas 1929	Foster 1997; Renfrew 1997	Renfrew *et al* 1986	Jones and Halstead 1993
Hordeum vulgare	x	42		214	x	6
Hordeum vulgare nudum		9				
Hordeum distichum	x					
Hordeum sp.						
Panicum miliaceum			x			
Secale cereale						
Triticum aestivum/durum	x			18		
Triticum dicoccum	x	x		741	x	5
Triticum monococcum	x	x		137	x	9
Triticum spelta		x				
Triticum sp.			x			
Triticum timopheevi?	x					
Cicer arietinum						
Lathyrus cicera						
Lathyrus sativus	x	98				
Lathyrus sp.		97				1
Leguminosae						
Lens culinaris	x	2701		33	x	1
Pisum sativum	x	1				
Pisum sp.		127				
Vicia ervilia	x			498	x	793
Vicia faba						
Ficus carica	x	57	x			
Vitis vinifera				184	x	
Camelina sativa						
Linum usitatissimum	x	2				
Amygdalus communis	x				x	
Arbutus Unedo						
Capparis sp.	x					
Coriandrum sativum						
Cornus mas	x	6		4		
Corylus avellana		1				
Crataegus spp						
Malva sylvestris				3		
Olea sp.					x	
Pistacia sp.					x	
Pistacia terebinthus	x	1		7		
Pistacia vera						
Portulaca oleracea	x					
Pyrus sp.		6				
Pyrus/Malus						
Quercus		x			x	
Rubus fruticosus	x	8				
Sambucus ebulus	x	1				
Sambucus sp.				1		
Vitis sp.						
Vitis sylvestris		57		26	x	
Aegilops sp.						
Astragalus sp.						
Avena sp.	x	1		5		1
Boraginaceae		1				
Bromus sp.	x			1		
Chenopodium album	x					
Chenopodiaceae	x					
Echium sp						
Fumaria sp.	x					
Galium aparine	x					
Galium sp.	x	18				
Galium spurium	x					
Graminae						
Lithospermum sp		11				
Lithospermum apulum						
Lithospermum arvense	x					
Lolium temulentum	x					
Medicago minima						
Plantago lanceolata						
Rumex sp.						

x=present

Table 5.8: Plant remains from Late/Final Neolithic deposits

Site	Ftelia	Saliagos	Kephala	Agora	Francthi	Lerne	Agios Georgios	Photoleivos	Stavroupoli	Agios Ioannis
Reference	Megaloudi and Marinval 2002	Renfrew 1968	Renfrew 1977	Hopf 1971	Hansen 1991	Hopf 1961, 1962	Sarpaki 1987	Renfrew 1973	Margariti 2002	Megaloudi unpublished
Hordeum vulgare	30		22				12	x	x	
Hordeum vulgare nudum	3			imprint						
Hordeum distichum		2			351					
Hordeum sp.	70	333					7			
Panicum miliaceum										2
Secale cereale										
Triticum aestivum/durum							1		x	
Triticum dicoccum	3	9			453		1		x	25
Triticum monococcum		1			57		1		x	5
Triticum spelta									x	
Triticum sp.		54					13	x		7
Triticum timopheevi?										
Cicer arietinum										
Lathyrus cicera	30000				x					
Lathyrus sativus			100							
Lathyrus sp.									x	
Leguminosae										
Lens culinaris	43				x		2		x	35
Pisum sativum					27				x	
Pisum sp.				imprint						
Vicia ervilia				imprint			1			
Vicia faba										
Ficus carica						1	2 fruits		x	30
Vitis vinifera										
Camelina sativa										
Linum usitatissimum										
Amygdalus communis										
Arbutus Unedo						1				
Capparis sp.										
Coriandrum sativum					2					
Cornus mas									x	
Corylus avellana										
Crataegus spp										
Malva sylvestris										
Olea sp.									x	
Pistacia sp.					x					
Pistacia terebinthus									x	
Pistacia vera										
Portulaca oleracea										
Pyrus sp.										
Pyrus/Malus										
Quercus										
Rubus fruticosus									x	
Sambucus ebulus										
Sambucus sp.									x	
Vitis sp.									x	
Vitis sylvestris					8			x		
Aegilops sp.										
Astragalus sp.										
Avena sp.										
Boraginaceae										
Bromus sp.										
Chenopodium album					x				x	
Chenopodiaceae										
Echium sp					91				x	
Fumaria sp.										
Galium aparine							1			
Galium sp.					x					
Galium spurium										
Graminae									x	
Lithospermum sp										
Lithospermum apulum					17					
Lithospermum arvense									x	
Lolium temulentum.		2							x	
Medicago minima					943					
Plantago lanceolata					3					
Polygonum aviculare									x	
Rumex sp.									x	
Setaria viridis										

Table 5.8: Plant remains from Late/Final Neolithic deposits

Site	Dimini	Rachmani Renfrew	Visvikis Renfrew	Pyrasos Renfrew	Sesklo Renfrew	Arapi	Pefkakia	Thermi Valamoti	Skoteini Mangaffa	Sarakinos Megaloudi in
Reference	Kroll 1981	1966	1966	1966	1966	Kroll 1983	Kroll 1983	1992	1993	press
Hordeum vulgare	x			415	x	x	x	x	42	137
Hordeum vulgare nudum	100		x				x			9
Hordeum distichum										
Hordeum sp.										56
Panicum miliaceum										
Secale cereale									3	
Triticum aestivum/durum		x					x	x	6	15
Triticum dicoccum	97		x	138	1000	x	x	x	5	48
Triticum monococcum	x		x	26		x	x	x	15	70000
Triticum spelta										
Triticum sp.								x	10	3058
Triticum timopheevi?										
Cicer arietinum	32									
Lathyrus cicera	8						x			
Lathyrus sativus	80						x	x	2	
Lathyrus sp.										4
Leguminosae	32					x		x	4	6
Lens culinaris	123	x				x	x	x		1
Pisum sativum	82				x			x		
Pisum sp.				6			x		1	
Vicia ervilia	13					x	x			
Vicia faba	x				x				1	
Ficus carica		40 fruits				x	x		13	197
Vitis vinifera						x	x			
Camelina sativa							x			
Linum usitatissimum						x	x			
Amygdalus communis	18				x		x			
Arbutus Unedo										
Capparis sp.										
Coriandrum sativum										
Cornus mas										
Corylus avellana										
Crataegus spp										
Malva sylvestris										1
Olea sp.	x									
Pistacia sp.								x		13
Pistacia terebinthus										
Pistacia vera				1						
Portulaca oleracea						x				
Pyrus sp.				x						
Pyrus/Malus									3	
Quercus				12			x			
Rubus fruticosus								x		
Sambucus ebulus										
Sambucus sp.										
Vitis sp.								x		1
Vitis sylvestris	x									
Aegilops sp.										1
Astragalus sp.									2	
Avena sp.						x	x			4
Boraginaceae									1	
Bromus sp.										
Chenopodium album										
Chenopodiaceae							x	x		
Echium sp										
Fumaria sp.						x	x	x		
Galium aparine										
Galium sp.										1
Galium spurium						x				
Graminae								x	5	
Lithospermum sp										
Lithospermum apulum										
Lithospermum arvense						x	x	x		
Lolium temulentum						x	x			
Medicago minima										
Plantago lanceolata										
Polygonum aviculare										
Rumex sp.							x	x		
Setaria viridis									1	
Sherardia arvensis										

Table 5.8: Plant remains from Late/Final Neolithic deposits

Site	Sitagroi Renfrew et al 1986	Kastanas Kroll 1983	Zarkos Jones and Halstead 1993	Pefkakia Kroll 1983	Eutresis Mylonas 1959	Skoteini Mangaffa 1993	Tirynth Kroll 1982	Lerna Hopf 1961, 1962	Debla Greig and Warren 1974	Myrtos Renfrew 1972	Argissa Hopf 1962	Synoro Willerding 1973
Hordeum vulgare	x	10,442	844	x			2	324		3 imprints	x	
Hordeum vulgare nudum								305			x	
Hordeum sp.		6 2f	50			10			imprints			
Panicum miliaceum		8										
Triticum dicoccum		459	161	x		27	1	5	imprints		x	
Triticum monococcum		586		x		31		6			x	
Triticum dic./monoc.			19			15						
Triticum spelta						6						
Triticum aestivum/durum		3				1						
Triticum sp.			5		x	12				1 imprints		
Cicer arietinum		1				5						
Lathyrus cicera		1						83				
Lathyrus sativus		5				2						
Lens culinaris		116					1	410			x	
Pisum sativum		1				8						
Pisum sp.								113				
Vicia ervilia		569	421	x			2	42			x	
Vicia faba		21				418	3	260				
Fabaceae		33					5				x	
Camelina sativa		1										
Linum usitatissimum		318									x	
Linum sp.								200				
Papaver somniferum		2										
Cornus mas		2										
Ficus carica		122		x			129	29				
Olea europaea							1		x	1		
Pyrus sp.		6										
Quercus	x	1686						4			x	
Rubus fruticosus		1										
Sambucus ebulus		7										
Vitis vinifera	x	71					19	1102		68		3 imprints
Alisma plantago		8										
Avena sp.		4	15				2		imprints		x	
Boraginaceae												
Bromus sp.		4							1+ imprints			
Chenopodiaceae		199									x	
Digitaria sanguinalis		2										
Galium spurium		35				2					x	
Poaceae		36		x								
Liliaceae						1						
Lithospermum arvense		63		x			2				x	
Lolium temulentum		203					1				x	
Malus sylvestris							1				x	
Medicago minima		7					1					
Medicago sp.											x	
Onopordum cf acanthium								101				
Papaver rhoeas												
Plantago lanceolata		3										
Polygonaceae		33									x	
Polygonum convolvulus		26									x	
Portulaca oleracea		2										
Rumex sp.											x	
Setaria viridis		1										
Typha sp.		20										

Table 5.9: Plant remains from Early Bronze Age deposits

Site	Agios Mamas	Argissa	Lerna	Zarkos	Pefkakia	Agora	Nichoria	Orchomenos	Chamalevri-Tzambakas House	Kouphovouno
Reference	Kroll 2003	Hopf 1962	Hopf 1961, 1962	Jones and Halstead 1993	Kroll 1983	Hopf 1971	Shay and Shay 1978	Vickery 1936	Sarpaki 1999	Megaloudi unpublished
Hordeum vulgare	x	x	138		x			x		1
Hordeum vulgare nudum		x	27			2 imprints				1
Triticum aestivum/durum		x			x					
Triticum dicoccum	x	x	46		x			x	x	2
Triticum monococcum	x	x			x					
Triticum spelta		x								
Lathyrus cicera			28		x					
Lathyrus sativus	x				x					
Lens culinaris	x	x	110		x				x	
Pisum sativum		x								
Vicia ervilia	x				x			x		
Vicia faba	x		210		x			x	x	
Camelina sativa	x									
Linum usitatissimum	x				x					
Ficus carica	x				x				x	
Olea sp.			2						x	6
Pistacia sp.					x				x	
Quercus	x			58	x					
Vitis sp.									x	2
Amygdalus communis									x	
Pyrus sp.									x	
Vitis vinifera	x				x	2 imprints				
Astragalus sp.		x								
Avena sterilis		x	4							
Avena sp.	x							x		
Bromus sp.			9							
Carex sp.		x								
Chenopodium sp.	x									
Galium spurium	x									
Celtis sp.									x	
Lithospermum arvense					x					
Lolium temulentum					x					
Malva sylvestris	x									
Medicago sp.									x	
Onopordum cf acanthium		x	188							
Poaceae					x					
Polygonaceae					x					
Rumex sp.		x								
Sambucus sp.									x	
Sheradia arvensis	x									1
Thymelaea hirsuta									x	
Trifolium sp.									x	

x=present

Table 5.10 : Plant remains from Middle Bronze Components

Site Reference	Mycenae Schliemann 1886	Palaikastro Bosanquet 1906	Nirou chani Evans 1900-1901	Iria Willerding 1973	Delphi Luce *et al.* forthcoming	The Citadel of Midea Shay et al. 1998	Archondico Valamoti 1997
Hordeum vulgare	x			7	3	1288	x
Hordeum vulgare nudum					3		
Hordeum distichum							
Hordeum sp.							
Graminae						4111	
Panicum miliaceum							
Secale cereale							
Triticum aestivum/durum					4	15	
Triticum dicoccum				1	3		x
Triticum monococcum					1	2	x
Triticum spelta							x
Triticum sp.	x	x					
Oryza sativa							
Cicer arietinum						70	
Fabaceae				x			
Lathyrus sativus/cicera							x
Lathyrus clymenum							
Lathyrus sativus						763	
Vicia sativa						12	
Leguminosae						5205	
Lens culinaris					2	92	X
Pisum sativum		x	x			14	
Pisum elatius		x					
Pisum sp.							
Vicia ervilia	x		x			439	x
Vicia faba			x			214	x
Cornus mas							x
Ficus carica					3	101	x
Ficus carica `fruits				7		28	
Ficus carica fragments						5746	
Olea europaea					3	74	
Olea europaea fragments						37	
Quercus sp.							x
Rubus fruticosus							x
Sambucus sp.							x
Pyrus sp.							
Pyrus/Malus							
Vitis vinifera					2	2	x
Vitis sylvestris							x
Bilderdykia convolvulus							x
Cyperaceae							x
Fumaria sp.							x
Galium sp.							x
Graminae							x
Lamiaceae							x
Lolium temulentum							x
Teucrium sp.							x
Amaranthus						2	
Chenopodium						1	
Galium						2	
Malva sp.							
wild grasses						x	

x=present

Table 5.11: Plant remains from Late Bronze Age deposits

46

Site	Dimitra Foster 1997; Renfrew 1997	Aghios Kroll 2003	Assiros Jones et al. 1986	Kastanas Kroll 1983	Dimini Megaloudi unpublished	Iolkos Jones 1982	Thermi Lamb 1936	Gla Jones 1995	Thebes Jones and Halstead 1993
Hordeum vulgare	55	x	x	1187		130			
Hordeum vulgare nudum				4					
Hordeum distichum				8					
Hordeum sp.									
Panicum miliaceum		x	x	577.639					
Secale cereale									
Triticum aestivum/durum	1		x	73					
Triticum dicoccum	163	x	x	652		6			
Triticum monococcum	9	x	x	10.751				1208	
Triticum spelta			x	567					
Triticum sp.								28	
Oryza sativa									
Cicer arietinum									
Fabaceae				70.08			x		
Lathyrus cicera									
Lathyrus clymenum									
Lathyrus sativus				39					
Lathyrus sp.									x
Leguminosae									
Lens culinaris	1			128					
Pisum sativum				15					
Pisum elatius									
Pisum sp.						24			
Vicia ervilia	126		x	246.978					
Vicia faba				21		551			x
Amygdalus communis									
Ficus carica		x		14					
Fragaria vesca				4					
Malus sylvestris							1fruit		
Olea europaea						1			
Pistacia sp.	1								
Pistacia terebinthus									
Prunus spinosa									
Punica granatum									
Pyrus sp.									
Pyrus/Malus					6				
Quercus				1		6			
Rubus fruticosus				8					
Sambucus ebulus				6					
Sambucus sp.									
Vitis sp.									
Vitis vinifera	8	x		582		12			
Vitis sylvestris	2								
Camelina sativa		x		324.448					
Linum usitatissimum		x		41					
Papaver somniferum		x		15					
Alisma plantago				176					
Astragalus sp.									
Avena sp.				30					
Boraginaceae									
Bromus sp.				171					
Capparis sp.									
Carex sp.									
Chenopodiaceae				432					
Chenopodium album									
Convolvulus arvensis				7					
Coriandrum sativum									
Cyperaceae				262					
Digitaria sanguinalis				365					
Echium									
Fumaria sp.									
Galium aparine									
Galium palustre									
Galium sp.								1	
Galium spurium				806					
Graminae				8869					
Hyoscyamus sp				2					
Lithospermum arvense				13					
Lolium temulentum				4016					
Malva sp				199					
Medicago sp.				1290					
Onopordon cf acanthium									
Papaver rhoeas							x		
Plantago lanceolata				3653					
Polygonaceae				476					
Polygonum aviculare									
Polygonum convolvulus				27					
Portulaca oleracea				387					
Rumex sp.									
Schoenus nigricans									
Setaria italica				2					
Setaria viridis				322					
Sheradia arvensis									
Solanum nigrum				8					
Teucrium				7					

x= present

Table 5.11a: Plant remains from Late Bronze Age deposits

Site	Akrotiri	Agora	Tirynth	Nichoria	Knossos	Aghia Triada	Chania	Therasia	Marmariani	Mallia
				Shay and Shay						Chapoutier and
Reference	Sarpaki 1992	Hopf 1971	Kroll 1982	1978	Jones 1984	Follieri 1979	Follieri 1982	Fouqué 1879	Vickery 1936	Charbonneaux 1928
Hordeum vulgare	x	imprint	658	x	1120	2		x		
Hordeum vulgare nudum		imprint								
Hordeum distichum	x		1							
Hordeum sp.			28							
Panicum miliaceum			10						x	
Secale cereale										
Triticum aestivum/durum			16		150	6				
Triticum dicoccum	x		1358		338	2			x	
Triticum monococcum	x		11		3					
Triticum spelta			2			2				
Triticum sp.				x						x
Oryza sativa			1							
Cicer arietinum			17	x ?						
Fabaceae				x						
Lathyrus cicera										
Lathyrus clymenum	x									
Lathyrus sativus			19		563	30				
Lathyrus sp.	x				93					
Leguminosae			34							
Lens culinaris	x		57		2	1		x		x
Pisum sativum	x		1		1188	1		x		
Pisum elatius										
Pisum sp.										
Vicia ervilia			1573		4	5				
Vicia faba			12		166		10			
Ficus carica	x		4394		6 fruits	60 fruits	7 fruits			
Fragaria vesca										
Malus sylvestris										
Olea europaea	x		185	x						
Pistacia sp.										
Pistacia terebinthus										
Prunus spinosa				x						
Punica granatum			2							
Pyrus sp.										
Pyrus/Malus										
Quercus				x						
Rubus fruticosus										
Sambucus ebulus			1							
Sambucus sp.										
Vitis sp.					4					
Vitis vinifera	x		165	x						
Vitis sylvestris										
Camelina sativa										
Linum usitatissimum			1							
Papaver somniferum			3							
Alisma plantago										
Astragalus sp.										
Avena sp.			15							
Boraginaceae										
Bromus sp.			1							
Capparis sp.										
Carex sp.										
Chenopodiaceae			58							
Chenopodium album										
Convolvulus arvensis										
Coriandrum sativum	x									
Cyperaceae			25							
Digitaria sanguinalis										
Echium			162							
Fumaria sp.			4							
Galium aparine					1					
Galium palustre										
Galium sp.										
Galium spurium										
Graminae			39							
Hyoscyamus sp										
Lithospermum arvense			72							
Lolium temulentum			69							
Malva sylvestris			26							
Medicago sp.			11							
Onopordon cf acanthium										
Papaver rhoeas										
Plantago lanceolata										
Polygonaceae			9							
Polygonum aviculare										
Polygonum convolvulus			1							
Portulaca oleracea										
Rumex sp.										
Schoenus nigricans	x									
Setaria italica										
Setaria viridis										
Sheradia arvensis	x									
Solanum nigrum										
Teucrium										

x= present

Table 5.11b: Plant remains from Late Bronze Age deposits

As *Tables 5.3* and *5.6* indicate, broomcorn millet was present at Greek archaeological sites as early as the Early Neolithic, although it does not seem to have played an important role at that time. A single grain of *Panicum miliaceum* is reported from the Aceramic levels of Argissa, but the chronology of its context is problematic (Hopf 1962b). In the Late Bronze Age the species was grown as a crop in its own right, at least at Assiros Toumba (Jones 1979; Jones et al. 1986; Wardle 1989) and at Kastanas (Kroll 1983). *Table 5.6* to *Table 5.11* clearly show that *Panicum miliaceum* is present mainly at sites in northern Greece, while in the southern part of the country millet was present only in Late Bronze Age Tirynth (Kroll 1982), and possibly in Marmariani (Tsountas 1908; Vickery 1936). It seems that the species was never established in southern Greece, where millets were regarded as exotic and barbaric and may have been considered the food of the lower class (Kroll 2000; Amouretti 1986).

Sufficient evidence for the presence of foxtail millet comes from Kastanas, where the species is first identified in its wild form *Setaria viridis*. Around 1000 B.C. its cultivated form *Setaria italica* emerged (Kroll 1983). *Tables 5.10* to *5.12* indicate that *Setaria italica* emerged in northern Greece during the Bronze Age and became an established crop at the end of the Late Bronze Age.

In Classical Greece *kenchros* (κέγχρος), broomcorn millet, and *melini* (μελίνη) or *elimos* (ἔλυμος), foxtail millet, are known and are mentioned on the stelai of the Hermokopidai in Attica, but they were regarded as barbarian food (Amouretti 1986). Both species were used boiled, like rice, and millet bread is also mentioned (André 1981). Herodotus describes the fields of foxtail millet in the region of Turkmenistan and compares the "exotic" rice of India with the "large-seeded millet" (3.117)[1].

According to Theophrastus, millets are summer crops: "broomcorn millet is the robuster plant while foxtail millet is sweeter and less robust" (*Hist. pl.* 8.4.3.)[2]. *Panicum miliaceum* was cultivated in Laconia, Thrace, and Cilice, if we are to believe Xenophon (*Anab.* 2.4.13), and Hippocrates advises readers to use a gruel of barley and millet against hemorrhoids (*Des mal. aig.* 513)

Rye (*Secale cereale* L.)
Secale cereale is a characteristic crop of temperate and northern Europe, as it is winter hardy, resistant to drought, and can grow in acid or sandy soils (Zohary and Hopf 2000). The species is endemic to southwest Asia and seems to have come into Europe as a tolerated weed sometime during the Neolithic (Behre 1992).

Rye is rich in protein and can be baked into a dark-colored bread that can be preserved for quite a long time (Kröber-Grohne 1987). Rye grains and green plants can also used as animal fodder, for the preparation of rye whiskey, and in beer brewing (Zohary and Hopf 2000; Kröber-Grohne 1987).

Rye was never a crop in prehistoric and protohistoric Greece. Rye is reported from the Late Neolithic levels of Skoteini Cave, but the finds are limited into three grains (Magaffa 1993). A few rye grains are also reported from Bronze Age and Protogeometric Kastanas and Kalapodi (Kroll 1983, 1993) but the number of finds indicates that the species was only a cereal weed. The Attic climate was too warm and dry for rye to be significant, except as a weed, and Attic Greek has no word corresponding to *sikale*, the modern word for rye (Sallares 1991).

Galen, writing in the second century A.D., suggests that rye was an important crop in Thrace and Macedonia (Sallares 1991), but the species did not become widely cultivated until the Byzantine period, a change probably related to the expansion of the medieval cities. Large amounts of rye are reported from the 13th- and 14th-century A.D. levels of Aghios Mamas near Olynthos on Chalkidike (Kroll 1999), but no other archaeobotanical information is available for the medieval period.

Oats (*Avena* ssp.)
Common oat (*Avena sativa* L.) was a major cereal crop in traditional Old World agriculture and in northwest Europe the species was cultivated as a principal grain crop (Zohary and Hopf 2000). The high protein value of oat makes it a staple in the human diet. *Table 5.15* indicates that oats have been present in Greece since the Aceramic and Early Neolithic periods. Archaeobotanically it is not possible to distinguish between common oat (*Avena sativa*) and the wild forms *Avena fatua* and *Avena sterilis* (see chapter 4, section G). Oats occur in small quantities in the archaeobotanical assemblages, and they do not appear to have been deliberately cultivated; it is more likely that they were weeds. Theophrastus describes oats as "wild and uncultivated things" and considers them emmer weeds (*Hist. pl.* 8.9.2). Galen (2nd century A.D.) describes oat cultivation in Mysia in Asia Minor, and Servius, writing in the late Roman Empire, mentions that oats were cultivated in Thrace in his time (Sallares 1991).

Rice (*Oryza sativa* L.)
Rice (*Oryza sativa* L.) is a species of eastern and southern Asia and was probably introduced to Greece after the expedition of Alexander, as literary references to rice do not predate him. Strabo (15.21-22) mentions the rice of India that, according to Aristobulus, has grains similar to those of wheat. Chrysippus of Tyana describes a rice cake called *orizitis plakous* (ορυζίτης πλακοῦς), but he transmits no recipe for it (Ath. *Deipn.* 647e). Galen recommends rice pudding for invalids (*On the Properties of Foods* 1.17).

A single rachis identified as rice (*Oryza sativa*) is reported from the Late Bronze Age levels at Tirynth (Kroll 1982). This find is still unique, and the archaeobotanical evidence so far does not indicate rice cultivation in Greece, at least not before Alexander's expedition.

---

[1]   All Herodotus translations are from Godley 1921-1924
[2]   All Theophrastus translations are from Hort 1916

Sites	Kastanas PG	Nichoria PG	Iolkos PG	Kalapodi PG	Iolkos G	Kalapodi G	Agora Athens G	Nichoria G	Delphi G	Krania G
Reference	Kroll 1982, 1983	Shay and Shay 1978	Jones 1982	Kroll 1993	Jones 1982	Kroll 1993	Hopf 1971	Shay and Shay 1978	Luce et al. forthcoming	Margariti 2002
Hordeum vulgare	2396		805	4443	364	66				x
Hordeum vulg. var. nudum	6									
Panicum miliaceum	61.732				1					
Secale cereale	136									
Triticum aestivum/durum	87			5302	7	25			2	x
Triticum dicoccum	948			244	214	11			1	x
Triticum monococcum	320				15				1	x
Triticum spelta	333				8					
Triticum sp.	1470				355			x		
Lathyrus sativus	12			3075	6	1				
Lens culinaris	102			728	38	13				x
Pisum sativum	20			6						x
Vicia ervilia	290		1030	222	5	8			2	x
Vicia faba	19			8		3			1	
Ficus carica	285			8		12	x		5	x
Olea europaea				5		5		x	12	x
Punica granatum										x
Vitis vinifera	417			10		6	x	x	3	
Camelina sativa	780			8						
Linum usitatissimum	43			2						
Papaver somniferum	1376			28						
Apium graveolens	5									
Cucumis melo	2									
Citrullus lanatus										x
Cornus mas	8									
Corylus avelana										x
Crataegus sp.	1									
Fragaria vesca	119									
Malva sylvestris	86									
Portulaca oleracea	253									
Prunus spinosa	3	1								
Prunus sp.								8		
Pyrus sp.	4									
Quercus sp.	27	4						7	1	
Rubus fruticosus	104									
Sambucus ebulus	829									
Vitis sp.										x
Agrostema githago	97									
Alisma plantago-aquatica	345									
Astragalus sp.										
Avena sp.	25			15	7	2				
Boraginaceae										
Bromus sp.	273			2		4				
Chenopodiaceae	646									
Cynodon dactylon	46									
Daucus type	1									
Digitaria sanguinalis	86									
Echinochloa crus-galli	712									
Fabaceae	190	2				8		7		
Fumaria sp.	5									
Fyoscyamus sp.	33									
Galium aparine	2									
Galium spurium	364				4					
Graminae	200									
Juniperus sp									1	
Lamiaceae	39									
Lithospermum	32									
Lithospermum arvense	400		2							
Lolium temulentum	680				78					x
Medicago sp.	62									
Plantago lanceolata	41									
Polygonacae	401									
Polygonum convolvulus	261									
Rumex sp.										x
Setaria glauca	72									
Setaria italica	116									
Setaria viridis	279			1		2				
Solanum nigrum	301									
Teucrium chamaedrys	16									
Verbena officinalis	17									
Ventenata dubia	1329									

Table 5.12 : Plant remains from Protogeometric and Geometric deposits

Site	Delphi	Ipsili	Heraion Samos	Kalapodi	Phylla Vrachos
Reference	Luce *et al*. forthcoming	Megaloudi unpublished	Kucan 1995	Kroll 1993	Coulton et al. 2002
Hordeum vulgare	92		21	54	
Hordeum sp.	28				
Triticum aestivum/durum	31		1	12	
Triticum dicoccum	10		1		
Triticum monococcum	4		5		
Triticum spelta					
Lathyrus sativus	11				
Lens culinaris	24		1		
Pisum sativum	5				
Vicia ervilia	25				
Vicia faba	6				
Amygdalus communis			20		
Cydonia oblonga	1				
Ficus carica	34		118.155		
Olea europaea	80	20	520		
Punica granatum	1		1076		
Vitis vinifera	21		7.175		1
Papaver somniferum			49		
Amaranthus lividus			1182		
Anethum graveolens			5		
Apium graveolens			562		
Citrullus lanatus	1		1		
Coriandrum sativum			44		
Cucumis melo			486		
Hibiscus esculentus			1		
Lactuca serriola			45		
Beta vulgaris			9		
Capparis spinosa			1		
Cornus mas		3			
Corylus avellana			302		
Laurus nobilis			1		
Lupinus humulus	1				
Malva sp.			1044		
Morus nigra			180		
Myrtus communis			316		
Pistacia terebinthus			98		
Portulaca oleracea			240		
Prunus persica			1		
Quercus sp.	5		160		
Rubus fruticosus			918		
Vitex agnus castus			52.717		
Several herbs, flowers,wild grasses			x		

Table 5.13 : Plant remains from Archaic deposits

Site Reference	4th cent. BC Nichoria Shay and Shay 1978	5/4th cent. BC Lerne Hopf 1961,1962a	4th cent. BC Limenas Thasos Megaloudi 2005	5th cent. BC Corinth Bookidis et al. 1999	5th cent. BC Kastanas Kroll 1982, 1983	4th cent. BC Kalapodi Kroll 1993
Hordeum vulgare					2	15
Hordeum sp.				98		
Panicum miliaceum				1	3	
Triticum aestivum			1	28		5
Triticum dicoccum					2	4
Triticum monococcum					2	
Triticum sp.				37	26	
Bread remains			x			
Cicer arietinum				1		
Fabaceae			2			
Lathyrus sativus						27
Leguminoseae				16		
Lens culinaris				70	2	2
Pisum sativum					2	
Pisum sp.				3		
Vicia ervilia				4	9	3
Vicia faba						2
Ficus carica				41 (5 fruits)	4	3
Olea europaea	4	2	1	522		
Punica granatum			3	1		
Vitis vinifera	1		22	47	4	7
Allium sativum			55			
Capparis spinosa				1		
Juglans regia			2			
Malva sylvestris			1			
Quercus	2					
Vitis sp.				1		
Avena sp						2
Chenopodiaceae				1	4	
Fumaria officinalis				1		
Gramineae				47		
Lamiaceae				4		
Lithospermum arvense					39	

Table 5.14: Plant remains from 5th and 4th cent. BC deposits

B. Pulses

Pulses are annual legumes with high economic value. They are able to improve the fertility of the soil because of a symbiotic bacterium (*Rhizobium radicola*) that stimulates the growth of nitrogen-capturing root nodules. By rotating or mixing legume crops with cereals the farmer is able to maintain soil fertility. Pulses, unlike cereals, are not parched at any stage of their processing and they are often consumed as soup or porridge; thus they are less likely to be preserved in archaeological assemblages, and for a long time they were not considered to have been as important as cereals in the prehistoric diet. Recent archaeobotanical finds, however, contradict this assumption: the Late Neolithic site of Ftelia on Mykonos has yielded large quantities of *Lathyrus cicera*, while cereals seem to have been a secondary crop (Megaloudi and Marinval 2002). Pulses are also very well represented at Late/Final Neolithic Dikili Tash and Arkadikos (Valamoti 2004). In Bronze Age levels at Kastanas more than 100,000 remains of bitter vetch (*Vicia ervilia*) were identified, which indicates the important role of legume cultivation, at least at that site (Kroll 1983). Sarpaki, in her study of the role of legumes in prehistory (1992), underlined the importance of legumes in prehistoric Greece and concluded that an agricultural system could not have succeeded without legume cultivation. Sallares (1991, p.

301), supports this view, suggesting that cereals and legumes were probably grown together on the same field and not rotated. Literary and archaeobotanical evidence indicates that legumes were used regularly throughout antiquity, although they were probably not considered favorite foods (Flint-Hamilton 1999).

In this section I present the legume species that, according to the archaeobotanical evidence, seem to have played an important role in the prehistoric and protohistoric economy (*Table 5.16*).

Chickpea (*Cicer arietinum* L.)

Chickpea (*Cicer arietinum*) is a high palatable seed legume that has long been cultivated in the Mediterranean basin, western India, and Ethiopia. India produces 85% of the world's chickpeas today, followed by the Mediterranean countries and Ethiopia. The species does not tolerate cool regions and grows well in rocky limestone soils.

The wild progenitor of cultivated chickpea would be *Cicer arietinum* ssp. *reticulatum*, a species restricted to southeastern Turkey, and it must have been brought into cultivation in the central part of the Near East (Zohary and Hopf 2000). *Cicer arietinum* must have reached Europe together with the other Near Eastern grain crops (Zohary and Hopf 2000).

Species	AN	EN	MN	LN/FN	EBA	MBA	LBA	PG	G	A	C
N of components	5	9	10	26	14	10	26	6	4	5	6
Avena ssp	20	33.3	60	30.4	28.6	20	7.7	33.3	25	20	16.7
Agrostemma githaco	0	0	0	4	0	0	4	16.7	0	20	0
Bromus ssp	20	22.2	10	7.7	21.4	10	7.7	33.3	25	0	0
Chenopodium album	0	0	20	15.4	0	0	0	0	0	20	0
Chenopodiaceae	0	33.3	20	7.7	7.1	10	7.7	16.7	0	40	33
Convolvulus arvensis	0	0	0	0	0	10	4	16.7	0	20	0
Fumaria ssp	0	22.2	20	11.5	14.3	10	7.7	16.7	0	0	16.7
Fumaria offcinalis	0	0	0	0	0	0	0	0	0	20	0
Galium aparine	0	11.1	20	7.7	0	0	7.7	0	0	20	0
Galium spurium	0	11.1	0	7.7	7.1	10	4	16.7	25	20	0
Galium ssp	20	11.1	10	15.4	7.1	0	7.7	0	0	0	0
Lithospermum arvense	0	11.1	20	23.1	21.4	20	7.7	33.3	25	20	16.7
Lolium temulentum	0	22.2	30	19.2	21.4	20	11.5	50	50	40	33.3
Lolium remotum	0	0	0	4	7.1	0	0	0	0	0	0
Medicago minima	0	0	0	4	0	0	0	0	0	20	0
Medicago ssp	0	0	10	7.7	14.3	0	4	16.7	0	0	0
Papaver rhoias	0	0	0	0	0	0	4	0	0	20	0
Plantago lanceolata	0	0	0	7.7	7.1	0	7.7	16.7	0	20	0
Polygonum aviculare	0	0	10	7.7	14.3	0	4	16.7	0	20	0
Setaria viridis	0	0	0	7.7	7.1	0	4	16.7	0	0	0
Sheradia arvensis	0	0	0	4	7.1	20	4	16.7	0	0	0

Table 5.15: Percentage of Appearances of Weeds per component

AN: Aceramic Neolithic, EN: Early Neolithic, MN: Middle Neolithic, LN/FN: Late Neolithic, Final Neolithic, EBA: Early Bronze Age, MBA: Middle Bronze Age, LBA: Late Bronze Age, PG: Proto-Geometric, G: Geometric, A: Archaic, C: Classic

Species	AN	EN	MN	LA/FN	EBA	MBA	LBA	PG	G	A	C
N of components	5	9	10	26	14	10	26	6	4	5	6
Cicer arietinum	0	11	0	4	14	0	8	17	0	20	17
Lathyrus cicera	0	11	30	19	7	0	8	0	0	0	0
Lathyrus sativus	0	22	10	23	14	20	15	33	25	0	33
Lens culinaris	60	67	90	65	36	20	35	33	75	60	33
Pisum sativum	0	22	20	31	14	10	23	33	50	0	17
Vicia ervilia	20	44	50	31	43	30	27	67	50	40	50
Vicia faba	0	0	0	12	43	30	19	50	25	20	17

Table 5.16: Percentage of Appearances of Legume species per component

AN: Aceramic Neolithic, EN: Early Neolithic, MN: Middle Neolithic, LN/FN: Late Neolithic, Final Neolithic, EBA: Early Bronze Age, MBA: Middle Bronze Age, LBA: Late Bronze Age, PG: Proto-Geometric, G: Geometric, A: Archaic, C: Classic

In Greece chickpeas are reported from 6th-millennium B.C. Otzaki and Sesklo in Thessaly (Kroll 1983), Late Neolithic Dimini (Kroll 1979), and Late Neolithic Zeas Cave on Naxos (Flint-Hamilton 1994). In the Early Bronze Age the species is reported from Kastanas (Kroll 1983), Skoteini Cave (Mangaffa 1993), and Tirynth (Kroll 1982). K. Vickery (1936) reports the presence of chickpeas from Early Bronze Age Rachmani and Gona, as well as from Late Bronze Age Aghia Triada in Crete. In protohistorical Greece chickpeas are reported only from the Protogeometric levels of Kalapodi (Kroll 1993) and from Nichoria (Shay and Shay 1978). The archaeobotanical evidence so far suggests that chickpeas were cultivated in Greece but were probably not a staple food, and their popularity grew with time.

In Classical Greece *Cicer arietinum* is identified as *erebinthos* (ερέβινθος). Theophrastus advises that in order to "make chickpeas large they bid one moisten the seed while still in the pods, before sowing" (*Hist. pl.* 2.4.2). The same author also comments that sowing two crops of chickpea every year exhausts the soil, and he considers chickpeas quick to flower and mature and destructive to some weeds, and "above all and soonest caltrop" (*Hist. pl.* 8.1.4, 8.7.2). Chickpeas are often cited in Aristophanes' comedies: in the *Acharnians* (801) the pig seller feeds chickpeas and figs to his pigs; in the *Ecclesiazusae* (606), Praxagoras claims that, according to the principles of equality, people will have in abundance all they could want, including chickpeas. Chickpeas were served both as a staple and as a dessert, roasted or fresh, if they were young and tender (Ath. *Epitome* 54e). According to Pliny, chickpea gruel was used to leaven barley bread (*HN* 18.103).

Despite the frequency of chickpeas in Classical written sources, archaeobotanically, chickpeas are reported in Classical deposits in only one instance: in the 5th-century B.C. sanctuary of Demeter and Kore at Corinth (Bookidis et al. 1999). It is not easy to conclude whether the rarity of chickpeas in archaeobotanical assemblages reflects reality, or whether it is due to taphonomical bias, and only further archaeobotanical studies could answer the question. The available macrofossil evidence so far indicates that chickpeas were appreciated, but were probably not a regular staple food like lentils or bitter vetch.

Grass pea (*Lathyrus sativus* L.)
Grass pea (or chickling vetch) is an annual plant that grows well in dry places and in poor soils. Grass pea was traditionally cultivated in Spain, France, and Italy (Townsend 1994, in Kislev 1989), and was a staple for poor people in 18th-century France (Toussaint-Samat 1987). Today the species is mainly produced in India and is used as fodder, but is also consumed by humans, especially in times of famine. In India, people from the lowest classes still receive *Lathyrus sativus* in lieu of wages (Flint-Hamilton 1999, p. 382).

In Greece, grass pea used to be a staple called *fava* (φάβα) made by the grounded seeds of the plant. At present the species is cultivated on the island of Euboea, where it is known as *lathouri* (λαθούρι) and is used as an animal feed. *Lathyrus* sp. can be highly toxic if consumed in large quantities, as the species contains the neurotoxic amino acid BOAA that causes lathyrism in humans, a neurological syndrome that causes spastic paraplegia of the legs (Hansen 1999; Marinval 1986; Jean-Blain and Grisvard 1973). Lathyrism continued to afflict people in Western Europe until World War II, and today there are still outbreaks in regions of Bangladesh, China, Ethiopia, and India (Flint-Hamilton 1999). The harmful effects can be avoided if *Lathyrus* seeds are soaked and boiled at high temperatures, and the disease is reversible to some

extent if treated early in its outbreak (Hansen 1999; Jean-Blain and Grisvard 1973).

In Greece, *Lathyrus sativus* has been identified archaeobotanically at Prodromos, dating back to 6000 B.C. (Halstead and Jones 1980). *Lathyrus sativus/cicera* is also reported from Middle Neolithic Limenaria on Thasos (Megaloudi, forthcoming). Grass pea is well represented at Late Neolithic Dimini (Kroll 1979). On the Final Neolithic site of Ftelia on Mykonos, large quantities of another species of grass pea, *Lathyrus cicera*, were discovered, which indicated that the species was grown as a crop in its own right, at least at that site (Megaloudi and Marinval 2002; Megaloudi et al. 2003).

In Classical Greece wild grass pea (*Lathyrus cicera*) was identified as *aphaki* (αφάκη) and grass pea (*Lathyrus sativus*) as *lathyros* (λάθυρος) (Dalby 1996). Grass pea is frequently mentioned in the comic writers Anaxandrides and Alexis (André 1981). The species was consumed roasted or boiled (Plin. *HN* 18.98). Gruel from grass pea was used for leavening (Sen. *Ep.* 18.10). According to Pliny (*HN* 27.95), grass pea seeds soaked in water were used to cure dropsy and draw away bile, but could be harmful to the stomach if eaten without soaking.

Lentils (*Lens culinaris* Medik.)
Lentils (*Lens culinaris*), together with wheat and barley, are among the founder crops of Neolithic food production that spread throughout the eastern Mediterranean. Today the species is a basic component of Mediterranean agriculture and is also grown in India, Pakistan, Ethiopia, and the Near East (Zohary and Hopf 2000). Lentils are palatable and very nutritious (25% protein), and serve as a substitute for meat in traditional peasant communities. In modern Greece, lentils are considered a valuable source of iron.

Cultivated lentil (*Lens culinaris*) shows close morphological affinities to wild *Lens orientalis*, a small pulse that is found in the Near East (Zohary and Hopf 2000, p. 95) and is thought to be the wild progenitor of cultivated lentil.

In Greece lentils have been identified at Franchthi Cave as early as the Upper Paleolithic period (Hansen 1991), where the increase in the average size of the lentils in the Mesolithic period could indicate that domesticated lentil was present at the cave as early as the Mesolithic period—although it is not possible to know whether lentils were domesticated at Franchthi or whether they were introduced along with the domesticated cereals (Hansen 1991, pp. 58–59). Lentils have been identified at many prehistoric and protohistoric sites in Greece and the species was a common component in the everyday diet from the Neolithic period onwards (*Tables 5.6* to *5.14*).

According to Theophrastus (*Hist. pl.* 2.4.2; 8.8.6), lentils, as well as other pulses, may become "cookable" and "uncookable" depending on harvesting and soil conditions, as well as on climate and especially the direction of prevailing wind. He also comments that "the same piece of land, tilled in the same manner produces sometimes seeds that are cookable and sometimes seeds that are uncookable" (8.8.6) and advises that "to make lentils vigorous they plant the seeds in dung" (2.4.2). K. Flint-Hamilton notes that Theophrastus may have been observing the action of mycotoxins, and if lentils were harvested or winnowed on damp days or if they are stored in damp conditions, this could result to uncookable seeds (Flint-Hamilton 1999, p. 376).

Lentils were very common in Classical Greece, as is clear from the literary references. In Aristophanes' comedies lentils are frequently mentioned but they seem to be a food of the lower class, a food that symbolizes poverty: Philocleon in *Wasps* eats too much of the snack of lentils that Bdelycleon offers him, and develops a stomachache (*Vesp.* 811, 984); the sausage seller in *Knights* sees lentils in his oracle (*Eq.* 997); and Chremulus in *Wealth* comments that the gigolo will no longer eat lentil soup, now that he is wealthy (*Plut.* 1004). The lentil soup called *phake* (φακή) was an everyday staple, a food of workers that was unlikely to be seen at rich men's feasts (Dalby 1996). Lentils do make several appearances in Athnenaeus' *Deipnosophistae*, however, where they are served as a side dish in several forms and are even used in bread making, for "lentil bread" (*Deipn.* 4.156 and 4.158e).

Bitter vetch (*Vicia ervilia* L.)
Bitter vetch (*Vicia ervilia*) is a small plant that grows in the Mediterranean basin and the Near East. Today the primary producer of bitter vetch is Turkey (Zohary and Hopf 2000). The seeds of bitter vetch are bitter-tasting and the species contains toxins that are harmful for horses and pigs—but not for ruminants such as cows and sheep, for which the legume is an excellent fodder. Bitter vetch is also harmful for humans in its raw state, but its toxins are easily eliminated by cooking (Grmek 1994; Jean-Blain and Grisvard 1973). In modern times bitter vetch is mainly used as a fodder, but it is also consumed by humans in times of famine. Gruel of bitter vetch and cereals was used in bread making in Greece during the "Great Famine" of the winter of 1942–1943, during World War II (Luce et al., forthcoming).

In Greece, *Vicia ervilia* is fairly common at prehistoric settlements, where its mode of storage suggests that it was a crop legume for humans and not exclusively an animal fodder (*Tables 5.6 to 5.11*). In historical deposits bitter vetch *orovos* (ὄροβος), is reported from the sanctuary of Demeter and Kore at Corinth and from the sanctuary of Artemis at Kalapodi (Bookidis et al. 1999; Kroll 1983). Since very few archaeobotanical studies have been conducted at Classical sites, it is not easy to determine how frequently and in what way bitter vetch was used during later periods.

Bitter vetch was consumed roasted or boiled and, as was the case with chickpeas, gruel from the species was used to leaven barley bread (Plin. *HN* 14.103). Consumption of bitter vetch in Classical Greece seems to have been limited to the poorer, lower class; Demosthenes comments that during the Decelean War, the Athenians became so poor that "vetches were sold as food" (*Against Androtion* 22.15). This is confirmed by his contemporary Alexis, who comments that bitter vetch was a food designated for the poor (*CAF* 2.447).

Theophrastus knew of the poisonous properties of bitter vetch and he comments that if "one sows vetches in spring they become harmless and are not indigestible like those sown in autumn" (*Hist. pl.* 2.4.2). Pliny, like Theophrastus, determines the toxicity of the plant by the time of year it is sown (harmless if sown in early spring and dangerous if sown in autumn and late spring; *HN* 18.139). This toxicity could be related to toxic fungi that grows in late spring and early autumn but do not flourish in colder weather (Flint-Hamilton 1999, p. 379), although this hypothesis needs further investigation. Theophrastus advises that in order to protect radishes from spiders bitter vetch should be sown among the crop (*Hist. pl.* 7.5).

According to Hippocrates the seeds of bitter vetch are a source of strength and give a color of health (*Du rég.* 45.2). He comments that the consumption of raw or boiled vetch can cause flatulence and pain (*Acut.* 18) and mentions illnesses arising from excessive consumption of bitter vetch during a subsistence crisis at Ainos in Thrace in the late 5th century B.C.

Aristotle advises that cattle be fattened on vetch (*Hist. an.* 8.7.10). According to Pliny, an antidote to a poisonous venom engraved on the temple of Asclepius of Cos included vetch meal (*HN* 20.264). Pliny attributes to vetch healing properties against pimples and spots, while painful urination, flatulence, liver problems, and digestive difficulties can be relieved by eating roasted vetch mixed with honey (*HN* 22.151). In Galen's time, vetch was mainly used to feed cattle; men consumed the plant only in period of famine (*On the Properties of Foods* 1).

Broad bean (*Vicia faba* L.)
Broad bean (*Vicia faba*) is an annual plant that belongs to the principal pulses of Old World agriculture. The plant grows well in warm Mediterranean climates, as well as in the most temperate parts of Europe and Asia (Zohary and Hopf 2000). Because *Vicia faba* is rich in protein (containing 20% to 25%), in some Asian and Mediterranean countries the plant is the principal source of protein for the poor. In Greece the species is a common food known as *koukia* and is also used for green manure or in maslin with other crops.

Vicia faba causes the disease known as favism, an hemolytic anemia found in people presenting a genetic

55

deficiency of the red blood cell enzyme G6PD (Grmek 1994). The G6PD deficiency is more frequent among men than women (by a factor of 6:1), and although it has been observed worldwide it mainly affects people living around the Mediterranean basin (Kattamis et al. 1969). Favism generally occurs within several hours of consumption of broad beans, but the reaction can be delayed for up to nine days. Soaking the beans and removing the seed-coat may alter their toxic effects, as the seed-coat has the higher concentration of toxins (Hansen 1999; Grmek 1994).

Broad bean has been reported from Late Neolithic Dimini (Kroll 1979) and Sesklo in Thessaly (Renfrew 1966; Kroll 1983). Broad bean was found in important quantities at Delphi in Protogeometric levels (Luce et al., forthcoming), and to a small extent at Kastanas and Kalapodi (Kroll 1983, 1993). It is possible that broad beans were cultivated in small plots in gardens (as *Vicia faba* is a demanding species in terms of water) and fresh pods were plucked as a fine vegetable. Sarpaki (1992) argues that the rarity of broad bean in archaeobotanical assemblages might represent poor preservation, rather than its unpopularity as a food. The seeds of *Vicia faba* are large and they cannot easily be preserved by carbonization as they tend to explode or crumble.

Literary evidence regarding broad bean, which was called *kuamos* (κύαμος), indicates that the species was cultivated and consumed throughout antiquity. According to Theophrastus the species fertilizes the soil and for that reason "the people of Macedonia and Thessaly turn over the ground when it is in flower" (*Hist. pl.* 8.9.1). He also reports that broad bean requires more days than other crops to sprout and in some places " they take as much as fifteen days or even twenty" (8.1.5). We learn from Athenaeus that broad beans were included on the menu at fine meals (*Deipn.* 4.131) and were served as a dessert mixed with figs (4.139).

Vicia faba was widely used medicinally and Dioscorides recommends gruel of broad bean against coughing, renal insufficiency, and diarrhea (Fournier 1947). Pliny reports that broad bean strengthens the voice and can be used against colic, boils, burns, and swellings of testicles; the ashes of the plant mixed with pig's lard are recommended for chronic pains of the joints, while the boiled husks provide relief from constipation (*HN* 22.140).

In spite the popularity of *Vicia faba*, ancient taboo regarding the consumption of the species persisted—an aversion that could be related to the medical syndrome of favism. Pausanias, visiting the sanctuary of Demeter at Pheneus (8.15.3), reports that Demeter presented to the Pheneatians a variety of legumes as a gift but she specifically excluded broad beans. According to Herodotus (2.37) the Egyptians refused to eat broad beans and their priests could not even look upon them. The Pythagoreans refused to touch the bean vines as they considered that the souls of the dead were housed into the

beans (Plin. *HN* 18.118). Pythagoras, as he was trying to escape Syracusan soldiers, came upon a field of broad bean vines and preferred capture to crossing the field (Diog. Laert. *Pythagoras*).

Pea (*Pisum sativum* L.)

Pea (*Pisum sativum*) is a small legume well adapted to both warm-Mediterranean and cool-temperate climates and is today cultivated in temperate Europe, Ethiopia, parts of Russia and China, and the northwestern United States. The species grows in light soils with sufficient rainfall but it can also yield on heavy soils if they are well drained. Peas are used fresh or dried for human consumption and for green manure. In Greek popular medicine a meal from peas was applied to wounds to relieve pain (Arnold et al. 1993). According to Theophrastus pea is one of the several crops that must be sown late (*Hist. pl.* 8.1.4), and Pliny advises that pea should be sown in autumn or spring as long as the plants have plenty of sun, because they are sensitive to cold (*HN* 18.123). In Classical Greece, pea was known as *pisos* (πισός), and it was the main constituent of *etnos* (έτνος), a soup that was also made of lentils (Dalby 1996).

Pisum sativum appeared in Greece alongside wheat and barley as early as the 7th millennium B.C. The species is reported from the Early Neolithic site of Nea Nikomedeia (van Zeist and Bottema 1971), but it seems that wild pea (*Pisum sativum* ssp. *elatius*) was present at Franchthi Cave as early as the 8th millennium B.C. (Hansen 1991).

C. Industrial plants

In this section are included plants that produce oil, fiber, and/or dyes. Cultivation of these plants must have been undertaken in the early stages of agriculture, but the evidence for the beginnings of their domestication is still insufficient.

Charred seeds of oil plants, such as flax (*Linum usitatissimum*) and gold of pleasure (*Camelina sativa*) are not easily preserved in archaeological deposits as the high oil content causes the seed to burst when charring. Various archaeological sites, however, have yielded significant quantities of charred seeds of *Linum usitatissimum* and *Camelina sativa*, suggesting that their remains are not scarce at sites where the species played a prominent role in the economy.

Sesame (*Sesamum indicum*) was highly prized for its oil, which keeps fresh for a long time without turning rancid. The species is mentioned in Linear B tablets. Herodotus (1.193.4) reports that the inhabitants of Babylonia consumed sesame oil rather than olive oil. Aristophanes talks of sesame folded into a cake (*Peace* 869), although this passage has been doubted (Dalby 1996). Theophrastus categorizes sesame, along with the millets, as one of the main summer crops (*Hist pl.* 8.1.1), and he remarks that sesame oil receives rose perfume better than other oils because of its higher quality (*De odoribus*

4.20). Archaeobotanically, sesame is a rare find. The species is reported from Late Bronze Age Akrotiri (Sarpaki 1987) and from the 2nd-century A.D. Dioikitirion at Thessalonica (Mangaffa 1998).

Seeds of the oil plant *Lallemantia* are reported from three Bronze Age sites in northern Greece: Mandalo, Archondiko, and Assiros (Jones and Valamoti 2005). At all three sites, the seeds were found in significant concentrations in storage contexts, suggesting that they were deliberately stored for use by the inhabitants. Smaller quantities of *Lallemantia* have been found in Middle and Late Bronze Age Aghios Mamas (Kroll, forthcoming) and Bronze Age Kastanas (cited in Jones and Valamoti 2005). The seeds of the plant are rich in oil and can be used for food, lighting, medicine, and as a tanning agent or varnish (Hedrick 1972). None of the *Lallemantia* species are native to Greece or to Europe, indicating that the plant was initially imported (Jones and Valamoti 2005). This seems to have happened in the early Bronze Age, and the plant continued to be used into the Late Bronze Age. The discovery of *Lallemantia* seeds at Bronze Age sites in northern Greece attests to long-distance contacts with communities to the east during the Bronze Age, and would suggest that the increased importance of oil production during the Bronze Age was not restricted to southern Greece, as is commonly believed (Jones and Valamoti 2005).

Linum usitatissimum and *Cannabis sativa* were important fiber crops. Flax and hemp stems were retted and broken in order to free the fibers. Flax is well documented in Greek archaeobotanical assemblages (see below). The method of obtaining hemp fiber is similar to that used for getting linen from flax, and the fibers are not easy to distinguish from linen. Herodotus also noticed this, writing that one not used to telling hemp and linen apart would not even notice the difference (4.74). Hemp is known only from literary evidence, as no physical remains of the species are recorded so far. Barber (1991) reports the recovery of hemp fabric scraps from Trakhones (Attica) dated to 5th century B.C. This piece, however, seems to have been imported, as it was accompanied by a cloth made of cotton, a plant that had not yet reached Greece. According to Herodotus (4.74–75) the Scythians of the Black Sea region breathed the fumes of burning *Cannabis* as a part of a purification ritual. Hemp was not grown in Greece in Herodotus' time, but in the 4th century B.C. there was a need for hemp in Greek communities that used it for ropes for the navies; this need had led to a trade in hemp in the Euxine (Forbes 1987, p. 59). In Hellenistic times the species was grown in Greece: Pausanias reports hemp cultivation in Elis about A.D. 170 (Forbes 1987).

Cotton (*Gossypium* sp.) seems to have arrived in Greece with the expedition of Alexander the Great and it was a rare and expensive commodity. Literary evidence indicates that the Greeks were familiar with the cotton tree. Herodotus (3.106, 7.65) reports that in India there were wild trees bearing wool "exceeding in beauty...that of a sheep, the natives use it for making their clothes" and that "the Indians [in Xerxes' army] wore cotton dresses." He also describes a corselet worked with cotton and gold that was sent to Athena as an offering by the pharaoh Amasis in the 6th century B.C. (3.47). According to Theophrastus the island of Tylos in the Persian Gulf (modern Bahrain) produced the "wool-bearing" tree (cotton plant) in abundance (*Hist. pl.* 4.7.7), and he adds that this tree was also found in India and Arabia (4.7.8). The diffusion of cotton cultivation and of its processing technologies had reached Greece in Hellenistic Times (Zohary and Hopf 2000; Barber 1991; Forbes 1987).

Another fiber plant was the common nettle (*Urtica dioica*), which was also used for food and in medicine. Evidence of its use as a fiber plant comes from Denmark around 500 B.C. and from Germany in the Middle Ages (Roche-Bernard 1993). No ancient Greek authors refer to these fabrics.

Lime wood (*Tilia platyphillos* Scop.) was used for ropes as it was easily " bent because its sap is viscid" (Theophr. *Hist. pl.* 1.5.5). This information is confirmed by Pliny, who reports that the Greeks used lime wood to make ropes (*HN* 19.31).

In the field of dyes, one of the most important red dyes was kermes, a dye extracted from the body of female insect, *Kermococcus vermilio* Planch., that lives on the kermes oak (*Quercus coccifera*). The color of kermes ranges from brilliant red to scarlet. According to Theophrastus "all the kinds (oaks) produce galls" (*Hist. pl.* 3.8.6), and in another passage he mentions that the kermes oak "...besides its acorns bears a kind of scarlet berry"(3.16). In the Hellenistic period kermes was used to dye wool, leather, and silk. It was applied as a vat-dye along with Egyptian alum and urine to bind the dye to the fiber (Forbes 1987, p. 105).

Cheaper forms of red dye were madder, extracted from the roots of the plant *Rubia tinctorium,* and archil, produced from lichens. We learn from Pliny that madder was widely used in dyeing woolens and leather (*HN* 19.47–48). Dioscorides reports that the root of madder is red and fit for dyeing and in Italy and Caria the plant was sown among the olives (*MM* 3.160).

A high-quality blue dye was woad, made from the leaves of *Isatis tinctoria*. Herodotus reports (1.203) that the inhabitants of the Caucasus lived on wild fruits of *Isatis tinctoria* and manufactured a clothing dye from the chopped-up leaves mixed with water. A cheaper blue dye was indigo, which was produced from *Indigofera tinctoria,* but it did not become common until Hellenistic times (Forbes 1987). Saffron, an orange-yellow dye extracted from the dried stigmas of the crocus flower (*Crocus sativus*), was also popular. Saffron was also known as a seasoning for food, a use that is widespread in

Greece today. Although no physical remains of the species have been recovered from the archaeobotanical assemblages, Minoan pottery and frescoes from the Late Bronze Age Akrotiri (*Xesté* 3) depict the picking of *Crocus* flowers. Theophrastus describes saffron crocus as "herbaceous in character," with a "large and fleshy root that loves to be trodden on and grows fairer when the root is crushed into the ground by foot" (*Hist. pl.* 6.6.10).

In the following section are discussed in detail species that appear with relative frequency in the archaeobotanical assemblages mentioned in this work.

Olive tree (*Olea europaea* L.)
The olive tree is part of the *Oleacea* family and the genus *Olea* includes 40 species spread across the five continents. In the Mediterranean region, the only species found is *Olea europea* (Zohary and Hopf 2000). The olive, while not a demanding species, is particularly well suited to the climate in the Mediterranean, where it is a characteristic component of maquis vegetation. Olive does not tolerate cold winters (temperatures below 3° C), and the highest altitude at which it can be found is 600 m above sea level.

The history of olive domestication is a crucial question for archaeological and palaeoenvironmental research. Archaeological and archaeobotanical studies can contribute to a better understanding of the origins—both chronological and geographical—of olive domestication and of the diffusion of its cultivation across the Mediterranean. Genetic studies have shown that the selection of cultivars occurred in different genetic pools, supporting the hypothesis that olive domestication occurred in many locations in the Mediterranean basin (Besnard and Bervillé 2000; Besnard et al. 2002). Kislev (1995) conducted morphological studies of intact olive stones from Kfar Samir, an Israeli Chalcolithic site (3700 B.C.), and suggested the existence of an olive-oil industry prior to the beginning of the domestication process. Morphometric analysis applied on olive stones from wild and cultivated populations of various Mediterranean origins and from archaeological assemblages of Spanish, French, and Italian settlements suggests an early and autochthonous olive domestication in the northwestern Mediterranean (Terral et al. 2004). The appearance of cultivated forms in the Chalcolithic/Bronze Age seems to confirm that farming and selective practices have been in operation at least since that time (Terral et al. 2004).

Olives and vines were part of the Mediterranean polycultural triad (along with wheat) and remains of the two species occur in many protohistorical and historical deposits. The domesticated olive tree in Greece has its origins in the second millennium (Runnels and Hansen 1986), but some scholars believe that the tree was already cultivated on Crete by the Early Minoan period, in the third millennium B.C. (Blitzer 1993). On Crete, palynological evidence from Tumbakion (Bottema 1980) and from the Akrotiri peninsula near Chania (Gennett

1982; Moody 1987) showed that the olive tree was present in the Middle Neolithic period and became more common during the Late Neolithic. Moody (1987) reports *Olea* in Tersana from 6000 to 3500 BP. In Moody's diagram, *Olea* pollen is not found in the lowest sample; the curve then develops a maximum of about 40% before it decreases towards a low percentage around 3500 BP.

The pollen diagram from a core collected near Asi Gonia, in the Idi Mountains, at 780 m above sea level (Atherden and Hall 1994; 1999) dates back to about 1500 BC. Atherden and Hall correlated the Asia Gonia diagram with the sociopolitical periods of the last 1500 years on Crete. The olive pollen appearing 5700 BP is contemporaneous with a decline in deciduous and evergreen oaks pointing to a decrease in oaks growing on the foothills of the mountains towards the coast. At the same time, indicators of crop cultivation and animal husbandry appear or increase. Palynological evidence from the coastal lowland of northwestern Crete in the area of Lake Kournias indicates that *Olea* pollen appears around 6200 BP and around 5700 BP the species became settled on the island (Bottema and Sarpaki 2003). According to Bottema and Sarpaki (2003, p. 737) *Olea europaea* did not occut in Crete by origin but the species was very likely brough to the island at the second half of the holocene.

Olive stones were discovered in many Early Minoan sites (Blitzer 1993), but the material cannot be classified as wild or domesticated, since no detailed examination of the morphology of olive stones has been conducted. On the site of Myrtos (Early Minoan II: 2700/2650–2150 B.C.) numerous wood prunings from what are thought to have been cultivated olive plants were discovered (Rackham 1972).

A thorough account of all archaeobotanical finds of olive from the south of Greece, and in particular from Crete, has been assembled by Y. Hamilakis (1996), who finds no substantial evidence to support the hypothesis that tree crops were cultivated systematically from the Early Minoan Period. Outside of the occasional use of olive trees, the systematic use of olive oil seems to have started in the second palace period (1750/1720–1490/1470 B.C.) and increased during the "post-palatial" period (1490/1470–1075/1050 B.C.). That olive was a fundamental element of the agricultural economy on Crete by the second millennium B.C. (Middle Minoan period) is also confirmed by the early Linear A tablets and sealings found in several sites on Crete on which olives are recorded; in some cases (e.g., at Aghia Triada) olives were probably used as payment to laborers (Was 1973). Clay lamps using liquid fuel (probably olive oil) appear at many Early Minoan sites (Warren 1972) and they became common objects throughout Crete during the Middle Minoan period (Evans 1921–1935). Blitzer (1993, p. 172) compares processing installations from Minoan Crete with the contemporary stone press beds found at Maroni on

Cyprus, dated to ca. 1300 B.C., and sees them as indicative of an expansion of olive-oil production by a centralized Mycenaean authority as part of growing eastern Mediterranean trade. Other scholars, however, note that although similar press beds have been found in Crete (at Knossos and Palaikastro), none dating to the Bronze Age have been found on the Greek mainland (Runnels and Hansen 1985, p 305; Sallares 1991, p. 306).

The *Olea* values in Bronze Age pollen cores from mainland Greece are of great interest because they indicate olive cultivation during this period (Bottema 1974; Turner and Greig 1975; Genet 1982; Jahns 1993). Curiously, the same evidence indicates a decrease in olive pollen during the beginning of the Iron Age (1050–700 B.C.); evidence of its cultivation appears again much later, in the Archaic period. The silence of the ancient written sources (such as Homer and Hesiod) on the culinary use of olive oil, the disappearance of oil lamps in the beginning of the Iron Age, and their reappearance in the 8th century B.C. led some scholars to the conclusion that the Homeric world did not cultivate olives but used imported oil (Hehn-Schrader 1911). The absence of oil lamps could indicate, however, a low production of olives without suggesting the abandonment or interruption of olive cultivation. In 10th-century B.C. layers at Delphi, olive stones longer than 10 mm have been found—a size that, according to the archaeobotanist of the site, suggests cultivation (Luce et al., forthcoming), although the increased size of olive stones is no longer considered a criterion for domestication (Terral et al. 2004). In the same area the pollen record presents an almost continuous curve, with no interruption during the Dark Ages (Luce et al., forthcoming). Moreover, the *Olea* values from the Argissa plain in the Argolid indicate olive cultivation during the Geometric period (Jahns 1993).

At the beginning of the 8th century B.C. the planting of olive trees and the export of olive oil became widespread and made the olive tree *the* tree of the Greeks in the 5th century (Amouretti 1986). Society responded to exterior market opportunities through the creation of specialized olive-oil production centers. In Classical deposits remains of olive stones were reported from the 7th-century B.C. layers at the sanctuary of Hera on Samos (Kučan 1995) and at the 5th-century B.C. sanctuary of Demeter and Kore in Corinth (Bookidis et al. 1999).

Olive oil was an ingredient in bread making and was served as a snack on bread, in place of butter (Ath. *Deipn.* 2.56b–f). But olive oil was not used only for culinary purposes; it was widely used in the fabrication of perfumes, cosmetics, and textiles, and also as a lamp oil. For a fuller discussion of the uses of olive oil, see Amouretti 1986.

Flax (*Linum usitatissimum* L.)

Flax (*Linum usitatissimum*) is an annual crop that until recently was the principal oil and fiber source in the Old World. Its geographical distribution from the Atlantic coast of Europe to Russia and India indicates that the species is not very demanding in terms of soil and climatic conditions, but grows better in humid temperate zones (Ewers 1989).

The seeds of *Linum* contain about 40% oil. In peasant communities linseed was used as a source of edible oil, but the oil is better suited to household purposes as it dries like a lacquer and provides a high-grade lamp oil. The seeds can be used in cooking—intact, ground, or crushed—and were used in antiquity as an aromatic garnish on loaves (Ath. *Deipn.* 111a). The fibers for spinning are obtained from fiber-cell bundles that run the length of the stem and form a ring in the cortex (Zohary and Hopf 2000). The stems are harvested before the maturation of the seed; next they are dried and then immersed in water for retting (the microbial decomposition of the pectin connecting the fibers with other tissues of the stem). After retting the flax is dried and further processed at leisure. The entire process as it was carried out in the 1st century A.D. is well described by Pliny (*HN* 19.3.16).

Flax was first used in its wild form *Linum angustifolium*, a species widely distributed in the Mediterranean basin, North Africa, Near East, and the Caucasus (Ewers 1989). In Greece the oldest linseed remains were retrieved from Early Neolithic Thessaly (Otzaki and Sesklo; see Kroll 1983, 1991). The earliest records for flax as a crop, however, are provided by the Late Neolithic assemblages from Arkadikos, Makriyalos, and Mandalo (Valamoti 2004); these finds suggest that the cultivation of the species was practiced in northern Greece from at least the 6th millennium B.C. Other finds of the species are shown in *Tables 5.6* to *5.12*.

Gold of pleasure (*Camelina sativa* (L.) Crantz)

Gold of pleasure, or false fax (*Camelina sativa*), was an important oil crop in eastern and central Europe until the 1940s. Today the species is a relic oil plant that is no longer cultivated. *Camelina* seeds contain 25% to 40% edible oil that was mainly used to season food. Gold of pleasure can also be used as fodder and as a medicinal plant; its seeds are thought to have laxative properties and relief burnings of the skin (Fournier 1947).

Camelina sativa is closely related to a variable aggregate of wild and weedy forms distributed over Europe and southwest Asia, *Camélina microcarpa* (Zohary and Hopf 2000). Distinction between cultivated varieties of *Camelina sativa* and the wild and weedy forms is not always possible; it seems that the length of the seeds is the main identification criterion, as cultivated seeds are at about 1.5 and 2 mm long (Zohary and Hopf 2000).

In Greece the oldest remains of *Camelina sativa* are reported from Late Neolithic Pefkakia in Thessaly but the find is limited to one seed (Kroll 1983, 1991). *Table 5.17* suggests that the species became common in northern Greece sometime during the Bronze Age. By the first millennium B.C. the species became a considerable oilseed crop, as it has been found in Kastanas (Kroll 1983) and to a lesser extent in Kalapodi (Kroll 1993). Like flax, charred seeds of *Camelina sativa* are highly perishable but the seed fragments can easily be recognized in archaeological deposits due to their typical shape. *Tables 5.17* and *5.18* indicate that *Camelina sativa* finds are limited to the northern parts of Greece; it seems that olive was the main source of oil for central and southern Greece, where other oil plants, such as gold of pleasure and poppy, do not appear at archaeological sites.

Opium poppy (*Papaver somniferum* L.)
Opium poppy is an annual plant with white-spotted petals and a large ovoid capsule. *Papaver somniferum* is not native to Greece and is thought to have originated in the Iberian peninsula (Zohary and Hopf 2000). The species is grown mostly for opium, which is obtained from the latex released by the plants after their unripe capsules are gashed (Zohary and Hopf 2000). The seeds of the plant have no narcotic properties; the fluid contained in the bud that becomes opium is present only before the seeds are fully formed. Poppy seeds are used as a flavoring in confections, pastry, and other baking, but they can also be pressed for oil. A first cold pressing yields a clear, edible oil; a second pressing under heat produces an inferior, colored oil that can be used in painting and for industrial purposes. In Greek popular medicine, an herbal tea made of the petals and the capsules was used to calm a cough (Arnold et al. 1993).

Archaeobotanically, *Papaver somniferum* is rather well documented. In historic contexts from Greece, opium poppy remains were discovered in a Protogeometric context in the sanctuary of Kalapodi (Kroll 1993); at Kastanas, in the same period, poppy remains represent 7.21% of the botanical remains, and the plant was probably used as a substitute for olive oil (Kroll 1983). At the Samian Heraion (7th century B.C.), 49 seeds of *Papaver somniferum* L. were discovered in a waterlogged deposit, and it seems that the species was used for its narcotic properties (Kučan 1995).

Papaver somniferum and its hypnotic qualities were well known in antiquity and the plant was regarded as magical or poisonous. The ancient Greeks portrayed the divinities of Sleep, Night, and Death as wreathed with poppies or carrying poppies in their hands. In statuary Apollo, Demeter, Aphrodite, Kybele, and other gods often wear poppy wreaths on their heads or carry poppy bouquets, with or without stalks of wheat, in their hands. According to the legend, Demeter, in despair over Pluto's abduction of her daughter Persephone, ate poppies to forget her pain and to sleep. The poppy became one of the symbols of Demeter, and Theocritus states that in the temple of Demeter Alois, the goddess bore poppies on her head (*Id.* 1.157).

Poppy is frequently mentioned in the ancient literature and the plant was used in various ways, as a hypnotic or a culinary plant. Hesiod (8th century B.C.) reports that the poppy was brought for cultivation to a city near Corinth and that this city then received the name Mekoné (from the Greek word *mékon,* "poppy") because of the extensive cultivation of the plant in the surrounding area (*Theog.* 11.535–537). This prehistoric name was later replaced by Sikyon.

In the *Iliad,* Homer compares a hero falling in battle to a poppy full of seeds, drooping in the rains of spring (*Il.* 9.302–308). In the *Odyssey,* Helen obtains from the Egyptian Polydamas a drug called *nepénthes,* and gives it to Telemachus and his comrade to make them forget their grief (*Od.* 10.220–232). This drug could be related to opium poppy. Around 1500 B.C. *Papaver somniferum* may have reached Egypt, where opium was celebrated for its medicinal uses (Hobbs 1998). Diodorus Siculus, referring to Homer's *nepénthes,* reports that in his days the women of Egypt used the drug because only the women of Dispolis had, in very ancient times, discovered this antidote to anger and grief (1.97.30). Theophrastus, referring to the same passage, comments that the land of Egypt was among the places that produced this drug, but he does not give further information regarding the species mentioned by Homer (*Hist. pl.* 9.15.1.). He reports that there are various plants called poppy, and he lists "the black or horned poppy, the poppy called rhoias, and the Herakleian poppy" (*Hist. pl.* 9.12.3–5). None of these species can be identified as *Papaver somniferum* L., but opium poppy was not unknown to Theophrastus.

As regards the extraction of the poppy juice, Theophrastus writes that poppy is the only plant from which the juice is extracted from the head and not from the stalks, and this juice, called *mekónion,* is collected straight into vessels (*Hist. pl.* 9.8.2). He reports that Thrasyas of Mantineia had discovered that an easy and painless death could be obtained from the juice of hemlock or of poppy (*Hist. pl.* 9.16.8). This use of the plant is confirmed by Herakleides of Pontus, writing in the 4th century B.C. He comments that on the island of Keios those who reached a certain age—especially women—voluntarily put an end to their life by drinking the juice of poppy or of hemlock, in order to avoid the illness and pains of old age (On Governments, *FGrH* II.215, IX 3). Pliny was the first to use the term *opium* to describe the juice of the poppy that the ancient Greeks called *mekónion;* he comments that the juice of black poppy is hypnotic and, if taken in large doses, induces death through sleep and it is called *opium* (*HN* 20.19.53).

Papaver somniferum was an important component of ancient medicine. Hippocrates mentions the poppy in numerous passages concerning the concoction of pharmaceutical preparations. He distinguishes between the white, fire-red and black poppy.

Species	AN	EN	MN	LA/FN	EBA	MBA	LBA	PG	G	A	C
N of components	5	9	9	19	8	4	10	4	3	3	3
Camelina sativa	0	0	0	5.3	12.5	25	30	50	0	0	0
Linum usitatissimum	0	11.1	22.2	21.1	12.5	50	20	50	0	0	0
Olea ssp	20	11.1	0	10.5	12.5	25	0	0	0	0	0
Olea europaea	0	0	0	0	0	0	20	50	33.3	66.7	33.3
Papaver somniferum	0	0	0	0	12.5	0	20	50	0	0	0

Table 5.17: Percentage of Appearances of Industrial plants per Component (northern Greece)

AN: Aceramic Neolithic, EN: Early Neolithic, MN: Middle Neolithic, LN/FN: Late Neolithic, Final Neolithic, EBA: Early Bronze Age, MBA: Middle Bronze Age, LBA: Late Bronze Age, PG: Proto-Geometric, G: Geometric, A: Archaic, C: Classic

Species	AN	EN	MN	LA/FN	EBA	MBA	LBA	PG	G	A	C
N of components	0	0	1	7	6	6	7	2	1	2	3
Camelina sativa	0	0	0	0	0	0	0	0	0	0	0
Linum usitatissimum	0	0	0	0	16.7	0	6.3	0	0	0	0
Olea ssp	0	0	0	0	16.7	16.7	0	0	0	50	0
Olea europaea	0	0	0	0	16.7	18.8	50	0	100	100	100
Papaver somniferum	0	0	0	0	0	0	6.3	0	0	50	0

Table 5.18: Percentage of Appearances of Industrial plants per Component (southern Greece)

AN: Aceramic Neolithic, EN: Early Neolithic, MN: Middle Neolithic, LN/FN: Late Neolithic, Final Neolithic, EBA: Early Bronze Age, MBA: Middle Bronze Age, LBA: Late Bronze Age, PG: Proto-Geometric, G: Geometric, A: Archaic, C: Classic

Species	AN	EN	MN	LA/FN	EBA	MBA	LBA	PG	G	A	C
N of components	5	9	10	26	14	10	26	6	4	5	6
Arbutus unedo	0	0	10	4	0	0	0	0	0	20	0
Cornus mas	0	33.3	10	19.2	14.3	0	4	16.7	0	40	0
Crataegus ssp	20	0	0	0	0	0	0	16.7	0	20	0
Fragaria vesca	0	0	0	0	0	0	4	16.7	0	20	0
Juniperus ssp	0	0	0	0	0	0	0	16.7	0	40	16.7
Malus sylvestris	0	0	0	0	0	0	4	0	0	0	0
Pistacia ssp	20	11.1	30	19.2	14.3	10	0	0	0	0	0
Pistacia terebinthus	0	22.2	28	19.2	7.1	0	0	0	25	20	0
Prunus spinosa	0	11.1	0	0	0	10	4	33.3	0	20	0
Pyrus ssp	0	0	0	7.7	7.1	0	4	16.7	0	20	0
Quercus ssp	40	55.6	30	15.4	14.3	40	4	33.3	0	40	0
Rosa ssp.	0	0	0	4	0	0	0	0	0	40	0
Rubus fruticosus	0	11.1	10	15.4	14.3	0	4	16.7	25	20	0
Sambucus ebulus	0	0	0	7.7	7.1	0	7.7	16.7	0	0	0
Sambucus ssp	0	11.1	0	7.7	7.1	0	0	0	0	0	0
Vitis sylvestris	0	33.3	40	27	0	10	0	0	0	20	0

Table 5.19: Percentage of Appearances of Wild fruits per Component

AN: Aceramic Neolithic, EN: Early Neolithic, MN: Middle Neolithic, LN/FN: Late Neolithic, Final Neolithic, EBA: Early Bronze Age, MBA: Middle Bronze Age, LBA: Late Bronze Age, PG: Proto-Geometric, G: Geometric, A: Archaic, C: Classic

In terms of therapeutic efficacy he mentions the unripe (*On Internal Diseases* 12), the ripe (*Mul.* 192), and the baked poppy (*Nat. mul.* 58). Hippocrates dismisses the magical attributes of poppy juice, *mekónion*, but acknowledges its usefulness as a narcotic and styptic in treating internal diseases, coughing, diseases of women, and epidemics (*Nat. mul.* 33; *Epid.* 2.18).

Dioscorides distinguishes between the flowing poppy that "sheds its flower rapidly and has narcotic properties" and the cultivated or garden poppy, the seeds of which are used in baking bread (*MM* 4.64.1, 3; *MM* 65.1–7)[3]. He also provides instructions on the proper extraction of the poppy juice (*MM* 4.35.7). Dioscorides reports that the leaves and the capsules of wild poppies, boiled in water, induce sleep; the poppy juice "when…cooled and dried and taken in small quantities like vetch is harmless, induces sleep, aids digestion, relieves cough and stomach troubles, but when more of it is taken, it plunges one into lethargic sleep" (*MM* 4.64.1–3). Similar reflections can be found in Galen's work *Medicorum Graecorum*; he mentions that "poppy juice is the strongest of the drugs and when it is soaked in boiling water can induce a deadening sleep" (13.273).

D. Fruit trees and nuts

Fruits trees were an important element of food production in Greece. Like grains and pulses, the first trees seem to have been brought into cultivation in the Near East (Zohary and Hopf 2000). Arboriculture seems to have started relatively late in Greece, however—at the end of the Neolithic period of the beginnings of the Bronze Age, if not later. The emergence of arboriculture was a long and gradual process, and all the stages have not yet been defined. Bringing the trees into cultivation demanded above all an evolution in the mentality of the population so that they could respond to the new challenges that came along.

Plant remains retrieved from archaeological excavations indicate that wild fruits were frequently collected from Upper Paleolithic times, as it was the case at Franchthi Cave (Hansen 1991). The Greek landscape was extremely rich and a large amount of fruits was gathered from the wild. *Table 5.19* presents the percentages of appearances of wild fruits per cultural component. The present evidence indicates that fruit gathering was a common practice in Greece from at least the Aceramic Neolithic and was therefore not infrequent as has been recently proposed (see Perles 2002).

Elder and Dane wort (*Sambucus nigra* L. and *Sambucus ebulus* L.) are identified in Greek archaeobotanical assemblages from at least the Early Neolithic in Thessaly and Macedonia (Hopf 1962b; Kroll 1981, 1983; Valamoti 1995, 2004). The species became more frequent in Iron Age, as is clear at Kastanas (Kroll 1983). It seems that

Sambucus fruits were collected from the surroundings of the site and were probably used in wine making (Kroll 1983).

Pears (*Pyrus* sp.) were in Greece at least as early as the Mesolithic period, as they were gathered from the wild at Franchthi Cave (Hansen 1991). The wild pears (*Pyrus amygdaliformis*) at Franchthi were probably consumed raw by humans, or they may have been cooked with cereals and eaten as a porridge. Finds of fruits or seeds that were identified as pears are reported from Late Neolithic Dikili Tash (Mangafa 1990), Dimini (Kroll 1979), and Sitagroi (Renfrew et al. 1986), as well as from Mycenaean Dimini (Megaloudi, in preparation). The spread of cultivated pears may have come through the grafting of cultivated clones onto wild roots, and the beginning of the process may have taken place in Anatolia (Zohary and Hopf 2000, pp. 177–178). Theophrastus (*Hist. pl.* 1.14.4, 2.1.2) describes three cultivated varieties of pear and mentions propagation by grafting. Wild and cultivated pears are distinguished by both Dioscorides and Galen. Dioscorides (*MM* 1.168.85) states that the long-ripening wild pear, *akhras*, has a more binding force than the cultivated type and the ashes of the wood help those intoxicated by eating mushrooms. Cultivated pear, *apios*, was associated with the cult of Hera, who was sometimes called *Hera Apia* (Brosse 1989).

Cornelian cherry (*Cornus mas* L.) occurred in Greece at least in the Early Neolithic (*Table 5.19*), as stones of the species have been reported from Neolithic and Bronze Age sites in Macedonia and Thessaly (Valamoti 2004; Margariti 2002b; Valamoti 1995; Renfrew 1997; Kroll 1983; Jones and Halstead 1980; Renfrew 1973; van Zeist and Bottema 1971). According to Homer the companions of Odysseus were fed with cornelian cherry fruits when Circe changed them into pigs (*Od.* 10.242). The wood of cornelian cherry was highly prized in antiquity. It was used to make javelins for hunting and Theophrastus compares its hardness with that of horn (*Hist. pl.* 3.12.1). The Lycians were equipped with bows cut from cornelian cherry wood (Hdt. 7.92), and according to Pausanias (3.13.5) the Trojan horse was made from cornelian cherry wood taken from the sacred wood of Apollo on Mount Ida in Troas. Legend says that the prophet Teiresias guided himself with a stick of cornelian cherry, which he chose on account of its hardness. Modern shepherds in the remote mountains of Greece still use crooks made of the hard wood of *Cornus mas*.

Remains of *Pistacia* sp. occur relatively often in archaeobotanical assemblages from Greece. Turpentine tree, or terebinth pistachio (*Pistacia terebinthus* L.), is a shrub that produces turpentine, a resin widely used in the cosmetics industry. The plant is also used in the production of dyes. The violet galls that cover the tree in winter yield a deep yellow dye that was used in Hellenistic times for coloring silk material imported from the Orient. *Pistacia terebinthus* appeared in Greece at

---

[3] All Dioscorides translations are from Wellmann 1914

least as early as the Middle Neolithic. An important quantity of *Pistacia terebinthus* nuts was discovered at the site of Limenaria on Thasos; this find indicates a primitive "technical" use of the plant in Greece as early as the 5th millennium B.C. (Megaloudi, forthcoming). Another species of the genus *Pistacia*, widespread in Greece, is the evergreen mastic tree (*Pistacia lentiscus* L.). The species produces a resinous gum that was used in antiquity as a chewing gum (Polunin and Huxley 1965). Dioscorides tells us (*MM* 1.91) that this transparent gum was also used for attaching false eyelashes to eyelids. Today a variety of this shrub, called *Chia,* is cultivated on the island of Chios for its resinous gum, which is used to flavor chewing gum. Theophrastus says that the oil obtained from the mastic tree is suitable for flavoring wine (*Hist. pl.* 9.1–2, 4–7).

Walnuts (*Juglans regia*) and hazelnuts (*Corylus avelana*) do not occur frequently in archaeobotanical assemblages. A single fragment of a walnut shell was found in a grave of the 4th century B.C. in the necropolis of Thasos (Megaloudi 2005). The walnut is absent from the palynologial records of the Neolithic and appears suddenly around 1500 B.C. (Bottema 2000). Unfortunately, the palynological evidence does not give a clear picture of the origin of the walnut or the direction of its distribution. On the site of Lake Trichonis in western Greece, the emergence of the walnut coincides with the presence of volcanic ash from the eruption of the Thera volcano (modern Santorini). The collapse of Minoan civilization and the ascendance of the Mycenaean kingdoms could have favored contact with Asia Minor (modern Turkey), and thus may have brought about the rapid distribution of walnuts. People may have found it impossible to grow crops in the soils that had been poisoned by volcanic deposits, and large fruit trees (such as walnuts), which suffered less in those conditions, may have been rapidly developed (Bottema 1980, 2000). In Archaic Greece the walnut tree was associated with the cult of Dionysus and was seen as a symbol of fecundity. Later on, the species was dedicated to chthonian divinities—the *Keres*—that in Classical Greece were related to violent death (Brosse 1989). This belief survived into medieval times in Europe, when the walnut tree was considered to be the tree of the devil and of sorcerers (Benzi and Berliocchi 1999).

Corylus avelana is a common component of the oak forests of temperate Europe, the Caucasus, and northern Turkey, and the Caspian belt of Iran (Zohary and Hopf 2000). The hazelnut is a species of high nutritional value and its nuts are easy to store and transport. It can also be used for its oil. When the European hazelnut was taken into cultivation, it was planted both for its nuts and for its wood, which was used for the preparation of hurdles and walking sticks (Zohary and Hopf 2000). In Greece hazelnuts are reported from a Late Neolithic deposit at Dikili Tash (Matterne 1993) and from a Protogeometric level in Krania in the region of Pieria (Margariti 2002) as

well as at the Samian Heraion (7th century B.C.) (Kučan 1995). Theophrastus (*Hist. pl.* 3.2.1, 3.15.1–2) places hazelnuts among the cultivated species, and it was probably cultivated during the Classical period. The cultivation of the species was probably introduced in Italy by Greek colonists (7th and 6th century B.C.) making use of the existing varieties of the species, although it is not yet clear when the domestication of *Corylus avelana* was started.

The conquests of Alexander brought great and lasting changes to Greece: Greek culture was spread through the Near East, and new species, some of them originating in China, traveled westward to Italy and Greece. The peach (*Prunus punica*), the apricot (*Prunus armeniaca*), the citrus (*Citrus medica*), and the cherry ((*Prunus avium/cerasus*) are species that appear to have come to Greece during Hellenistic times and have been grown there ever since. All these species however, are known from literary sources and almost no archaeobotanical evidence is yet available. The only sample comes from the 7th century B.C. sanctuary of Hera on Samos, where a piece of peach was found (Kučan 1995). The presence of peach at the Heraion does not suggest cultivation of the species at that time; *Prunus persica* was probably imported. This find and its context (sanctuary), however, indicate that peach was known to Archaic Greece and was probably considered as an "exotic" species reserved for special occasions.

Archaeobotanical evidence regarding quince (*Cydonia oblonga*) is ambiguous. A quince pip is reported from the layers of the 7th and 6th centuries B.C. in Delphi (Luce et al., forthcoming), but its morphology indicates that it could also be an apple pip. If it is a quince pip, then we have the first archaeobotanical evidence of this species in Greece. According to Zohary and Hopf (2000) the quince, which originated in the East, arrived in Europe only in the Classical period. Akkadian records of the late 2nd millennium however, list quinces (Postgate 1987). This fact led A. Dalby (1996) to suggest that the Minoans introduced the species into Greece. The Greek name of the fruit, *kydoni,* suggests a Cretan origin (Kydonia was the ancient name for the city of Chania in Crete), but there has been no archaeological evidence support for this hypothesis.

In the following section are highlighted in greater detail some fruit and nut species that aer regularly recorded in the archaeobotanical assemblages considered in this book. Some of the species presented here are retained because they seem to have had a special symbolic meaning.

Acorns (*Quercus* sp.)

Numerous species of oaks (*Quercus* sp.) exist and *Quercus* remains (such as acorns) are often found at archaeological sites. Acorns are considered to be astringent and "bitter" due to the tannin they contain. Tannin concentrations can vary considerably among oak species and even among the trees within a single oak species; thus some acorns are considered to be "sweet" and are referred to in the literature as "edible" acorns (Mason 1995). All acorns can be made edible, however, if the tannins are removed or neutralized by boiling or roasting the acorns.

Acorns are found at sites throughout Europe dating from Mesolithic times to the medieval period. In Greece acorns are found at Aceramic Neolithic levels in Thessaly (Renfrew 1966, 1989; Kroll 1983, 1991; Vickery 1936) and they continued to be used throughout prehistory. In Early Bronze Age layers at Kastanas a concentration of 1700 acorn remains has been found; according to the archaeobotanist of the site the acorns were designated for human consumption (Kroll 1983). The use of acorns in the human diet has parallels in the Balkans; at Bronze age Raskopanitza in Bulgaria acorns were found mixed with einkorn and barley grains on a saddle quern, and it has been suggested they were being ground into flour together (Renfrew 1969). Evidence for human consumption of acorns is available in written sources. Strabo (3.3.7) reports that in mountainous northern Spain people lived on acorn bread for much of the year. Acorns were also consumed in the mountainous district of Arcadia in the Peloponnese, as we hear from Herodotus (1.66) and Pausanias (8.4). Written sources imply that the consumption of acorns was an ancient custom that survived only in remote areas. Acorns were consumed in 5th-century B.C. Athens, however, and according to Aristophanes they were eaten roasted together with chickpea as a relish (*Peace* 137).

Acorns are nutritionally similar to cereals, being a source of carbohydrates, and are known to have been an important staple in Eastern North America and Japan (Mason 1995). In Roman mythology the goddess Ceres, who introduced cereals to mankind, is said to have been the first to replace their original food of leaves and grass with the acorn (Ov. *Fast.* 4.399). However, the discovery of acorns in archaeological contexts cannot always be taken as evidence that they were used for human food. *Quercus* remains could have been used as tanning agents, or they might have had a medicinal function for both humans and animals. Dioscorides attributed healing properties to acorns (*MM* 1.142) and in modern Greece the leaves and the fruits of *Quercus coccifera* and *Quercus sempervirens* are considered to be an astringent and are administered against diarrhea (Arnold et al. 1993). Acorns are eaten by a wide range of domestic and wild animals, and may also have been used as an animal feed, especially for pigs (Mason 1995). It has been suggested that concentrations of acorns at an archaeological site might indicate human consumption, as animals would forage for their own acorns (Jorgenesen 1977; Renfrew 1973; Kroll 1983; Vencl 1985). Ancient sources, however, do describe the collection of large quantities of acorns as feed for animals and their processing to remove the astringent tannins (Cato A*gr.* 54.1.60). Ethnographic parallels from Spain and

southeastern Turkey have shown that acorns are collected to be fed to animals (Mason 1992, 1995). Thus it is difficult to obtain with certainty good direct evidence for the role of acorns at an archaeological site, and more archaeobotanical data are necessary to make reliable conclusions.

Chaste tree (*Vitex agnus-castus* L.)
Chaste tree (*Vitex agnus-castus*) is a shrub that grows up to 3 m high with dark green leaves and small sweet-scented flowers. The plant grows next to streams, gullies, and damp places near the sea. The species is also known as Monk's pepper and its fruit yields a spicy edible oil that is often used to spice up various foods in modern Greek cuisine.

The Latin name of the plant *agnus-castus* do not derive from the Latin *agnus,* "sheep," but from the Greek *hagnos* (αγνός), meaning "chaste" (Latin *castus* = "chaste"). According to Dioscorides (*MM* 1.135) the species is called *agnus* because women wishing to affirm their chastity at the annual festival in honor of Demeter (Thesmophoria) would lie on couches made from branches of the tree. In Sparta the statue of Asclepius was made of chaste-tree wood and the god was called *Agnitas*, "the chaste" (Paus. 3.14.7).

A chaste tree ornamented the entrance to the temple of Hera on Samos and Pausanias lists that tree, along with the oak sacred to Zeus at Dodona, as the oldest trees living at that time (8.23.5). This shrub was sacred to Hera, the guardian of marriage, who was probably born under a chaste tree. In this context should be placed the 52,717 mineralized remains of *Vitex agnus-castus* discovered at the 7th-century Samian Heraion (Kučan 1995).

The wood of the chaste tree is very flexible and when Prometheus was delivered from his suffering by Hercules (or Chiron) he commemorated his bondage by putting on a wreath made of *Vitex agnus-castus* (Baumann 1993). Achilles used the flexible stems of the chaste tree to bind the two sons of Priam found tending sheep on Mount Ida (Hom. *Il.* 2.105) and the same species was used by Odysseus to tie his companions under the bellies of sheep in order to escape from the cave of Polyphemus (*Od.* 9.427).

Grape vine (*Vitis vinifera* L.)
The second species of the famous Mediterranean triad, the vine (*Vitis* sp.) occurs in archaeological deposits from the Early Neolithic period (Renfrew 1971). The species prefers the Mediterranean climate but tolerates cold and humidity better than the olive tree (Zohary and Hopf 2000). The cultivated grape vine is closely related to an aggregate of wild forms distributed over Europe and western Asia, *V. vinifera* ssp. *sylvestris* (Zohary and Hopf 2000). *Sylvestris* vines are indigenous in southern Europe, the Near East, and the southern Caspian Belt (Zohary and Hopf 2000). The boundary between

cultivated grape vine and wild forms is not easy to determine, as the spontaneous crossing between wild plants and cultivars has been repeatedly found. Morphological differences between wild and cultivated varieties exist (see *Chapter 4, Section G*).

According to some scholars grape cultivation did not start before the Early Bronze Age in southern Greece and the late Bronze Age in the north (Hansen 1988). Other scholars suggest a proto-culture of the species as early as the Late Neolithic (Renfrew 1973, 1995; Kroll 1991). Although this hypothesis is not accepted by all scholars, the find of 184 domesticated grape pips (*Vitis vinifera*) in the Late Neolithic levels of Dimitra in Macedonia lends strength to the theory that the vine was being domesticated in northern Greece in the Late Neolithic period (Renfrew 1997).

The earliest archaeological evidence for wine making belongs to Early Bronze Age Myrtos (Renfrew 1972) and Early Helladic Aghios Kosmas in Attica (Renfrew 1971). Grape skins consistent with wine pressing are reported from Dikili Tash, dated to the second half of the 5th millennium B.C. (Mangaffa et al. 2003); although wine production cannot be proved, these remains may represent the earliest indication of wine production in the broader Mediterranean area. Wine was a luxury item, locally produced in rural areas and closely linked to feasting and ceremonial activities (Hamilakis 1996, 1999; Renfrew 1972). Its consumption is related to the appearance of small cups and jugs in the archaeological record in the Early Bronze Age (Renfrew 1972). It has been suggested that Minoans and Mycenaeans distinguished both red and white wine (Stanley 1982, pp. 577–578), but at the present stage of research no evidence exists to confirm this hypothesis.

The vine was a creation of the god Dionysus and in the Homeric poems wine it always accompanies a meal. The three constituents of a proper Greek meal were *sitos* (bread), *opson* (meat), and *oinos* (wine) (Dalby 1996). Homer describes the Phaeacians gathering grapes from the vineyard, drying some for raisins and treading others to make wine (*Od.* 7.121–125). Hesiod advises his brother Perses to dry grapes in September for ten days and then cover them for five more; afterwards he can fill vessels with "gifts of Dionysus" (*Op.* 611–613). Theophrastus defines the vine as a tree species because "a tree is a thing which springs from the root…and it cannot easily be uprooted…for instance olive, fig, vine" (*Hist. pl.* 1.3.1). He advises flavoring wine with spices because "(wine) has a special property of assimilating odors" (*De odoribus* 3.7–13).

In Classical Greece vineyards were a symbol of the prosperity and the "good life," and prosperity and grape-processing scenes appear frequently on Attic black- and red-figure vessels of the 5th and 4th century B.C. In Aristophanes' *Peace* (308), the goddess Peace is described as "most loving of the vine" and Trygaeus

greets the goddess with the appellation "giver of the grapes" (520). The importance of the grape vine in Classical Greece can also be seen in the cruical role of wine in the symposium. According to Athenaeus wine was mixed with snow in order to keep it chilled (*Deipn.* 3.124c–d). Wine also played an important role in medicine, and Dionysus, the patron god of wine, was called "physician" (Curtis 2001). Hippocrates attributes to wine qualities of hot and dry and says that it acts as a purgative (*Du rég.* 2.52).

Grapes were an integral part of religious services and carbonized grape pips have been retrieved from sacrificial and funeral contexts.[4] Wine was often used to quench burnt offerings on the altar and as an offering to the dead. This ancient custom still exists in many parts of Greece today. In Thasos, for example, a priest pours red wine onto the body of the deceased prior to final interment. Once the body is buried, the wine pitcher used to anoint the corpse is smashed over the coffin.

Fig (*Ficus carica* L.)

The fig (*Ficus carica*) is a fast-growing crop (with production starting 3–4 years after planting) that seems to have been part of food production in the Mediterranean basin since at least the Early Bronze Age (Zohary and Hopf 2000). The species grows on stony ground, often near water or on well-watered land, but its spreading root system and small leaf area make it ideal for semiarid conditions. The complicated pollination of *Ficus carica* and the climatic requirements of the species must have been known at least as early as the 4th century B.C., as they are mentioned by Theophrastus (*Hist. pl.* 2.2.4).

The cultivated fig tree shows a close morphological resemblance to an aggregate of wild and weedy forms that are distributed over the Mediterranean basin (Zohary and Hopf 2000). These spontaneous figs are considered to be the wild progenitor of the cultivated fig tree and they are natural components of the Mediterranean maquis formations.

Figs have a high sugar content and can be consumed dried or fresh. Figs are used for medicinal purposes; the fruits are considered to be laxative, and a beverage made from the leaves and fruits is administered against asthma and as a cough suppressant (Arnold et al. 1993).

In Greece figs are recorded at archaeological sites dating to the Early Neolithic in Thessaly (Hopf 1962; Kroll 1981, 1983), and they continued to be used throughout antiquity (*Tables 5.7* to *5.14*). According to Zohary and Hopf (2000). the species was brought into cultivation

---

4 Carbonized grapes were discovered at the sanctuary of Hera on Samos (Kučan 1995) and of Demeter and Kore in Corinth (Bookidis et al. 1999). They were also found in association with several grave offerings from the necropolis of Ctasos, dated from the 5th and 4th centuries B.C. (Megaloudi 2004; Megaloudi, in preparation) and offerings in the cemetery of Eleftherna in Crete (Megaloudi, in preparation).

sometime in the Bronze Age, at about the same time as the olive tree and the grape vine. The counts of fig finds at archaeological sites increase considerably by the Late Neolithic period (*Table 5.8*), indicating a more extensive use. In the same period whole fruits occur more frequently in the archaeobotanical assemblages throughout Greece.

It is still unclear whether these remains represent wild or domesticated figs, and to date no systematic study of their variable morphology has been carried out. Nevertheless, the aforementioned increase in fig frequency could indicate that the cultivation of the species did not begin during the Early Bronze Age, as is generally believed, but at the end of the Neolithic period.

The fig tree (*Ficus carica*) is depicted on the frescoes in Minoan Crete and the species is frequently mentioned in the Homeric poems (*Il.* 50.5; *Od.* 50.7, 50.11, 50.24). According to legend, Demeter caused the fig tree to spring from the soil in Athens, where olives, grapes, and figs were considered necessities of daily life. When the figs of Attica were presented as an exceptional delicacy to Xerxes, he resolved to conquer the country in which they grew (Baumann 1993). Figs make several appearances in Athenaeus' *Deipnosophistae* and were often parts of fine meals. Fig leaves, which were pickled to reduce their bitterness, were used as a wrapping in dishes similar to modern *dolmades* made of vine leaves (*Deipn.* 74d, 652b). In the *Letter to Diagoras,* Lynceus of Samos considers the fig an appetizer and says that figs should be served before dinner, "when the appetite is virgin" (cited in *Deipn.* 75c). Figs, like grapes, were part of religious services; whole carbonized figs have been retrieved from funeral contexts in Greece.[5]

Almonds *(Amygdalus communis* L.)

The cultivated almond (*Amygdalus communis*) is a characteristic species in Mediterranean environments. *Amygdalus communis* belongs to the *Rocasae* family and can grow on poor rocky soils (de la Taille 1985). The species is tolerant of most climates but is extremely susceptible to early spring frosts. It is a naturally occurring species in Greece but its fruits are bitter and toxic if it is not domesticated. The genus *Amygdalus* comprises 26 species distributed throughout southwest Europe and Asia and the cultivated almond is related to an aggregate of wild forms native to the Levant countries (Zohary and Hopf 2000).

Almonds are very nutritious, providing a valuable source of oil and protein. The kernels are eaten fresh or ground into flour. Almond oil can be used internally as a laxative, for coughs, and for hoarseness, and externally as an emollient (Hansen 1991; Fournier 1947). The oil of

bitter almond was the main ingredient in macassor oil, which was colored red with alkanet root and applied to hair (Grieve 1967, cited in Hansen 1991). In addition to that, the oil of bitter almond was used for making perfumed ointments. According to Theophrastus, (*Concerning Odors* 4.20) almond oil "loses its virtue and keeps for a shorter time" if not used rapidly. Dioscorides (*MM* 1.176.86) mentions that the root of the bitter almond, if bruised and soaked in water, removes facial blemishes caused by sunburn. He also notes that almond, ground and applied in a poultice with rosewater and vinegar, provides relief from headache.

In Greece almonds have been collected from the wild since the Upper Paleolithic; they have been found at Franchthi Cave (Hansen 1991) and the species occurs at several sites throughout the Neolithic period (*Table 5.20*). Almonds were also part of ritual offerings. They are reported from the 7th century Samian Heraion (Kučan 1995) as well as from several funeral offerings discovered in the 4th-century B.C. layers of the necropolis on Thasos (Megaloudi, in preparation).

Pomegranate (*Punica granatum* L.)

The pomegranate (*Punica granatum*) is a deciduous bush or small tree that was highly prized in traditional Mediterranean horticulture. The species grows well on stony ground and in warm climates and is today cultivated in western and central Asia, northern India, and in the Mediterranean countries. Pomegranate fruits contain numerous seeds and are covered with a juicy flesh that can be eaten fresh, or whose juice can be extracted. Grenadine (pomegranate juice) is a common souring agent in southern Europe and western Asia. *Punica granatum* can be used in medicine both for its own perceived curative qualities and for its use as an ingredient for medicinal recipes (Fournier 1948). The bark of the pomegranate tree may also be used as a very strong purgative, although several side effects are reported (Leclerc 1927).

The Greek name for pomegranate is *roia* or *roa.* Some scholars (Andre 1956) believe that this word derives from the verb *réo* (flow), to indicate the astringent properties of the fruit in ancient medicine (Dioscorides, *MM* 1.110 ; Plin. *HN* 23.106). In Latin the fruit was known as either *malum punicum* or *malum granatum* (André 1985). The adjective *punicus* refers to Carthage, a Phoenician colony in northern Africa that according to Pliny (*HN* 13.112) was the origin of the species. The wild ancestor of the cultivated pomegranate, however, is well known: wild forms of *Punica granatum* grow in the southern Caspian belt, in northeastern Turkey, and in Albania and southern Serbia, and the domestication of the species by clone propagation brought about an increase in fruit size (Zohary and Hopf 2000).

The earliest evidence of pomegranate use in Greece comes from the Mycenaean levels (Late Bronze Age) of Tirynth in southern Greece (Kroll 1982). Later finds are

---

[5]   For species retrieved from funeral contexts see Megaloudi 2004; whole carbonized figs were discovered in large quantities in funeral contexts at Eleftherna in Crete (Megaloudi, in preparation).

reported from Geometric Krania at Pieria (Margariti 2002b), a layer of the 8th century B.C. in Delphi (Luce et al., forthcoming), the 7th century B.C. sanctuary of Hera in Samos (Kučan 1995), and that of Demeter and Core in Corinth, dated to the 5th century B.C. (Bookidis et al. 1999). A more recent occurrence of the species comes from a grave of the 4th century in the necropolis of Thasos (Megaloudi 2004).

Punica granatum was a symbol of fertility and life and was venerated in the cult of Hera, mother of Gods, protectress of marriage and childbirth (Baumann 1993). According to Pausanias (2.19.3), at the sanctuary of Hera at Argos stood a chryselephantine statue of the goddess holding a pomegranate in her hand. The species was also sacred to both Aphrodite and Athena. In Greek mythology pomegranate is associated with the story of the abduction of Persephone. Persephone was condemned to remain beneath the earth for half of every year because by eating a pomegranate in the underworld she had involuntarily married Hades (*Hom. Hymn Dem.* 372, 412).

Hippocrates (*Mul.* 1.75) administers for fever after childbirth a mixture of pomegranate juice and lentil flour that is cooked with cumin, salt, oil and vinegar, and then given to the patient cold. In this case the pomegranate may have been operating on a symbolic level, their many seeds promoting fertility (King 1995). This symbolic meaning of the fruit can be seen in another recipe designated to promote conception: it consists of pomegranate juice mixed with the milk of a woman suckling a male child.

E. Vegetables, herbs, and spices

Vegetables, herbs, and spices must have been essential in the ancient diet as ingredients in stews and soups and as fresh relishes. Archaeobotanical evidence regarding these species is scarce as vegetables—plant parts such as leaves, roots, or tubers—are highly perishable and are unlikely to be preserved through carbonization (Megaloudi 2005). Written sources regarding vegetables and condiments are precious sources of information, but they are often ambiguous. For an analysis of the role of vegetables, herbs, and spices retrieved from archaeological contexts and for the literary evidence the reader is referred to Megaloudi 2005.

Carrot (*Daucus carota* L.)
The carrot (*Daucus carota*) is a vegetable that grows in the temperate zones of the world. Two main types of cultivated carrots are recognized: an eastern type that grows in Afghanistan, Iran, and Turkey and is considered the primitive cultivar, and a western type that is mainly cultivated in the Mediterranean basin (Zohary and Hopf 2000).

In Greece carrot seeds were found at Iron Age Kastanas (Kroll 1983) but the species does not seem to be very popular in ancient times. Theophrastus (*Hist. pl.* 9.15.5–8, 9.20.2) refers to a species called *daukos,* but this name recurs in other passages and could belong to another plant (Hort 1916–1926, p. 293, not. 4). It seems that before imperial times the roots of carrot were not used as distinct from the seed and the leaves (Ath. 371b). Some scholars argue that the *staphylinos* mentioned by Dioscorides, whose aromatic root is being used both as food and for medicine, is *Daucus carota* (Körber-Grohne 1987). According to Dioscorides carrot leaves can be administrated as a remedy against tumors (*MM* 3.52). Carrots as we know them today, with red, swollen, aromatic, and nutritionally rich roots, are mentioned only in the 1st century A.D. as an appendix to the description of the plant (Dalby 1996). Carrots with a thick red root are also depicted in the illustration of Dioscorides' codex, which was drawn in Constantinople around A.D. 500. This illustration indicates that carotene-containing cultivars first appeared sometime between the 1st and 6th centuries A.D.

Okra (*Hibiscus esculentus* L.)
Okra (*Hibiscus esculentus*) is an herbaceous plant that probably originated in tropical parts of Africa (Germer 1985). Other scholars suggest an Egyptian origin of the species since it is reported from archaeological contexts in Egypt dated to the 2nd millennium B.C. (Hermann 1983, cited in Kučan 1995).

The edible part of the species is the unopened flower bud (capsule). These parts, pickled in vinegar, are consumed as a staple in modern Greece. In some cases roasted grains of the plant can be brewed and used as a coffee substitute.

As regards the extraction of the poppy juice, Theophrastus writes that poppy is the only plant from which the juice is extracted from the head and not from the stalks, and this juice, called *mekónion,* is collected straight into vessels (*Hist. pl.* 9.8.2). He reports that Thrasyas of Mantineia had discovered that an easy and painless death could be obtained from the juice of hemlock or of poppy (*Hist. pl.* 9.16.8). This use of the plant is confirmed by Herakleides of Pontus, writing in the 4th century B.C. He comments that on the island of Keios those who reached a certain age—especially women—voluntarily put an end to their life by drinking the juice of poppy or of hemlock, in order to avoid the illness and pains of old age (On Governments, *FGrH* II.215, IX 3). Pliny was the first to use the term *opium* to describe the juice of the poppy that the ancient Greeks called *mekónion;* he comments that the juice of black poppy is hypnotic and, if taken in large doses, induces death through sleep and it is called *opium* (*HN* 20.19.53).

The okra has been known in Greece at least since Archaic times, as it is reported from the 7th century B.C. Samian Heraion. (Kučan 1995). It is not clear, however, that the species was used for culinary purposes.

Species	AN	EN	MN	LN/FN	EBA	MBA	LBA	PG	G	A	C
N of components	5	9	10	26	14	10	26	6	4	5	6
Amygdalus communis	0	11.1	20	19.2	0	0	4	0	0	20	0
Corylus avelana	0	0	0	4	0	0	0	0	25	20	0
Ficus carica	0	33.3	30	42.3	28.6	20	34.6	66.8	75	60	50
Morus nigra	0	0	0	0	0	0	0	0	0	20	0
Myrtus communis	0	0	0	0	0	0	4	0	0	20	0
Punica granatum	0	0	0	0	0	0	4	0	25	40	33
Vitis vinifera	0	0	0	11.5	50	50	31	83.3	50	60	86.3

Table 5.20: Percentage of Appearances of fruits/nuts per Component

AN: Aceramic Neolithic, EN: Early Neolithic, MN: Middle Neolithic, LN/FN: Late Neolithic, Final Neolithic, EBA: Early Bronze Age, MBA: Middle Bronze Age, LBA: Late Bronze Age, PG: Proto-Geometric, G: Geometric, A: Archaic, C: Classic

Species	AN	EN	MN	LN/FN	EBA	MBA	LBA	PG	G	A	C
N of components	5	9	10	26	14	10	26	6	4	5	6
Anethum graveolens	0	0	0	0	0	0	4	16.7	0	20	0
Apium graveolens	0	0	0	0	0	10	4	16.7	0	20	0
Capparis ssp	0	0	0	4	0	0	0	0	0	0	0
Capparis spinosa	0	0	0	0	0	0	0	0	0	20	16.7
Citrullus lanatus	0	0	0	0	0	0	0	0	25	40	0
Coriandrum sativum	0	0	0	4	0	0	4	0	0	20	0
Cucumis melo	0	0	0	0	0	0	7.7	16.7	0	20	0
Daucus ssp	0	0	0	0	0	0	4	16.7	0	0	0
Portulaca oleracea	0	22.2	0	4	7.1	0	4	16.7	0	20	0
Raphanis raphanistrum	0	0	0	0	0	0	4	0	0	20	0

Table 5.21: Percentage of Appearances of legumes/condiments per Component

AN: Aceramic Neolithic, EN: Early Neolithic, MN: Middle Neolithic, LN/FN: Late Neolithic, Final Neolithic, EBA: Early Bronze Age, MBA: Middle Bronze Age, LBA: Late Bronze Age, PG: Proto-Geometric, G: Geometric, A: Archaic, C: Classic

Purslane (*Portulaca oleracea* L.)

Purslane is an annual vegetable with fleshy succulent leaves and small yellow flowers. The plant is very common in Greec, growing in gardens and disturbed areas (Dimitrakis 1999). Purslane is a useful leafy plant that produces small black edible seeds. The plant can be eaten fresh or cooked and has no bitter taste at all. In Greek popular medicine, purslane is used as a remedy for constipation and inflammation of the urinary system (Arnold et al. 1993).

It seems that *Portulaca oleracea* was widely used in Greece, as archaeobotanical remains of the plant are a common find at many prehistoric sites (*Table 5.21*). In historical contexts, purslane seeds were retrieved from a Protogeometric layer at Kastanas (Kroll 1983) as well as from the 7th-century B.C. Samian Heraion (Kučan 1995), where 240 seeds were recovered from a waterlogged deposit.

Theophrastus (*Hist. pl.* 7.1.2) names purslane (*andrákhne*) as one of the several summer pot herbs that must be sown in April (*Munichion*). Medicinally, purslane was very much appreciated in antiquity. Its extensive healing properties were thought so reliable that Pliny advises wearing the plant as an amulet in order to expel all evil (*HN* 20.120). According to Dioscorides (*MM* 11.150), migraines, respiratory problems, indigestion, and other digestive difficulties can be easily relieved by eating boiled purslane. Today, in fact, the plant is recognized to be an excellent source of Omega-3 fatty acids and it is used medicinally for high blood pressure, blood clotting, or inflammations.

Wild lettuce (*Lactuca serriola* L.)

Wild lettuce is an annual or biennial leafy plant used as a salad or as a cooked vegetable. The species is a weed in the Mediterranean basin and the Near East and it is the closest wild relative of cultivated lettuce, or *Lactuca sativa* L. (Zohary and Hopf 2000).

Archaeobotanical evidence of *Lactuca serriola* in Greek archaeological contexts is scant. Forty-five uncarbonized seeds of wild lettuce were retrieved from a waterlogged deposit at the 7th-century B.C. sanctuary of Hera on Samos (Kučan 1995). The plant can be eaten as a salad, despite its sour taste, but its presence in the Samian Heraion is not related to such a use. The plant was probably used for its soporific properties during the ritual that took place in the sanctuary (Kučan 1995).

Theophrastus reports that wild lettuce, *thridakíni*, has a shorter stem than the cultivated form, *thrídax*, and that, as the plant matures, it becomes spinous (*Hist. pl.* 7.6.2.). The juice of wild lettuce was considered to be pungent and was used as a remedy against eye ulcers (*Hist. pl.* 7.6.2). Theophrastus distinguishes different kinds of cultivated lettuce: the white kind, which is sweeter and more tender, the flat-stalked, the round-stalked, and the Laconian (*Hist. pl.* 7.4.5). He comments that the round-stalked lettuce is like the wild variety because of its abundant milky juice and its small leaves (*Hist. pl.* 7.4.5). He also reports that the juice of wild lettuce is extracted from the stalks and is collected with a piece of wool (*Hist. pl.* 9.8.2). Wild lettuce does contain a bitter milky juice that can be extracted with a simple cut of the stem and used as a drug. In antiquity this property of the plant was known, and lettuce was considered a good regulatory and soporific drug, one that checked sexual desire. Amphis in *Lamentation* reports that if a man consumes lettuce, he will not be able to "accomplish his desires...and he might twist and turn the whole night long instead of acting like a man" (Ath. *Deipn.* 2.68–69c)[6]. Ancient poets considered that lettuce produces impotence, and according to Eubulus, Aphrodite laid out dead Adonis in a lettuce bed, so "lettuce is dead men's food" (Ath. *Deipn.* 2.69d). The Pythagoreans called lettuce "eunuch" because it causes urination and relaxes sexual desire (Ath. *Deipn.* 2.69e). Similarly, Pliny (*NH* 19.48) distinguishes, among the different kinds of lettuce, a white variety of the plant called by the Greeks "poppy lettuce," "from its abundance of juice with a soporific property."

Coriander (*Coriandrum sativum* L.)

Coriander is an annual shrub native to western Asia and northern Africa but widespread in the Mediterranean region (Polunin 1980). The plant is cultivated for its aromatic seeds, which can be used as a condiment or for medicinal purposes, as a stimulant and carminative (Fournier 1947).

Coriander seems to have been cultivated in Greece at least since the 2nd millennium B.C. In Linear B tablets, the species is referred to as being cultivated for the manufacture of perfumes, and it appears that it was used in two forms: its seed were used as a spice and its leaves as a flavoring herb (Shelmerdine 1985). Archaeological evidence from the same period seems to corroborate the

Linear B tablets; the large quantities of the species retrieved from an Early Bronze Age layer at Sitagroi in Macedonia could point to the cultivation of the species at that time (Renfrew 1973); at Late Bronze Age Akrotiri, 46 seeds of coriander were found in a crop of *Lathyrus clymenum* L. and, while they were considered weeds of cultivation, they could have been cultivated independently elsewhere (Sarpaki 1992). In historical contexts from Greece, we know of only one occurrence of the species: 44 uncarbonized coriander seeds were found in a waterlogged deposit at the Samian Heraion, dated to the 7th century B.C. (Kučan 1995).

We learn from Theophrastus that coriander seeds were sown in July (*Metageítnion*) but the plant germinates with difficulty and only when it is moistened (*Hist. pl.* 7.1.2–3). The species is especially sensitive to hot weather, which makes the coriander leaf *koréannon*, "mildewed" (*Hist. pl.* 7.5.4). Coriander was a popular component of ancient Greek cooking. According to Athenaeus, coriander mixed with asparagus and marjoram gives distinction to smoked fish (2.68b), and Zenon, in his recipe for lentil soup, recommends using half of a coriander seed (4.157–158b). In Aristophanes' *Knights* the sausage seller announces proudly that he bought all the coriander seeds that were on the market and "gave it to them...as seasoning for their anchovies" (*Eq.* 680). Medicinally, coriander can be used in a variety of ways. According to Dioscorides, it has a cooling effect when applied with bread to an ulcer and its seeds mixed with wine help to expel worms (*MM* 3.71.305).

Caper (*Capparis spinosa* L.)

Caper is a biennial spiny shrub that bears rounded, rather fleshy leaves and big pinkish-white flowers. It is native to the Greek archipelagos and it grows wild on walls or in rocky coastal areas throughout the Mediterranean region (Dimitrakis 1999; Polunin 1980). Caper is cultivated for its use as a pickled condiment that was very much appreciated in antiquity. The edible part of the plant is not the fruit but the unopened flower buds. These parts, pickled in brine, are used in salads and sauces. Semimature fruits and young shoots may also be pickled for use as a condiment or in medicine. Today, in Greek popular medicine, a herbal tea made of caper root and young shoots is considered to be beneficial against rheumatism (Arnold et al. 1993).

Capers are most commonly represented in archaeological levels in the form of carbonized seeds, and rarely as flower buds and fruits. In prehistoric and historic contexts from Greece, capers are represented only in the form of seeds. Caper seeds are reported from the Mesolithic levels of Franchthi Cave (Hansen 1991) and in the Late Neolithic site of Makri in Thrace (Efstratiou et al. 1998). They were found at the 7th-century B.C. Heraion on Samos (Kučan 1995) and at the Sanctuary of Demeter and Kore at Corinth, dated to the 5th century B.C. (Bookidis et al. 1999). Flower buds of caper are extremely perishable and unlikely to survive charring;

---

6   All Athenaeus translations are from Gulick 1927

this could explain their absence from archaeological contexts. In any case, the use of pickled caper flower buds is a modern conjecture of ancient use. Seeds of caper could be used in ancient times for medicinal purposes or as food. Akgül and Özcan (1999) argue that the seeds of *Capparis sicula* L. and *C. spinosa* L. are rich in protein, oil, and fiber and might have been a valuable food in the past. Medicinally, caper seeds could be used in a variety of ways. Dioscorides (*MM* 2.204t) provides instructions on the use of the sprouts, roots, leaves, and seeds of capers in the treatment of strangury and inflammatory conditions.

Much attention is paid to capers by Athenaeus in *Deipnosophistae:* they appear as a common hors d'oeuvre accompanying raw smoked fish (4.133c), and the species figures in the list of seasonings in the melting-pot of Alexis (4.170b). According to Pliny, caper was cultivated (*HN* 19. 48.163). Theophrastus comments that, as the caper is "especially wild in character," its fruits ripen better in the wild state (*Hist. pl.* 3.2.1). This raises the question of whether cultivation of the plant started in the period between the 4th century B.C. and 1st century A.D. Archaeobotanically, there is not sufficient evidence to support the cultivation of the species, as caper remains are still very few. All the *Capparis* findings in archaeological contexts from Greece are referred to as *Capparis spinosa* L., a spontaneous hybrid between *C. orientalis* L. and *C. sicula* L. (Rivera et al. 2002). In Greece, capers grow wild in coastal areas, and the archaeobotanical remains of this species could point to the gathering of ripe fruits and not to its cultivation—at least not before the 4th century B.C.

Celery (*Apium graveolens* L.)

Celery is a biennial plant, native to the Mediterranean area, that grows in moist places, especially near the sea (Pelt 1993). It is a particularly useful vegetable, as it can be eaten raw in salads or as an hors d'œuvre, as a cooked vegetable, or in soups, and its seeds can be used as a seasoning. Celery is also recommended for its digestive properties, and in the Greek islands a tea made of celery leaves is used as a remedy for kidney stones (Arnold et al. 1993). The oil that can be extracted from its seeds is commonly used in the cosmetic industry. Archaebotanically, *Apium graveolens* has been found in a 9th-century B.C. layer at Kastanas (Kroll 1983) as well as at the 7th-century B.C. Heraion on Samos (Kučan 1995). In the latter instance, 23,595 seeds of a wild variety of celery (*Apium nodiflorum* L.) were retrieved. *Apium nodiflorum* is an element of the Samian landscape, growing naturally around the sanctuary. The presence of both *Apium gravaeolens* and *Apium nodiflorum* at the Heraion is not related to any culinary use; the plants were probably used by visitors to the sanctuary for garlands (Kučan 1995).

In Homer's *Iliad*, the Myrmidons' horses graze on wild celery that grows in the marshes of Troy (*Il.* 2.776), and in the *Odyssey* meadows of violet and wild celery surround Calypso's cave (*Od.* 5.72–73). In the 4th century B.C., Theophrastus suggests that celery seeds should be tied up in a cloth before sowing in order to provide a larger crop (*Hist. pl.* 7.3.6). When celery is transplanted, he advises that the plant is hammered down with a peg and the hole filled with dung and soil (*Hist. pl.* 7.3.6).

In Classical antiquity, several varieties of cultivated and wild celery were known (Amigues 2002). Theophrastus reports three varieties of wild celery: the horse celery *hipposélinon*, the marsh celery *eleiosélinon*, and the mountain celery *oreosélinon*, all of which "differ both from one another and from the cultivated kind" (*Hist. pl.* 7.6.3). It seems that horse celery and marsh celery, mixed in sweet white wine, were used as a remedy in case of kidney stones, and mountain celery mixed in dry wine was given for diseases of women (*Hist. pl.* 7.6.3).

It is interesting to note that in ancient literature "curly" celery is often compared to the curly hair of women; Lucian (*Amores* 26) describes the hair of a woman as being "curlier than the celery in the meadow." Theocritus makes a similar reference (*Id.* 20.23). The curly celery described in these sources can be related to the "close and curly" celery that Theophrastus lists among the cultivated varieties of the plant (*Hist. pl.* 7.4.6).

However, celery was above all a wreath plant and a chthonian symbol. According to legend, the plant sprouted from the blood of Kadmilos, father of the Cabers, chthonian divinities celebrated in Samothrace, Lemnos, and Thebes. The spicy odor and the dark color of its leaves made the celery a chthonian symbol, and it was closely related to the cult of the dead. In Classical Greece, celery leaves were used as garlands for the dead. The wreaths of the winners at the Isthmian Games were first made of celery, before being replaced by crowns of pine. According to Pliny (*HN* 19.46), the garland worn by the winners of the sacred contest at Nemea was also made of celery.

Garlic (*Allium sativum* L.)

Garlic is a perennial plant used widely as a culinary herb. It is a corm, made up of several cloves enclosed within the white "skin" of the parent corm. Garlic is maintained by vegetative propagation since most garlic cultivars are sterile (Karg 1991). The wild ancestry of garlic is not definitely established. *Allium longicuspis* is the most probable candidate for the ancestor of the cultivated variety. This species is a native of central Asia and it is mainly found in northern Iran and southeastern Turkey (Zohary and Hopf 2000). According to A. de Candolle (1883), in the 19th century the steppelike formations of Kirghizistan were the only regions in which garlic seemed to grow wild. Today, it is believed these territories were probably the source of both the cultivated and the weedy forms.

Because if its pungency, the species is generally regarded as a flavoring agent rather than a vegetable in its own right. The characteristic odor and the spicy taste of garlic are due to allicin, a substance that is contained in the underground part of the plant and is produced when garlic is crushed or chewed (Fournier 1947; Couplan 1983). Aside from its culinary uses, the plant may be used as an antiseptic, a stimulant, and an expectorant (Fournier 1947).

In Greece, the botanical evidence regarding this species is very scarce. We know of only one occurrence: 55 carbonized garlic cloves were found in a grave of the 4th century in the necropolis of Thasos. This sample included 18 whole garlic gloves ranging from 15 mm to 19 mm in size. The dimensions of the gloves suggest that the remains probably belong to the cultivated variety *Allium sativum* L. (Megaloudi 2004).

According to Herodotus (2.125), garlic figured among the food provisions given to the workers that built the Chaeops pyramid, but this information has been doubted (Manniche 1999). We know from Theophrastus (*Hist. pl.* 7.4.11) that, at the end of the 4th century B.C., garlic (*skórodon*) was propagated from seed or from the planting of individual cloves. He describes a plant named *móly* that grew on Mount Kyllene and had a "round root like an onion and a leaf like squill" (*Hist. pl.* 9.15.7). According to Theophrastus, this plant was the *móly* mentioned by Homer and was used "against spells and magic arts" (*Hist. pl.* 9.15.7). In Homer's *Odyssey, móly* is the antidote that Hermes gives to Odysseus to protect him from the spells of Circe; Homer describes the plant as being "black at the root but its flower was like milk" (*Od.* 10. 302–306). This raises the question whether the Homeric *móly* and the *móly* of Theophrastus were cultivated garlic—and if so, whether garlic was cultivated since Homeric times. Amigues (1995), in her comparative study of the plants called *móly* in ancient texts, concluded that both Homeric *móly* and the *móly* of Theophrastus are *Allium sativum* L. In this case, we could assume that garlic was a component of ancient vegetable gardens at least since Homeric times.

Dioscorides (in Plin. *HN* 2.152) reports an Egyptian variety of undivided garlic used by sorcerers and magicians (Meeks 1993). In Classical Greece, the plant was appreciated both as a magical plant and as a garnishing herb. According to Theophrastus (*Hist. pl.* 7.4.11), garlic was the principal ingredient in *mittotós*, a kind of sauce similar the *skordaliá* eaten in Greece today. In Aristophanes' *Acharnians* garlic enrages those who eat it; Theorus says to Dikaiopolis: "How dare you touch them, when they are garlic-primed?" (166). It appears that humans, like cocks, were supposed to fight better when primed with garlic. In *Thesmophoriazusae* an adulterous wife chews garlic before her husband returns home, so she can avoid kisses (494–496).

Medicinally, garlic seems to have been something of a panacea. Hippocrates, Dioscorides, and Galen recommend it (Andre 1956) and Pliny (*HN* 10.50–57)

notes its healing properties as an antiseptic (applied to caries or used as a remedy against lung infections).

Garlic was closely related to the cult of Hecate, a chthonian divinity and patron of sorcerers (see Theocr. *Id.* 2). In Theophrastus' *Characters* (16), garlic was placed on the piles of stones at crossroads, as a supper for Hecate and the Superstitious: "if he observes anyone feasting on the garlic at the crossroads, he will go away, pour water over his head, and, summoning the priestesses, bid them carry a squill or a puppy around him for purification." Hecate was the symbol of every occult power, and pathogenic microbes were thought to be "bad spirits"; garlic, a highly antiseptic plant, was believed to protect against bad spirits and consequently against microbes. This belief has survived in eastern Europe, where garlic cloves suspended in windows are supposed to keep the vampires out of the houses (Collectif 1964). Similar beliefs about garlic have survived in everyday life in modern Greece. For example, when an adult looks at a baby, a vulnerable creature, he or she symbolically spits and says "*skórda*" (the Greek word for garlic cloves), or someone receiving a compliment says "garlic into your eyes"; in both instances mention of garlic aims to repel evil.

Melon (*Cucumis melo* L.)
The cultivated melon (*Cucumis melo*) belongs to the Curcubitaceae family and is a variable crop that includes sweet and unsweet varieties. The ancestor of the species is well defined. The cultivated melon is closely related to a variable group of wild and weedy melons that are distributed over the subtropical and tropical parts of Asia, Africa, and Australia and are mainly identified as *Cucumis callosus* (Kirkbride 1993, in Zohary and Hopf 2000). This species is closest to the melon cultivars raised in western Asia and the Mediterranean basin. *Cucumis melo* was probably brought into cultivation in southwest Asia or in Egypt (Zohary and Hopf 2000).

At present the earliest discovery of the cultivated melon in Europe comes from Greece. Three seeds of the species were discovered at Tirynth in a layer dated to the 12th–11th century B.C. (Kroll 1982). Remains of *Cucumis melo* are reported from Kastanas in an Iron Age context (Kroll 1983) and from the 7th-century B.C. Samian Heraion (Kučan 1995). It is possible that Greek colonists introduced *melo* cultivation in Italy and the species was then taken into Gaul and the northern provinces of the Roman Empire (Marinval 2000).

In Classical Greece melon was known as *mélopeppon* (*Epit.* 58f; Ath. *Deipn.* 372b), probably the sweet muskmelon. Theophrastus does not provide any information on melons, but the discovery of almost 500 seeds of *Cucumis melo* at the sanctuary of Hera on Samos indicates that the Greeks were familiar with the species.

The cultivated melon can grow in warm and sunny environments and is a demanding species in terms of soil moisture. Thus its presence on an archaeological site indicates its cultivation in vegetable gardens.

Watermelon (*Citrullus lanatus* Thunb.)

Watermelon (*Citrullus lanatus*) is an annual species that has wild, cultivated, and feral forms. Its fruits are eaten raw and can also serve as animal fodder. The seeds yield an edible oil and can also be consumed roasted (Wasylikowa and van der Veen 2004). The ancestor of the modern cultivar has been thought to be wild forms of the species (*Citrullus lanatus* ssp.. *lanatus*) that grow today only in sub-Saharan Africa and are known under the local name *tsamma* (Wasylikowa and van der Veen 2004). The available archaeological information, however, does not support this conclusion (Zohary and Hopf 2000). Remains of cultivated watermelon have been found in Egypt dated to the 2nd millennium B.C., a time when farming was not yet practiced in southwest Africa.

In addition, the presence of 5000-year-old seeds of *Citrullus lanatus* in Libya indicates that a wild form of this species existed in the Libyan Sahara at that time (Wasylikowa and van der Veen 2004). This find raises the possibility that the domestication of *Citrullus lanatus* could have occurred somewhere in northern Africa (Wasylikowa and van der Veen 2004).

To date, the earliest record of *Citrullus lanatus* in Europe comes from Greece; seeds of the plant are reported from a Geometric layer at Krania in Macedonia (Margariti 2002b) and from an 8th-century B.C. layer at Delphi (Luce et al., forthcoming). *Citrullus lanatus* seeds have also been found at the 7th-century B.C. Samian Heraion (Kučan 1995).

Watermelon was known as *Sikyos pepon* in Classical Greece. Strangely, written sources (such as Theophrastus) provide little or no information regarding the species; thus the main evidence that watermelon was known in protohistoric and historic Greece comes from the archaeobotanical record. This contradiction is hard to explain at the present stage of research.

CHAPTER 6

PLANTS AND PEOPLE IN PREHISTORIC AND PROTOHISTORIC GREECE: A SYNTHESIS OF THE ARCHAEOBOTANICAL REMAINS

The earliest finding of plant remains at a Greek archaeological site goes back to 1878, when M. Kalokairinos discovered carbonized beans and peas in pithoi in the Bronze Age Palace of Knossos (see chap. 1). Seed determinations became frequent after the 1960s and even more so after the 1970s, with the introduction of systematic flotation. In *Chapter 4* I analyzed the problems of taphonomy and recovery bias; as a result of these problems seed samples are often heterogeneous, both qualitatively and quantitatively. We can attempt, however, to establish patterns for the primary edible plants that have been used in Greece from the Neolithic to Classical period, based on the archaeobotanical remains.

Here I provide a survey of the archaeobotanical data retrieved from the archaeological sites considered in this work (*Chapter 4*). These data concern the primary plant foods (cereals, pulses, fruits, and nuts) that have been recorded in the aforementioned archaeobotanical assemblages. I present the data with a view to examining changes that might be seen in the types of plant foods present and discussing what roles various foods might have played.

It is important to note that I do not discuss here the origin of agriculture, an issue that has been treated at length by many scholars (e.g., Childe 1925; Clark 1952; Binford 1968; Flannery 1969; Ammerman and Cavalli-Sforza 1984; Rindos 1984; Runnels and Van Andel 1988; Cauvin 1989). In the Aegean, taphonomic biases and unequal recovery techniques can lead to widely differing interpretations of the subsistence economy, and there is a difference of opinion about whether the Aegean sites were established by immigrants from the Near East, or developed from an indigenous population (see Dennel 1983; Lewthwaite 1986; Runnels and van Andel 1988; for a discussion on the origin and spread of agriculture in the Aegean, see Hansen 1991; Kotsakis 1992; van Andel and Runnels 1995).

A. Early Neolithic (6700/6500–5800/5600 B.C.)

Archaeobotanical data concerning the Early Neolithic are provided from nine archaeological sites that correspond to 7% of the total number of sites considered in this book (*Figures 4.17b* and *4.18*).

The principal crops of Early Neolithic agriculture are cereals and pulses (*Table 5.6*). Barley seems to be the most common cereal at that time and both varieties are present: *Hordeum vulgare nudum* and *Hordeum vulgare*.

Hulled barley (*Hordeum vulgare*) is identified at 56% of the Early Neolithic settlements considered in this book; naked barley (*Hordeum vulgare nudum*) is well documented on the site of Nea Nikomedeia in Macedonia (van Zeist and Bottema 1971), but there is no archaeobotanical evidence of the species in southern Greece. Two-rowed barley (*Hordeum distichon*) is present in the Aceramic levels at Thessaly but its use decreases considerably in the following periods (*Table 5.5*). Since there is no significant difference in the edaphic or climatic requirements of the two species, the decreased usage of two-rowed barley cannot be attributed to environmental changes. It seems that the Neolithic farmers gradually abandoned two-rowed barley and replaced it with six-rowed barley because the latter can yield three times as much grain (Körber-Grohne 1987). Other scholars (e.g., Hansen 1991) explain the change by arguing that it represents a gradual shift in cultural preference.

Hulled wheats *Triticum dicoccum* and *Triticum monococcum* are very well represented in the sites dated to the Early Neolithic. Free-threshing wheats are cultivated on a very limited scale during the first phases of the Neolithic period; the rarity of free-threshing species such as bread wheat may be related to their greater vulnerability in storage or to their more demanding soil and edaphic requirements—or to a combination of both.

Legumes are well represented in terms of both frequency of occurrence and percentage of seeds. The principal species are lentils (*Lens culinaris*), bitter vetch (*Vicia ervilia*), and peas (*Pisum sativum*) (*Table 5.6*). Added to these are two new species, grass pea (*Lathyrus sativus*) and probably chickpea (*Cicer arietinum*). A large deposit of grass pea was discovered at Prodromos 2 (Jones and Halstead 1980). One site (Otzaki Magoula; see Kroll 1983) has produced chickpea dated to that period. This find, however, is limited to a single seed that could be intrusive.

The available archaeobotanical evidence suggests that cereals and pulses are the main components of the Early Neolithic diet. Cereals predominate at every site sampled, except Nea Nikomedeia, and this level of representation may lead to the assumption that cereals were produced and stored on a larger scale than legumes. We must take into account, though, that cereals are often parched at some stage of their processing, which increases their chances of preservation in archaeological contexts. On the other hand, pulses do not require charring and are consequently less prone to carbonization than cereals. This could explain the under-representation of legumes in archaeological contexts.

Ethnographic parallels indicate that the combination of cereals with pulses would have been a good risk-avoidance strategy, since pulses seem to withstand periodic droughts better than cereals (Forbes 1989). Crop diversification can be a viable economic strategy for coping with crop failure in bad years.

Pistachio, almonds, and pears were used since the Upper Paleolithic period, as they are found at the Upper Paleolithic and Mesolithic levels at Franchthi Cave (Hansen 1991). With the arrival of the Early Neolithic, cornelian cherry, acorns, figs, and wild grape are added to the aforementioned species (*Table 5.6*). At Balomenos Toumba figs, pistachio, and blackberries are well represented in terms of seeds percentages, which indicates that wild plants played an important role in the diet, at least at that site (Sarpaki 1995). Among the weeds the main species recorded are *Avena, Bromus, Lolium, Fumaria, Portulacea,* and *Galium* (*Table 5.6*). These species could have been collected as fodder or as complementary food for humans; the leaves of *Portulacea, Galium,* and *Stellaria* are edible and can be used as salad. *Portulaca oleracea, Chenopodiaceae, Lolium, Avena,* and *Bromus* may indicate a winter sowing, a common practice in the Mediterranean climate.

To summarize the data on crop diversity in Early Neolithic Greece, glume wheats (*Triticum dicoccum* and *Triticum monococcum*) and hulled barley (*Hordeum vulgare*) are the main crops. Among pulses, lentil (*Lens culinaris*) is the principal legume, followed by bitter vetch (*Vicia ervilia)* and pea (*Pisum sativum*). Two new species appear in the Early Neolithic, grass pea (*Lathyrus sativus*) and probably chickpea (*Cicer arietinum*). A variety of wild fruits and nuts were used, including fig, pear, grape, acorns, cornelian cherry, pistachio, and almonds (*Table 5.6*).

Agriculture was developed by 9,000 B.P. in the Near East with a complex of crops consisting of glume wheats (einkorn and emmer), two-rowed and six-rowed barley, lentils, peas, and vetch (Tell Aswad, Cayönü: van Zeist and Bakker-Heeres 1985; Tell Abu Hureyra: Hillman 1975). The same range of species is recorded in the Aegean sites from about the 7th millennium B.C. Whether this was the result of a rapid colonization movement across the Aegean, slow diffusion through a wave of advance both overland and by sea (Hansen 1991), or an indigenous development is not possible to say.

B. Middle Neolithic (5800/5600–5400/5300 B.C.)

Archaeobotanical information on the Middle Neolithic is available from ten archaeological contexts, corresponding to 8% of the sites considered in this book (*Figures 4.17b* and *4.18*).

With the Middle Neolithic there is no significant change in the nature of plant species (*Table 5.7*); the period seems to be a time of stability in terms of plant resources. Simple products fulfill the fundamental needs, as it is evidenced by the archaeobotanical remains. Wheat—emmer (*Triticum dicoccum*) and einkorn (*Triticum monococcum*)—seems to be the most common species with hulled six-rowed barley (*Hordeum vulgare*) second. Naked barley (*Hordeum vulgare nudum*) decreases considerably in that period and is identified only at the settlement of Limenaria (Megaloudi, forthcoming). There is no specific ecologic reason for choosing naked barley (*Hordeum vulgare nudum*); the species is considered more advantageous than hulled barley, however, as the latter needs rigorous dehusking before use (Kroll, pers. comm.). It is not always possible to distinguish between hulled and naked barley; the kernels of naked barley are recognized by their shriveled skin and by the furrow that stays narrow near the apex. Consequently, the under-representation of naked barley in the archaeobotanical assemblages could be due to problems of identification.

Broomcorn millet (*Panicum miliaceum*) it is identified in the Middle Neolithic levels of Otzaki in Thessaly (Kroll 1983) and at Limenaria (Megaloudi, forthcoming). M. Hopf (1962b) reports a grain of *Panicum miliaceum* in a Preceramic level of Argissa, but the chronological attribution of this find is under discussion.

The archaeobotanical finds indicate that mixed crop was a common practice in Middle Neolithic agriculture. According to ethnographic works conducted at Amorgos, wheat and barley are usually grown as a mixed "maslin" crop, but this is often not the form in which they are consumed (Jones 1984; Jones and Halstead 1995). The two cereals can be separated by a combination of winnowing and sieving, a process that results in a wheat-rich fraction used for food and a barley-rich fraction kept for fodder. This can be a viable economic strategy for coping with bad years. At Toumba Balomenos, however, only einkorn wheat seems to have been cultivated (Sarpaki 1995). Among legumes, lentils (*Lens culinaris*) and bitter vetch (*Vicia ervilia*) are the principal species (*Table 5.7*). A large deposit of bitter vetch was discovered at Zarkos in Thessaly (Jones and Halstead 1993b; Becker 1991). The purity of the sample and the mode of storage suggests that bitter vetch was a crop legume for humans and not exclusively an animal fodder.

Cornelian cherry (*Cornus mas*), figs (*Ficus carica*), pistachio nuts (*Pistacia* sp.), blackberries (*Rubus fruticosus*), and acorns (*Quercus* sp.) are among the species that continue to be collected from the wild.

Weeds were scarce, as was the case in the Early Neolithic. *Galium aparine, Lithospermum arvense, Avena* sp., *Bromus* sp., and *Fumaria* sp. are the principal weeds of cultivation (*Table 5.7*). A large deposit of corn gromwell (*Lithospermum arvense*) was discovered at Achilleion (Renfrew 1989). According to the archaeobotanist of the site, the species had no specific use there. T. Tanaka (1976) notes that in Japan the young leaves are used in the spring as a boiled vegetable and J. Hansen (1991) proposes such a use of the species at Franchthi Cave.

C. Late and Final Neolithic (5400/5300–4700/4500 B.C. and 4700/4500–3300/3100 B.C.)

The Late Neolithic period sees a significant increase in the number of sites represented and species present (*Table 5.8*). Archaeobotanical information is available from 26 archaeological levels, which corresponds to 21% of the sites considered in this book (*Figures 4.17b* and *4.18*).

Hulled barley seems to be a common components of the Late Neolithic diet (*Table 5.8*). *Hordeum vulgare* is a very resistant species that can tolerate poor and dry soils, as well as some salinity; farmers would have quickly recognized these qualities. Two-rowed barley (*Hordeum distichon*) is identified only at the settlement of Makri in Macedonia (Efstratiou et al. 1998) and at Franchthi Cave (Hansen 1991); two impressions of the ventral side that probably belong to hulled two-rowed barley were also identified at the settlement of Saliagos, near Antiparos (Renfrew 1968). The replacement of two-rowed by six-rowed barley may reflect the selection of more productive species as farmers began to sow pure crops of barley rather than fields of mixed cereals.

With the Late Neolithic the finds of einkorn and emmer wheat increase: both species are identified almost at every site excavated. An important concentration of emmer wheat belonging to the Late Neolithic/Early Bronze Age transition was uncovered at Sesklo (Renfrew 1966). The size and the purity of the emmer finds seems to indicate a specialization in growing a crop well suited to the environment. This was not the case at Sarakenos Cave, where a large deposit of einkorn wheat was found in the Late Neolithic IIB (ca. 3800–3300 B.C.) levels of the cave (Megaloudi in press). The quantity and the purity of the einkorn samples clearly suggest its cultivation as a separate crop. There is no specific reason for choosing between emmer and einkorn wheat, as both species have the same ecologic requirements, and so the choice of einkorn over emmer could be attributed to cultural preferences (see *Chapter 4, Section A*).

Three new cereals appear in the Late Neolithic: spelt wheat (*Triticum spelta*), rye (*Secale cereale*), and timopheev wheat (*Triticum timopheevi*). Spelt wheat is identified at the Late Neolithic levels of Dikili Tash in Macedonia (Valamoti 2004; Matterne 1993). *Triticum spelta* is more winter hardy than other wheats and can be grown on poorly drained low-fertility soils; the species is a common crop in the Balkans and its presence only in Macedonia could suggest northern influences. Rye (*Secale cereale*) is reported from the Late Neolithic Skoteini Cave in Euboea (Mangaffa 1993). The limited number of rye findings indicates that the species could

not have been used for human consumption. This changes only in the Byzantine period as large quantities of rye have been discovered in Byzantine layers of the 12th and 14th century A.D. in Aghios Mamas on Chalkidike (Kroll 1999). Timopheev wheat (*Triticum timopheevi*) was identified at Late Neolithic sites in Macedonia (Valamoti 2004). The finds of timopheev wheat have parallels at the Balkans (site of Feudvar: Kroll, in preparation), and, as with spelt, its presence in Macedonia could suggest northern influence.

In the Late Neolithic the main crops, among pulses, seem to be lentils (*Lens culinaris*), bitter vetch (*Vicia ervilia*), grass pea (*Lathyrus sativus/cicera*), and peas (*Pisum sativum*) (*Table 5.8*) The cultivation of chickpea is well established at that period, as a large deposit of *Cicer arietinum* was uncovered at Dimini in Thessaly (Kroll 1979). Broad bean (*Vicia faba*) appears in the Late Neolithic. *Vicia faba* is an imposing plant that is quite resistant if sown in early spring when the soil is still moist from winter rain (Moule 1982).

Figs (*Ficus carica*) and vine could have been brought into cultivation already at the end of the Late Neolithic, to judge by the archaeobotanical evidence (see chapter 4, section D). Hazelnuts (*Corylus avelana*), pears (*Pyrus sp.*), elder and dane wort fruits (*Sambucus sp.*), capper (*Capparis sp.*), purslane (*Portulaca oleracea*), and coriander (*Coriandrum sativum*) are only some of the species that were gathered (*Table 5.8*).

D. Bronze Age: The first palaces in the Aegean

Despite the widespread feeling that the rise of the palaces was a gradual process that stretched over centuries, new questions have arisen in recent years concerning the role of agriculture in the rise of Mycenaean palace societies.

Various models have been proposed for changes in prehistoric subsistence with respect to the rise of Mycenaean society. These changes include a greater crop diversity, increasing crop purity and specialization, and intensification in land use resulting in the production of surplus. Renfrew in 1972 was the first to propose a theoretical model for the indigenous development of "civilization" in the Aegean, suggesting that wheat, olive, and vine comprised the Mediterranean triad in the Early Bronze Age, along with an increased number of cultivated legume species. This diversity allowed more marginal land to be exploited, resulting in increased production and greater security for farmers who could then begin to specialize in certain crops and produced a surplus that could be exchanged for other products. He states that "..the growth of the palaces has to be seen in the first instance as the development of redistributive centers for subsistence commodities, controlled by a well-defined social hierarchy. The emergence of Aegean civilization can be comprehended only if this central point is kept in view"(Renfrew 1972, p. 297).

Alternative models were suggested by C. Gamble and P. Halstead. Gamble (1979) envisages a manipulative, perhaps even forceful, elite that either coerced or cajoled the population into living in large nucleated settlements rather than in small farming villages. As a result, self-sufficient mixed farming became impracticable for many farmers because they were too far removed spatially from their landholdings. According to Halstead's model, (1981, 1986), since southern Greece's topography and climate differ appreciably over very short distances, reciprocal exchanges of this kind could be very effective even when practiced between populations living quite close to one another in space. This model of "social storage" furnishes a rationale for the production of surpluses as a form of insurance against short-term crop failure. At essentially the same time, Runnels and van Andel (1988) pointed out the weaknesses in Renfrew's emphasis on new developments in agriculture and suggested that Renfrew's alternative explanatory model based on trade provided the key to understanding the rise of complex society in the Aegean. The most recent extended treatment of the problem is by Manning (1995), who has argued in favor of an enhanced role of social factors at the expense of economic ones. Watrous (1987, 1994) has sought to revive the view that the Minoan palatial system owes more to Near Eastern models than has been generally conceded since Renfrew's first model.

All of the aforementioned models should be testable through the analysis of botanical remains, but at this time the available botanical data are not sufficient and no definite conclusions can be drawn (see also Hansen 1988). Some general tendencies, however, concerning the agricultural system of the Late Neolithic and the Bronze Age can be gleaned from the archaeobotanical record. *Table 5.8* indicates that there is an increase in crop diversity in the Late Neolithic, suggesting that many aspects of the agricultural system of the Bronze Age, such as crop diversity and crop purity, had already begun in the Late Neolithic. Crop specialization and surplus production demand an increased intensity in land use, with a subsequent production of surplus products and the facilities for storage of those products, that cannot be proved for the Late Neolithic. However it seems possible that the basis for such innovations dates back to that period and develops further during the Bronze Age.

D1. Early Bronze Age (3300/3100–2300/2200 B.C.)

Throughout the Bronze Age the same plant species are present. Farming is well established and simple products fulfill the fundamental needs (*Table 5.9*). The number of archaeobotanical studies concerning the Early Bronze Age period is 14, which corresponds to 12% of the total number of sites considered in this book (*Figures 4.17b* and *4.18*).

The main cereal crops of Early Bronze Age seem to be emmer wheat, hulled barley, and einkorn wheat. Free-threshing wheats are cultivated but on a limited scale,

while spelt wheat develops in popularity and becomes a well established crop, at least in northern Greece. A large deposit of broomcorn millet (*Panicum miliaceum*) was uncovered at Kastanas (Kroll 1983), indicating that the species was widely cultivated, at least at that site.

Bitter vetch (*Vicia ervilia*) and lentils (*Lens culinaris*) are the most common species among pulses. Broad bean finds (*Vicia faba*) increase in the Early Bronze Age and in some cases, such as the Skoteini Cave in Euboea, the species seems to be the principal crop (Mangaffa 1993).

It is possible that olive cultivation begins in southern Greece during the Early Bronze Age—although this has been doubted by some scholars (see *Chapter 4, Section C*). In northern Greece the main sources of oil seem to be oil crops such as gold of pleasure (*Camelina sativa*), poppy (*Papaver somniferum*), and flax (*Linum usitatissimum*). The later is a well-established crop at that time, as is clear from the archaeobotanical data of Kastanas, where *Lolium remotum*, a typical flax-weed, was identified (Kroll 1983).

Grape vine (*Vitis vinifera*) and figs (*Ficus carica*)—eaten fresh or dried, and as juices, wine, and vinegar—belong to the daily life of the Early Bronze Age communities. Other important species collected from the wild seem to be acorns (*Quercus sp.*), pistachio nuts (*Pistacia sp*), pears (*Pyrus sp.*), elder and dane wort fruits (*Sambucus sp.*), blackberries (*Rubus fruticosus*), and cornelian cherry (*Cornus mas*).

D2. Middle Bronze Age (2300/2200 B.C.–1700/1500 B.C.)

Archaeobotanical studies concerning the Middle Bronze Age number just 10, corresponding to 8% of the total number of archaeobotanical studies (*Figures 4.17a* and *4.18*). With the Middle Bronze Age there is no significant change in the general nature of the resources (*Table 5.10*).

Emmer wheat (*Triticum dicoccum*), einkorn (*Triticum monococcum*), and hulled barley (*Hordeum vulgare*) are the main cereal crops. Naked barley (*Hordeum vulgare nudum*) is reported in the Middle Bronze Age levels at Lerna (Hopf 1961, 1962a). Free-threshing wheats are still cultivated on a very limited scale; spelt wheat is reported only from Argissa, but this find has been doubted (Hopf 1962b).

Among pulses, bitter vetch (*Vicia ervilia*), broad bean (*Vicia faba*), lentil (*Lens culinaris*), and grass pea (*Lathyrus sativus*) seem to be the most common species (*Table 5.10*). At Aghios Mamas in Chalkidike (Kroll 2003), bitter vetch, lentils, grass pea, and broad bean were sown and stored separately, and probably prepared separately in the cooking of daily meals. Dishes made of pulses were either long-boiled stews or gruels. The Bronze Age was an era of boiled meals, with some stewed meat and broken marrow bones (Kroll 2003, p. 300). Pulses could have been an excellent accompanying of such meals.

The main oil crops of the Middle Bronze Age in northern Greece are gold of pleasure (*Camelina sativa*) and flax (*Linum usitatissimum*). The regularity of linseeds in the archaeobotanical material from Aghios Mamas indicates a rural linen production, at least at that site (Kroll 1993). In northern Greece there is no extensive production of olive oil, as is the case in the south. It seems that olive oil is a luxury product imported from southern Greece, and it is mainly used for cosmetic purposes (Kroll 1983, 2000).

Weeds are scarce: *Avena* sp., *Fumaria* sp., *Galium spurium*, *Lithospermum arvense*, *Lolium temulentum*, and *Sheradia arvensis* are the principal species, indicating a well-developed agriculture on fertile soils.

D3. Late Bronze Age (1700/1500 B.C.–1125/1100 B.C.)

The Late Bronze Age is very well documented in terms of archaeobotanical studies. Twenty-six studies are available for that period, which corresponds to 21% of the total number of sites considered in this book (*Figures 4.17b* and *4.18*).

The Late Bronze Age sees a significant increase in the number of species and in frequency of occurrence. Einkorn wheat (*Triticum monococcum*), emmer (*Triticum dicoccum*), free-threshing wheats (*Triticum aestivum/durum*), spelt wheat (*Triticum spelta*), broomcorn millet (*Panicum miliaceum*), and hulled barley (*Hordeum vulgare*) are the main cereals exploited by Late Bronze Age farmers (*Table 5.11*). This diversity in cereal crops is a viable strategy in case of crop failure, as it protects the farmers from a total loss of their harvest in a bad year. At Assiros Toumba in Macedonia, einkorn, broomcorn millet, and bitter vetch account for the largest percentage of the species and probably represent pure crops. Emmer and spelt wheat were mixed and probably represented maslin crops (Jones et al. 1986; Wardle 1989). It is also possible, however, that mixing occurred after the deposits were destroyed.

Among pulses, lentils (*Lens culinaris*) and bitter vetch (*Vicia ervilia*) are the principal species, followed by pea (*Pisum sativum*), broad bean (*Vicia faba*), and grass pea (*Lathyrus sativus/cicera*) (*Table 5.16*). *Lathyrus clymenum* is reported from Late Bronze Age Akrotiri and Knossos (Sarpaki and Jones 1990). The finds from Akrotiri were of stored caches, but the seeds from Knossos were found contaminating common pea deposits. In the same period seeds of another *Lathyrus* species, *Lathyrus ochrus,* are found in an LM II storage vessel at the Unexplored Mansion at Knossos (Jones 1992). *Lathyrus ochrus* (and *L. clymenum*) is grown for human consumption as well as for animal fodder. For human consmption the species is used in the dried split form with the testas removed and can be made into a kind of soup or gruel (Jones 1992).

In addition to the already existing fruit species, pomegranate (*Punica granatum*) and myrtle (*Myrtus communis*) are identified in the Late Bronze Age archaeobotanical assemblages (*Table 5.11*). In the same period melon (*Cucumis melo*) and probably carrot (*Daucus* sp.) are attested archaeobotanically. Their presence could be related to the existence of well-irrigated vegetable gardens.

As *Table 5.19* indicates, fruits and nuts continue to be collected from the wild: cornelian cherry (*Cornus mas*), mirabelle plum (*Prunus spinosa*), wild pears (*Pyrus* sp.), blackberries (*Rubus fruticosus*), acorns (*Quercus* sp.), elder and dane wort fruits (*Sambucus* sp.), strawberries (*Fragaria vesca*), and wild apples (*Malus sylvestris*) are some of the main species gathered.

E. Protogeometric and Geometric Periods (1050–700 B.C.) (see Megaloudi 2005b)

Archaeobotanical studies belonging to the Protogeometric and Geometric periods number just 10, corresponding to 8% of the total number of studies considered in this book (*Table 5.12*; (*Figures 4.17b* and *4.18*). The available evidence is scant and it is difficult to draw viable conclusions regarding the plant species of these periods. We can attempt here, however, a general overview of the food plants of Protogeometric and Geometric Greece.

There is sufficient archaeobotanical evidence to establish the use of at least six sorts of cereals in this period (*Table 5.12*): hulled barley (*Hordeum vulgare*), which is probably the main crop produced, followed by einkorn wheat (*Triticum monococcum*), emmer wheat (*Triticum dicoccum*), bread wheat (*Triticum aestivum*), spelt wheat (*Triticum spelta*), and millets (at least *Panicum miliaceum*). The increase in barley finds could indicate the need of protohistoric farmers to cultivate less rich soils in order to feed their communities. The importance of barley during that period is evidenced by the archaeological record: important quantities of barley remains are reported from the Protogeometric layers of Kastanas, Iolkos, Kalapodi, Delphi, and Nichoria. Hulled barley was discovered in a distinct concentration in a burnt Protogeometric floor at Iolkos (Jones 1982). The absence of any weed seeds indicates that barley was stored for human consumption and may reflect rigorous hand sorting (Jones 1982, p. 78). It seems that the crop played an important role in the economy of the site during that period. Important quantities of hulled barley were recorded at the sanctuary of Artemis and Apollo at Kalapodi (Kroll 1993). The finds were retrieved from a sacrificial context and according to the archaeobotanist of the site they could have been resulted from ritual meals.

A single seed of what appears to be barley is reported from a floor deposit at Nichoria, but as no other remains of the species or parts of the plant were found it is difficult to draw conclusions about the status of barley at

Nichoria (Shay and Shay 1978). At Delphi barley represents 7% of the the total number of plant remains in the 9th- and 8th-century levels of the sanctuary (Luce et al., forthcoming). It seems that the barley findings represent waste of food consumed by the visitors of the sanctuary during the time they spent there.

The available macrofossil data indicate that einkorn and emmer species continue to be widely used throughout the Protogeometric and Geometric periods, but barley and bread wheat develop considerably at that time and in some cases begin to replace emmer and einkorn. Bread wheat is a demanding crop in terms of soil moisture and nutrient requirements and it is a rarer find in Neolithic and Bronze Age Greece. In the Protogeometric period bread wheat is very well documented in Kalapodi and Delphi, where it even replaces other wheat as the main cereal besides barley. *Triticum aestivum* is a highly nutritious plant that is very rich in gluten and therefore the best suited for bread making. The increased number of bread wheat finds during the Protogeometric period could be related to culinary practices. In Kalapodi and in Delphi, in addition to the *Triticum aestivum* remains a large number of mortars and millstones was dicovered. Their presence is related to bread making and it seems that leavened bread—made of *Triticum aestivum*—starts to become very popular at this time.

In the Protogeometric period spelt wheat is discovered in small quantities at Kastanas and Kalapodi. It seems that the species was cultivated in Greece to a limited extent and it was never a main cereal. We have evidence of the use of broomcorn millet at Kalapodi, where an important concentration of *Panicum miliaceum* seeds was found in the Protogeometric layers of the sanctuary. Broomcorn millet was also discovered at Kastanas in layers dated to the same period. The distribution of the species is limited to the northern part of the country; in central and southern Greece, millets are regarded as exotic and barbaric and seem to be considered the food of the lower class (Kroll 2000). The predominant legumes cultivated are bitter vetch (*Vicia ervilia*), lentils (*Lens culinaris*), chickpeas (*Cicer arietinum*), peas (*Pisum sativum*), grass peas (at least *Lathyrus sativus* and *Lathyrus cicera*), and broad bean (*Vicia faba*). Lentils and bitter vetch are reported from Kastanas, Kalapodi, Delphi, and Iolkos.[1] In the latter, bitter vetch may have been contained in a small pottery vessel found broken nearby and it seems that the species resulted from a cleaned stored crop (Jones 1982). *Lens culinaris* and *Vicia ervilia* seem to be higly esteemed at that time, to judge by the frequency and the numbers of the findings. Chickpeas and peas are not missing in the Protogeometric period but they occur only in small quantities in Nichoria (chickpeas) and in Kalapodi (peas). The archaeobotanical evidence is still scant and at the present stage of research we have no evidence that *Cicer arietinum* and *Pisum sativum* formed important components of the subsistence agricultural

system in the Protogeometric and Geometric periods. Grass peas are reported from Kastanas and Delphi, as well as at Kalapodi, where the species is very well documented by the find of 3000 seeds of *Lathyrus sativus*. The species demands special care while growing as it needs a support for climbing, either cereal stalks or mechanical aids. It is more likely that the species was grown into gardens but sowing in the field cannot be excluded. *Lathyrus* sp. can be highly toxic if consumed in large quantities; it contains a neurotoxic amino acid (BOAA) that causes lathyrism in humans.

The main oil crops at this time seem to be poppy (*Papaver somiferum*), gold of pleasure (*Camelina sativa*), and flax or linseed (*Linum usitatissimum*). Among these species only flax is known to have been cultivated as early as the Early Bronze Age in northern Greece, either for its oil or for its fibers. Flax is well documented in the Protogeometric layers of Kalapodi and Kastanas, and flax, poppy, and gold of pleasure become the main oil crops of northern Greece (Kroll 2000; 1983). At Kastanas, flax is mainly used as a source of oil but an industrial use of the species (in clothing) cannot be excluded (Kroll 1983). The presence of *Lolium remotum* (a flax weed) at Kastanas clearly indicates that *Linum usitatissimum* is widely cultivated at that time, at least at this site. *Camelina sativa* becomes by the first millennium B.C. a considerable oilseed crop, as it appears at Kastanas (Kroll 1983) and to a lesser extent at Kalapodi (Kroll 1993). Like flax, charred seeds of *Camelina sativa* are highly perishable but the seed fragments can easily be recognized in archaeological deposits due to their typical shape. Gold of pleasure is a very resistant and productive crop and this must have been the main reason that the species becomes so important throughout the Iron Age. *Papaver somniferum* remains were discovered in a Protogeometric context in the sanctuary of Kalapodi; at Kastanas, in the same period, poppy remains represent 7% of the botanical remains, and the plant was probably used as a substitute for olive oil. Olive tree seems to be less important in northern Greece as olive stones are not recorded outside the range of olive cultivation. It seems that olive is the main source of oil for central and southern Greece, where other oil plants, such as gold of pleasure and poppy, are absent from the archaeological sites. Among fruits, we have ample evidence for the use of two species that seem to be predominant, fig (*Ficus carica*) and the grape vine (*Vitis vinifera*). Fig seeds are a common find at many sites in Greece from the Neolithic period onward. This is not surprising as a single fig contains several hundred seeds. In the Protogeometric levels fig seeds are reported from Kastanas, Kalapodi, Delphi, and Nichoria. At Delphi, in addition to the fig pips, remains of the fruit were discovered. Figs can be eaten fresh or dried and it is impossible to determine whether the charred fragments of figs or the seeds were derived from fresh or dried fruit. This distinction would be very useful as the discovery of dried figs would indicate a more systematic harvesting and processing of this fruit. Cultivated grape seeds are

---

[1]   At Iolkos only bitter vetch is reported.

reported from Kastanas, Kalapodi, Delphi, and Nichoria. The archaeobotanical evidence indicates that vine is cultivated at this time but it is difficult to determine the importance of viticulture in Protogeometric Greece through archaeobotanical remains alone. The counts of grape seeds suggest that grape is used at that time, but in small amounts. At the present stage of research a large wine industry cannot be proved. Vine production could have taken place in small vineyards, as it is still the case in many Mediterranean countries.

Watermelon (*Citrulus lanatus*) is reported from the Geometric levels (9th century B.C.) of Krania in the region of Pieria (Margariti 2002b) and its presence can be related to the expansion of vegetable gardens that appear already in the Late Bronze Age period.

F. Archaic period (700–500 B.C.)

Very few archaeobotanical studies are avalaible for Archaic Greece: only five sites have yielded archaeobotanical remains dated to that period and they come from sacrificial contexts (with the exception of the domestic deposits of Kastanas Toumba in Macedonia) (*Table 5.13*).

The available evidence suggests that hulled barley (*Hordeum vulgare*) is the principal cereal, followed by free-threshing wheat (*Triticum aestivum/durum*), emmer (*Triticum dicoccum*), and einkorn (*Triticum monococcum*) (*Table 5.5*). In the 8th- and 6th-century levels of Delphi, hulled barley represents 65% of the total finds of cereals (Luce et al., forthcoming). This is also the case at the sanctuary of Artemis and Apollo (?), at Kalapodi (Kroll 1993), where hulled barley and free-threshing wheat largely dominate the samples. Free-threshing wheat and barley had a major role in the cult of Apollo and Artemis. It has been suggested that *pelanos* (πέλανος), the fee that had to be paid for the consultation of an oracle, was originally a flat cake made of barley (?) and honey (Amandry 1950). According to Plutarch (*De Pyth. or.* 6.397A), Pythia burnt laurel and barley flower where the immortal fire was before descending to the adyton. The same author (*Quaest. Graec.* 9.292E) writes that at the 7 *Byzios* (February/March), which was dedicated to Apollo, it was common to consume *phthois;* this was a porridge that, according to Chrysippus of Tyana, was made of bread wheat, honey, and cheese (Ath. *Deipn.* 308f; 648b; 113a; 647c).

Lentils (*Lens culinaris*), bitter vetch (*Vicia ervilia*), broad bean (*Vicia faba*), and chickpeas (*Cicer arietinum*) are the most common species among pulses (at least at Kalapodi and at Delphi). Pulses contain a good supply of amino acids (e.g. lysine and tryptophan), in which cereals are deficient, and a diet based on a combination of pulses and cereals is very balanced.

Quince (*Cydonia oblonga*) is reported for the first time from the Archaic deposits at Delphi (Luce et al.,

forthcoming). A poem describing orchards of quinces (Ibycus of Rhegium 1.1; 6th century B.C.) is the only evidence of the presence of this species at that time in Greece.

The waterlogged deposits of the Samian Heraion (7th century B.C.) yielded a large quantity and variety of vegetables, herbs, spices, and flowers that could not have been preserved by carbonization (Kučan 1995). Most of those species must have been used at least since the Neolithic period, but the Archaic Samian Heraion yielded the first physical evidence of their use (in form of macro-remains). It is not easy to interpret the Samian remains since none of them was found in connection with a dining establishment, but it seems certain that some of these species were parts of ritual procedures.

It is interesting to note that there is no archaeobotanical evidence of laurel and incense at Delphi at that time (this was also confirmed by charcoal and pollen analysis; Luce et al., forthcoming). According to written sources Pythia chewed laurel and inhaled incense before giving the oracles (Amandry 1950). It seems that these materials were bought for the needs of the oracle and were not cultivated at Delphi, at least not before the 5th century B.C..

G. Classical period (480–323 B.C.)

Archaeobotanical evidence regarding the 5th and 4th centuries B.C. is limited to six sites (*Table 5.14*); among these sites sufficient evidence of plant remains comes only from three sacrificial contexts: the sanctuary of Artemis and Apollo at Kalapodi (Kroll 1993), the sanctuary of Demeter and Kore at Corinth (Bookidis et al. 1999), and the necropolis of Limenas on Thasos (Megaloudi 2004a, 2004b, in preparation). With so few sites it is not possible to draw any conclusion on the role of food plants, if we consider only the archaeobotanical remains. The plant specimens recorded in Greek sanctuaries, however, consist of typical Mediterranean species (wheat, legumes, fruits, and nuts) that were also components of daily diet in Greece at least since the Early Neolithic (see Megaloudi 2005).

Hulled barley (*Hordeum vulgare*) and free-threshing wheat (*Triticum aestivum/dururm*) dominate the samples at the sanctuary of Demeter and Kore at Corinth (Bookidis et al. 1999) and at Kalapodi (Kroll 1993). Barley seems to be very important in Archaic and Classical Attica. One of Solon's laws prescribed that those invited to dine in the Prytaneion at civic expense should have food made from barley on ordinary days and food made of wheat only on festival days (Sallares 1991, p. 314). Barley was the prize awarded to winners at the Eleusinian Games, and the Homeric *Hymn to Demeter* mentions the cultivation of white barley at Eleusis. Barley was also the common food at Sparta and the helots are said to have paid tribute to the Spartiates in barley rather than wheat (Sallares 1991).

Table 5.14 presents the main species recorded in the deposits dated to the 5th and 4th centuries B.C.

The archaeobotanical evidence for Classical Greece is too scant for any conclusions to be drawn. We do have sufficient evidence, however, of the composition of funeral plant offerings, as several pyres containing plant remains were discovered at the necropolis of Thasos (Megaloudi 2004a, 2004b, in preparation). The first physical evidence of garlic (*Allium sativum*) and walnut (*Juglans regia*) comes from funeral deposits on Thasos, where both species seem to play a part in the ritual.

CHAPTER 7

CONCLUDING REMARKS

This synthesis of Greek archaeobotanical data assembles for the first time material from the Neolithic to Classical Periods. For researchers interested in the ancient diet, this study is a useful research tool that allows one to examine trends and patterns in plant foods diachronically.

Figure 4.17b shows most of the sites that have produced plant remains; *Figure 4.18* shows the breakdown of sites into cultural components; I present each major period from which plant remains were recovered. The available macrofossil data indicate that the major sources of plant proteins did not change significantly through time. In the Early Neolithic the principal sources of plant protein are cereals (six-rowed hulled and naked barley, two-rowed barley, emmer, einkorn) and pulses (lentil, common pea, bitter vetch) with two new species added, grass pea and perhaps chickpea. Among the fruits and nuts, grapes, olive, cornelian cherry, acorns, blackberries, wild pears, and pistachio dominate. With the Middle Neolithic there is no significant change in the general nature of the resources, as the same range of species from the previous period continues to be exploited. The Late Neolithic sees a significant increase in the number of sites represented and the species present. In addition to the species previously represented, spelt wheat, rye, timopheev wheat, broad bean, and *Lathyrus clymenum* occur for the first time. In the same period there is evidence of vine domestication and the possibility of fig cultivation. Flax is cultivated in Macedonia, which suggests that the cultivation of the species was practiced in northern Greece from at least the 6th millennium. B.C.

Throughout the Bronze Age most of the same species are present. According to some scholars olive cultivation seems to begin in southern Greece during the Early Bronze Age (Blitzer 1993), while others put the beginnings of olive domestication somewhere in the 2nd millennium B.C. (Runnels and Hansen 1985; Hansen 1988; Hamilakis 1996). The main oil species for the Early and the Middle Bronze Age are gold of pleasure, poppy, and flax in northern Greece, and olive to the south. A new oil species, Lallemantia, appears as an imported oil plant in the Early Bronze Age and becomes a crop in the subsequent periods. The Late Bronze Age sees a significant increase in the number of species. Cereals and legumes are reported nearly in nearly equal proportions at Late Bronze Age sites. Certainly grape, olive, and fig continue to predominate among the fruits and nuts, and melon occurs for the first time in that period. At the same time, species that previously had been recorded only in northern Greece (e.g., spelt wheat, bromcorn millet, poppy) are also recorded at sites in southern Greece (e.g., Tirynth).

In Protogeometric and Geometric Greece, crops of the arable land can be grouped into cereals, pulses, oil plants and fruit trees. Free-threshing wheat, especially bread wheat, increases considerably and becomes—together with hulled barley—the major crop. Concerning pulses, there is no significant change as the same range of species—lentils, bitter vetch, peas, and grass pea—were exploited from the Neolithic through the Geometric period. However a slight expansion of the cultivation of a small-seeded variety of broad bean can be observed in the Protogeometric period. As to the exploitation of oil crops, the Bronze Age species persist and the main change can be seen in the case of Camelina sativa: the plant occurs regularly and in larger quantities in the Protogeometric/Geometric deposits. A new species, watermelon, occurs around the 9th century B.C.

In the Archaic and Classical Periods it is difficult to interpret the small amount of plant remains that have been uncovered at archaeological sites. The available evidence indicates that hulled barley and free-threshing wheats were the main species in both periods. Barley cakes were widely consumed and there are numerous references to them in written sources suggesting that they were everyday fare. In Classical Greece barley was used in the form of alphita and maza. Alphita is a porridge made of roasted ground barley that Pliny describes as a typical Greek recipe and maza is a mash of barley and wheat that was very common in Athens, at least until the end of the 4th century B.C.

The Hellenistic and Roman periods were not considered in this book. Only two archaeobotanical studies concerning Hellenistic times were in print at the time that I was writing this book. Archaeobotanical studies of sites dating to the Hellenistic period have been conducted recently, however, and the publication of these data will help advance our knowledge for that period. There is no archaeobotanical data concerning the Roman period in Greece, with the exception of a sacrificial context from Isthmia dated between A.D. 50 and 100 (Gebhard 1993). To talk about Roman times in Greece would be a mere transposition of knowledge about practices elsewhere in the Roman world.

Plant products have always played a vital role in the Aegean communities, being used mainly as food, but also as fuel, for building materials, in medications, and for several other uses, especially in ritual festivities. In the past, the cultivation of crop plants was the major occupation of most of the population, and it formed the major economic activity in preindustrial societies. Given the status of crop production, the study of plant remains should form a central part of any study of ancient civilizations.

The aim of this book has been to follow the evolution of food plant production in Greece throughout prehistoric and historic times; the results are based on the archaeobotanical studies conducted in the country during the last 100 years. In addition to the archaeobotanical evidence I have used literature references, when they were available, in an attempt to better understand how and in what context these species were used. Here I have addressed a general pattern of the use of plant species in Greece through time. It remains for future archaeobotanical researchers to investigate the validity of these patterns and to supply further samples for study.

REFERENCES

Abdalla, M. 1990. Bulgur an important wheat product in the cuisine of contemporary Assyrians in the Middle East, in Walker H. (ed) *Oxford Symposium on food and cookery 1989, staple foods.* Prospect Books, London pp. 27-37

Adams, R., and Simmons, D. 1993. Appendix. Botanical remains from Bronze age Marki-Alonia, Cyprus. *Reports Department Antiquities Cyprus* : 66-68.

Adam-Veleni, P., Ioannidou, E. and Mangafa, M. 1995. Ossa 1992. I kerameiki tou oikismou kai ta archaiovotanika kataloipa. To archaiologiko Ergo sti Makedonia kai Thraki, *AEMTH,* 6: 383-389.

Aitken, M. J., Michael, H. N., Betancourt, P. P. and Warren, P. M. 1988. The Thera Eruption: Continued Discussion of the Dating, *Archaeometry* 30: 164-182.

Akgül, A. and Özcan, M. 1999. Some compositional characteristics of capers (*Capparis spinosa*) seed and oil. *Grasas Aceites* 50 : 49-52.

Alexiou, S. 1958. Ein Frühminoisches Grab bei Lebena auf Kreta. *Archäologischer Anzeiger,* 1 / 4 : 2-10.

Alexiou, S. 1960. New light on Minoan dating. Early Minoan tombs at Lebena. *Illustrated London News,* 6 314 : 225-27.

Alonso i Martinez, N. 1997. *Agricultura a la plana occcidental catalana durant la protohistoria.* (Diss. Univ. of Lleida, Spain).

Amandry, P. 1950. *La mantique apollinienne à Delphes. Essai sur le fonctionnement de l'oracle.* 2 volumes. De Boccard, Paris.

Amigues, S. 1995. Des Plantes nommées Moly. *Journal des Savants* janvier-juin, 3-29.

Amigues, S. 2002. *Études de Botanique Antique.* Mémoires de l'Académie des Inscriptions et Belles-Lettres, 25, Paris.

Ammerman, A., and Cavalli-Sforza, L.L. 1984. *The Neolithic transition and the Genetics of Populations in Europe.* Princeton University Press, Princeton.

Amouretti, M.-C. 1986. *Le pain et l'Olivier dans la Grèce antique. De l'araire au moulin.* Centre de Recherche d'Histoire Ancienne 67. Annales Littéraire de l'Université de Besançon, Les Belles-Lettres, Paris.

André, J. 1981. *L'alimentation et la cuisine à Rome.* (1ère édition 1961). Les Belles Lettres, Paris.

André, J. 1985. *Les noms de plantes dans la Rome antique.* Les Belles Lettres, Paris.

André J. (ed. and trans.). Pliny: *Histoire Naturelle.* Les belles Lettres Paris.

Andreou, S., Fotiadis, M, and Kotsakis, K. 1996. Review of Aegean Prehistory, V : the Neolithic and Bronze age of Northern Greece. *American Journal of Archaeology,* 100: 537-597.

Arnold, H. J., Arnold-Apostolides, N., Gehu, J.M. and Gehu-Franck, J. 1993. Plantes utiles et médecine traditionnelle dans le Sud-Est égéen de la Grèce (îles de Karpathos, Kassos et Saria). *Colloques phytosociologiques,* 22. Bailleul : 1-55.

Arroba, D., Giacobini, G., Castelletti, L., Gardini, G., Merrigi, A., Ottoboni, A. 1999. Analisi di un corprolite rinvenuto nei livelli del Neolitico medio della Caverna delle Arene Candide. *Arene Candide* : 25-35.

Arroba, D., Murialdo, G. 2001. Le analisi palinologiche e paleocarpologiche, in : Mannoni T. and Murialdo G. (eds.) S. Antonino :Un insediamento fortifacto nella Liguria bizantina, Istituto internazionale di Studi Liguri. *Coll. Monografie Preistoriche ed Archeologiche XII*: 627-638.

Aström, P. and Hjelmqvist, H. 1971. Grain impressions from Cyprus and Crete. *Opuscula Atheniensia,* 10 : 9-14.

Atherden, M.A., and Hall, J.A. 1994: Holocene pollen diagrams from Greece, in: Bottema, S. and Heusser, C.J., guest editors, *Historical Biology, An International Journal of Paleobiology,* Sp. Issue vol. 9(1–2): 117–30.

Atherden, M.A. and Hall, J.A 1999: Human impact on vegetation in the White Mountains of Crete since ad 500. *The Holocene* 9, 183–93

Bakels, C.C. 1991. Western continental Europe, in: van Zeist, W., Wasylikowa, K. and Behre, K.E. (dir.). *Progress in Old world palaeoethnobotany.* Balkema, Rotterdam, pp. 279-298.

Bakels, C.C. 1997. De cultuurgewassen van de Nederlandse Prehistorie, 5400 v.C- 12v. C., in: Zeven A.C. (dir.). *De introductie van onze cultuurplanten en hun begeleiders, van het Neolithicum tot 1500 AD.*Vereniging voorLanbouwgeschiedenis, Wageningen, pp. 15-51.

Barber, E.J.W. 1991. *Prehistoric Textiles.* Princeton University Press.

Barker, G. 1985. *Prehistoring farming in Europe.* Cambridge University Press.

Baumann, H. 1993. *Greek Wild Flowers and Plant Lore in ancient Greece.* The Herbert Press, London.

Becker, C. 1991. Die Tierknochenfunde von der Platia Magoula Zarkou - neue Untersuchungen zu Haustierhaltung, Jagd und Rohstoffverwertung im neolithisch-bronzezeitlichen Thessalien. *Prähist. Zeitschr,* 66 (1) : 14-78.

Behre, K.E. 1992. The history of rye cultivation in Europe. *Vegetation History and Archaeobotany,* 1 (3) : 141-156.

Beijerinck, W. 1976. *Zadenatlas der Nederlandsche flora Ten Behoeve van de Botanie, Palaeontologie, Bodemcultuur on Warenkennis.* Backhuys and Meesters, Amsterdam.

Benzi, F. and Berliocchi, L. 1999. *L'histoire des plantes en Méditerranée. Art et Botanique.* Actes Sud, Motta.

Besnard, G. and Bervillé. A. 2000. Multiple origins for Mediterranean olive (*Olea europaea* L. ssp. *europaea*) based upon mitochondrial DNA polymorphisms. *Comptes Rendus de l'Académie des Sciences (Sciences de la Vie)*, 323 : 173-181.

Besnard, G., Khadari, B., Baradat, P. and Bervillé, A. 2002. *Olea europaea* (Oleaceae) phylogeography based on chloroplast DNS polymorphisms. *Theoretical and Applied Genetics,* 104: 139-44.

Betancourt, P. P. 1987. Dating the Aegean Late Bronze Age with Radiocarbon, *Archaeometry* 29: 45-49.

Betancourt, P. P. 1998. The Chronology of the Aegean Late Bronze Age: Unanswered Questions, in Balmuth, M. S., and Tykot, R. H. (eds.), *Sardinian and Aegean Chronology: Towards the Resolution of Relative and Absolute Dating in the Mediterranean* Oxford, pp. 291-296.

Betancourt, P. P., and Michael, H. N. 1987. Dating the Aegean Late Bronze Age with Radiocarbon: Addendum, *Archaeometry* 29: 212-213.

Berggren, G. 1969. *Atlas of Seeds and Small Fruits of Northwest European Plant Species Part 2 Cyperaceae.* Swedish Natural Science Research Council. Arlöv, Berlings.

Berggren, G. 1981. *Atlas of Seeds and Small Fruits of Northwest European Plant Species Part 3 Salicaceae - Cruciferae.* Swedish Natural Science Research Council. Lund, Berlingska Boktryckeriet.

Bertsh, K. 1941. *Früchte und Samen.* F. Enke, Stuttgart.

Binford, L. R. 1968. Post-Pleistocene adaptations, in: Binford, S. R. and Binford, L. R. (dir.) *New Perspectives in Archaeology.* Aldine, Chicago : 313-41.

Blitzer, H. 1993. Olive cultivation and oil production in Minoan Crete, in: Amouretti, M.-C. and Brun, J.-P. (eds.). La production du vin et l'huile en Méditerranée de l'âge du Bronze à la fin du XVIeme siècle. Symposium International, Aix en Provence *Bulletin de Correspondance Hellénique*, Supp. 25, Paris :163-175.

Boardman, S. and Jones, G. 1990. Experiments on the effects on charring on cereal plant components. *Journal of Archaeological Science,* 17 : 1-11.

Bookidis, N., Hansen, J., Snyder, L. and Goldberg, P. 1999. Dining in the sanctuary of Demeter and Coré at Corinth. *Hesperia,* 68 : 1-54.

Bosanquet, R.C. 1901-1902. Excavations at Palaikastro I. *Annual of the British School at Athens,* 8 : 286-316.

Bottema, S. 1974. *Late Quaternary vegetation history of northwestern Greece.* (Diss. Univ. of Groningen, Sweden).

Bottema, S. 1980. On the history of the walnut (*Juglans regia*) in southwestern Europe. *Acta Botanica Neerlandica,* 29 : 343-49.

Bottema, S. 2000. The Holocene history of walnut, sweet-chestnut, manna-ash and plane tree in the Eastern Mediterranean. *Pallas,* 52 : 35-59.

Bottema, S., Helbaek, H., Hjelmqvist, H. and van Zeist, W. 1983. Botanical Studies, appendix I. in: Aström, P. (ed.). The Cuirass tomb and other finds at Dendra.

Part 2 : excavations in the cemeteries, the lower town and the citadel. *Studies in Mediterranean Archaeology,* 4 : 43-44.

Bottema, S., and Sarpaki, A. 2003. Environmental Change in Crete: a 9000-year Record of Holocene vegetation history and the effects of the Santorini Eruption, *The Holocene* 13: 733-749.

Bouby, L. 2000. Agriculture et cueillette à l'âge du Bronze ancien dans la vallée du Rhône et en basse Auvergne in Leduc, M., Valdeyron, N. and Vaquer, J. (dir.) *Sociétés et espaces. Rencontres de Préhistoire récente. IIIe session (Toulouse 6-7 novembre 1998).* Archives d'Ecologie Préhistorique, pp. 201-210.

Bowman, A.R.A. 1966. *Studies on the heat induced carbonisation.* Unpublished undergraduate dissertation. Department of Agricultural Botany, University of Reading.

Braidwood, R. J. 1960. The agricultural revolution. *Scientific American,* 203 : 130-41.

Brinkkemper, O. 1993. Wetland Farming in the area to the south of the Meuse estuary during the Iron age and Roman Period, an environmental and palaeo-economic reconstruction. *Analecta Praehistorica Leidensia,* 24 : 1-226.

Brosse, J. 1989. *Mythologie des arbres.* Plon, Paris.

Browson, C. L. (ed. and trans.) Xenophon : *Anabasis,* C. L., Loeb Classical Library

Bruneton, J. 1996. *Plantes toxiques, végétaux dangereux pour l'Homme et les animaux.* Tec et Doc, Lavoisier, Paris.

Bulle, H. 1909. *Orchomenos.* Abhandlungen der Kaiserlichen bayerischen Akademie, Munich.

Buxó, R. 1989. Semences et fruits. Recherches sur les données carpologiques dans les niveaux antiques de Lattes : les procédures expérimentées sur la fouille, in: Py, M. (dir.). Introduction à l'étude de l'environnement de Lattes antique *Lattara,* 2 : 73-82.

Buxó, R. 1993. *Des semences et des fruits. Cueillette et agriculture en France et en Espagne méditerrannéenne du Néolithique à l'âge du fer.* (Diss. Univ. of Montpellier II, France).

Buxó, R. 1997. *Arqueología de las plantas. La explotación económica de las semillas y los frutos en el marco mediterráneo de la Península Ibérica.* Critica, Barcelone.

Cauvin, J. 1997. *Naissance des divinités, naissance de l'agriculture : La révolution des symboles au Néolithique.* CNRS, Paris.

Cavanagh, W.G., Mee, C.B. and Renard, J. 2001. Laconia, Sparta, Kouphovouno. *Annual Report of the British School at Athens* 2000-01: 28-9.

Cerceau, I. 1983. L'utilisation des ressources végétales dans les Cyclades aux périodes protohistoriques : un bilan des données publiées. *Les cyclades. Matériaux pour une étude de géographie historique.* Table Ronde. Université de Dijon, 11-13 septembre 1982. CNRS, Paris, pp. 75-80.

Cerceau, I. 1992. Les moyens de subsistance, in Treuil, R. (dir.). Dikili Tash. Village Prehistorique de

Macedoine Orientale I, Fouilles de Jean Deshayes (1961-1975) volume 1. *Bulletin de Correspondance Hellénique, Suppl.* 24 : 145-146.

Chapoutier F. and Charbonneaux J. (1928). *Fouilles exécutées à Malia.* Paris.

Childe, V. G. 1925. *The dawn of European civilisation.* London: Kegan Paul

Collectif 1964. *Encyclopédie du Monde Végétal.* Paris: Quillet.

Couplan, F. 1983. *Le régal végétal. Plantes sauvages comestibles.* Encyclopédie des plantes comestibles de l'Europe vol. 1. Debard, Paris.

Coulton, J.J., Metzger, IR, Sarpaki, A., and Wall-Crowther, S 2002. Chapter 7. Diet and environment, in: Sapouna- Sakellaraki, E., Coulton, J.J., and Metzger, I.R., (eds) The Fort at Phylla, Vrachos. Excavations and researches at a late Archaic fort in Central Euboea. *Brit School Athens suppl* vol 33. pp 89-98 .

Curtis, R. 2001. Ancient Food Technology. *Technology and Change in History* vol. 5. Brill. Leiden.

Dalby, A. 1996. *Siren Feasts; A history of food and gastronomy in Greece.* Routledge Publishing, New York.

Davis, P.H. 1965-1986. *Flora of Turkey and the east Agean Islands. Vols 1-10.* Edinburgh University Press, Edinburgh.

Dawkins, R.M., and Laistner, M.L. (1912-1913). The excavation of Kamares Cave in Crete. *British Scholl at Athens,* 19 : 1-34.

de Candolle, A. 1883. *Origine des plantes cultivées.* Fac-similé 1984, Jeanne Lafitte, Marseille.

de la Taille, R. 1985. *Les arbres à fruits secs. Amandier, châtaignier, noisetier, noyer.* Flammarion, Paris.

de Rougemont, G. M. 1989. *A field guide to the crops of Britain and Europe.* Collins. London.

Dennell, R. 1974. Botanical evidence for prehistoric crop processing activities. *Journal of Archaeological Science,* 1: 275-284.

Dennell, R. 1976. The economic importance of plant resources represented on archaeological sites. *Journal of Archaeological Science,* 3: 229-247.

Dennell, R. 1985. European Economic Prehistory: a New Approach. London Academic Press

Diamant, S. 1979. A Short history of Archaeological Sieving at Francthi Cave, Greece. *Journal of Field Archaeology,* 6 : 205-217.

Dimitrakis, K.G. 1999. *Agria fagosima chorta.* Kalliergitis, Athens.

Efstratiou, E., Fumanal, M.P, Ferrer, C., Urem Kotsos, D., Curci, A., Tagliacozzo, A., Stratouli, G., Valamoti, S.M, Dinou, M., Badal, E., Madella, M. and Skourtopoulou, K., 1998. Excavations at the Neolithic settlement of Makri, Thrace, Greece (1988-1996)- A Preliminary Report *SAGVNTVM,* 31: 11-62.

Ewers, M. 1989. *Linum usitatissimum* L. Le lin, une plante cultivée du Néolithique. Avec en annexe : L'homme et la femme sur la roche à Altlinster, par J. Engling (*Publ. Sect. Hist. Inst. Gr.-Ducal de* Luxembourg 2, 1846 : 95-103). *Bulletin de la Société Préhistorique Luxembourgeoise,* 11 : 169-202.

Evans, A. 1900-1901. The Palace at Knossos. *Annual of the British Scholl at Athens,* 7 : 1-120.

Evans, A. 1921-1935. *The Palace of Minos at Knossos.* Vols. I-IV. Macmillan. London.

Evans, J. D. 1968. Knossos Neolithic, part II : summary and conclusions. *Annual of the British Scholl at Athens* 63, : 267-76.

Evershed, R., Vaughan, S., Dubb, S.N. and Soles, J. 1997. Fuel for thought ? Beeswax in lamps and conical cups from late Minoan Crete. *Antiquity,* 71 : 979-985.

Flannery, K.V. 1969. Origins and Ecological Effects of Early Domestication in Iran and the Near East, in: Ucko, J., and Dimbleby, G.W. (eds) *The Domestication and Exploitation of Plants and Animals.* Aldine Publishing Company, Chicago, Illinois, pp. 73-100.

Flint-Hamilton, K. 1994. *The Palaeoethnobotany of the Zas Cave on Naxos.* (Diss. Univ. of Duke, USA).

Fouqué, F. 1879. *Santorini et ses éruptions.* Masson, Paris.

French, D. 1971. An experiment in Water-Sieving. *Anatolian Studies,* 20 : 59-64.

Forbes, H. 1989. Of grandfathers and grand theories : the hierarchised ordering of responses to hazard in a Greek rural community, in: Halstead, P. and Shea, J. O. (dir.). *Bad Year Economics. Cultural Resposnes to Risk and Uncertainity,* Cambridge University Press, Cambridge, pp. 87-97.

Forbes, R.J. 1987. *Studies in Ancient Technology,* vol. III, Leiden.

Ford, R. 1979. Palaeoethnobotany in American Archaeology, in: Schiffer, M. (ed.) *Advances in Archaeological Method and Theory 2.* Academic Press: New York, pp. 286-336

Follieri, M. 1979 (1985). Provviste Alimentari Vegetali in una Casa Minoica ad Haghia Triada (Creta). *Annuario della Scuola Archaeologica i Atene e delle Missione Italiane in Oriente* LVII N.S., 41 : 165-172.

Follieri, M. 1982. Cibi carbonizzati in Livelli Tardo Minoici a Canea (Creta Occidentale). *Studi Micenei ed Egeo-Anatolici* XXIII : 137-139.

Follieri, M. and Coccolini, G.B.L. 1979. Travi carbonizzate del palazzo minoico de Festos (Creta). *Annuario della Scuola Archaeologica i Atene e delle Missione Italiane in Oriente,* 57 NS 41 : 173-185.

Foster, C. 1997. Preliminary report on the examination of palaeo-ethnobotanical remains from Dimitra, N. Greece. Appendix 13, in: Grammenos G. *Neolithiki Makedonia,* Ipourgeio Politismou Dimosieumata tou Arxaiologikou Deltiou Ar. 56. Athens, pp. 217-219.

Fournier, P. 1947-48. *Le livre des plantes médicales et vénéneuses de France,* 1, 2 et 3. P. Lechevalier, Paris.

Frankel, D., and Webb, J. 2001. *The Marki Project.* http://www.archaeology.latrobe.edu.au/research/marki/flora.html.

Gamble, C. 1981. Social Control and the Economy, in: Sheridan, A., and Bailey, G. *Economic Archaeology* British Archaeological Reports 96, pp. 215-29.

Gebhard, E. 1993. The Isthmian Games and the sanctuary of Poseidon in the Early Empire, in: Gregory, T.E. (ed) The Corinthia in the Roman Period. *Journal of Roman Archaeology* Suppl. 8 : 78-94

Gennett, J. 1982. Three Holocene pollen records from southern Greece. *Palynology,* 6: 282.

Germer, R. 1985. *Flora des pharaonischen Ägypten.* Verlag Philip von Zabern, Mainz.

Germer, R. 1989. *Die Pflanzenmaterialien aus dem Grab des Tutankhamun.* Gerstenberg, Hildesheim.

Gerasimidis, A., and Athanasiadis, N. 1995. Woodland history of northern Greece from the mid-Holocene to recent time based on evidence from peat pollen profiles. *Vegetation History and Archaeobotany,* 4 : 109-116.

Gimbutas, M., Winn, S., and Shimabuku D. (dir.) 1989. *Achileion : A Neolithic Settlement in Thessaly, Greece 6400-5600 B.C.* Los Angeles, California.

Godley A. D. (ed. and trans.) 1921-25. Herodotus: *Historia.* 4 vols., The Loeb Classical Library.

Goldman, H. 1931. *Excavations at Eutresis in Boeotia.* Cambridge, Massachussets.

Grammenos, D. 1997. *Neolithiki Macedonia.* Ipourgeio Politismou Dimosieumata tou Arxaiologikou Deltiou Ar., 56. Athens.

Green, F.J. 1979. Phosphatic Minerazation of seeds from archaeological sites. *Journal of Archaeological Science,* 6 : 279-284.

Green, F.J. 1981. The development of crop husbandry, in: Jones, M. and Dimbleby, U. (eds.) *The environment of man : the Iron Age to the Anglo-saxon period.* British Archaeological Reports, British Series 87 Oxford, pp. 95-128.

Greig, J.R.A. 1974. Appendix : a report on plant impressions from Debla, Crete. *Annual of the British School at Athens,* 69 : 34.

Greig, J. 1991. The British Isles, in: van Zeist, W., Wasylikowa, K. and Behre, K. E. (dir.). *Progress in Old world palaeoethnobotany.* Rotterdam, Balkema : 299-334.

Greig, J.R.A., and Turner, J. 1974. Some Pollen Diagrams from Greece and their Archaeological Significance. *Journal of Archaeological Science,* 1 : 177-14.

Greig, J.R.A., and Warren, P. 1974. Early Bronze age Agriculture in Western Crete. *Antiquity,* 48 : 130-132.

Gulick, C. B. (ed. and trans.) 1927-41. Athenaeus: *Deipnosophistae,* The Loeb Classical Library, Cambridge.

Gummere, R. M. (ed. and trans.) Seneca : *Epistulae Moralis,* The Loeb Classical Library, Cambridge.

Gustafsson, S. 2000. Carbonized Cereal Grains and Weed Seeds in Prehistoric Houses- an Experimental Perspective. *Journal of Archaeological Science,* 27 : 65-70.

Haldane, C. 1991. Recovery and analysis of plant remains from some Mediterranean shipwrecked sites, in: Renfrew, J.M. (ed.). *New Light on early Farming. Recent Development in Palaeoethnobotany.* Edinburh University Press, pp. 213-223.

Halstead, P. 1977. Prehistoric Thessaly : the submergence of civilisation, in: Bintliff J.L. (dir.) *Mycenaean Geography.* British Association for Mycenaean Studies, Cambridge.

Halstead, P. 1981. Counting sheep in Neolithic and Bronze age Greece, in: Hodder, I., Isaak, G., and Hammond, N. (dir.). *Patterns of the Past : Studies in Honor of David Clarke.* Cambridge University Press, Cambridge, pp. 307-339.

Halstead, P. 1981b. From determinism to Uncertainty: Social Storage and Rise of the Minoan Palace, in: Sheridan, A., and Bailey, G. (eds). *Economic Archaeology* British Archaeological Reports 96, pp. 187-213.

Halstead, P. 1984. *Strategies for survival : an ecological approach to social and economic change in early farming communities of Thessaly, N. Greece,* (Diss. Univ. of Cambridge).

Halstead, P. 1989. The economy has a normal surplus : economic stability and social change among early farming communities of Thessaly, Greece, in: Halstaed, P. and Shea, O J. (eds.). *Bad Year Economics. Cultural Responses to Risk and Uncertainity.* Cambridge University Press.

Halstead, P. 1992 Agriculture in the Bronze Age Aegean. Towards a Model of Palatial Economy, in: Wells, B. (ed.). *Agriculture in Ancient Greece* Skrifter Utgivna av Svenska Institutet I Athen, 4, XLII, Stockholm, pp. 105-17.

Halstead, P. 1996. The development of agriculture and pastoralism in Greece. When, who and what? In: Harris, D. R. (ed.). *The origins and Spread of Agriculture and Pastoralism in Eurasia* London: UCL Press, pp. 296-309.

Halstead, P. 1999. Neighbours from hell? The Household in Neolithic Greece, in: Halstead, P. (ed.) *Neolithic Society in Greece. Sheffield Studies in Aegean Archaeology.* Shefield: Sheffield Academic Press, pp. 77-95.

Halstead, P., and Jones, G. 1980. Early Neolithic economy in Thessaly-some evidence from excavations at Prodromos. *Anthropologika,* 1 : 93-117.

Halstead, P., and Jones, G. 1987. Parartema 1 : Bioarchaeological Remains from Kalythies Cave, Rhodes, in: Sampson Ad. (ed.). *I Neolithiki Periodos sta Dodekanisa,* Ipourgeio

Hamilakis, Y. 1999. Food technologies/technologies of the body: the social context of wine and oil production and consumption in Bronze Age Crete. *World Archaeology* 31(1): 38-54.

Hamilakis, Y. 1996. Wine, oil and the dialectics on power in Bronze Age Crete: a review of the evidence. *Oxford Journal of Archaeology* 15(1): 1-32.

Hanf, M. 1983. *The arable weeds of Europe with their seedlings and seeds.* BASF United Kingdom.

Hansen, J. 1978. The earliest seed remains from Greece : Paleolithic through Neolithic At Francthi cave. *Berichte der Deutschen Botanischen Gesellscaft* 91 : 39-46.

Hansen, J. 1980. *The Palaeoethnobotany of Francthi Cave, Greece.* (Diss. Univ. of Minnesota).

Hansen, J. 1985. Palaeoethnobotany in Greece. Past, present and future, in: Wilkie, N.C., and. Coulson, W.D.E (eds.). *Contributions to Aegean Archaeology. Studies in honour of William A. Mc Donald. Publications in Ancient Studies, 1 :* 171-181 Minneapolis.

Hansen, J. 1988. Agriculture in the Prehistoric Aegean : Data versus Speculation. *American Journal of Archaeology,* 92 : 39-52.

Hansen, J. 1991. *The Palaeoethnobotany of Francthi cave.* Indiana Univ. Press.

Hansen, J. 1992. Francthi Cave and the beginnings of agriculture in Greece and the Aegean, in: Anderson-Cerfaud, P.C. (ed.). *Préhistoire de l'agriculture. Nouvelles approches expérimentales et ethnographiques,* CNRS, Paris : 231-247 (Monographie du CRA, no 6).

Hansen, J. 1999. Konispol Cave : Plant remains, in : Betancourt, P.P., Karageorghis, V., Laffineur, R., and Niemeier, W.D. (eds.). Meletemata, Studies in Aegean Archaeology. Presented to Malcolm H. Wiener as he enters his 65th Year. *Aegaeum 20 Annales d'archéologie égéenne de l'Université de Liège et UT-PASP :*, pp. 333-338.

Hansen, J., and Renfrew, J.M. 1978. Paleolithic-Neolithic seed remains at Francthi Cave, Greece. *Nature,* 271 : 349-352.

Hansen, J., Bookidis, N., and Snyder, L. 1996. Foods of ritual dining at the Sanctuary of Demeter and Coré at Corinth. *American Journal of Archaeology,* 100 : 341-342.

Harris, D. R., and Hillman, G. C. 1989 *Foraging and Farming: The Evolution of Plant Exploitation.* London: Unwin Hyman.

Harlan, J. R. 1995 *The Living Fields: Our Agricultural Heritage.* Cambridge: University Press

Hawes, H. B. 1909. *Gournia, Vasiliki and other Prehistoric sites on the Isthmus of Hierapetra.* Philadelphia.

Hedrick, U. P. 1972. *Sturtevant's Edible Plants of the World.* New York.

Helbaek, H. 1959. Domestication of food plants in the Old World. *Science,* 130 : 365-372

Hehn, V. and Schräder, O. 1911. *Kulturpflanzen und Haustiere in ihrem Übergang aus Asien nach Griechenland und Italien sowie in das übrige Europa : historisch-linguistische Skizzen.* Gebr. Borntraeger, Berlin.

Hepper, F. N. 1990. *Pharaoh's Flowers. The Botanical Treasure of Tutankhamun.* Thames and Hudson, London.

Heron, C., Nemcek, N., Bonfield, K. M., Dixon, D., and Ottaway, B. S. 1994. The chemistry of Neolithic beeswax. *Naturwissenschaft,* 81 : 266-269.

Hiscks, R. D. (ed. and trans.). Diogenes Laertius: *Pythagorae,* The Loeb Classical Library, Cambridge.

Hillman, G. 1975. The Plant remains from Tell Abu Hureyra. A preliminary report, in: Moore, A.M.T., Hillman, G. and Legge, A. J. (eds.) The excavation of Tell Abu Hureyra. *Proceedings Prehstory Society,* 41 : 70-73.

Hillman, G. 1978. On the origins of domestic rye- *Secale cereale :* the finds from aceramic Can Hasan III in Turkey. *Anatolian Studies,* 28 : 157-174.

Hillman, G. 1981. Reconstructing crop husbandry practices from charred remains of crops, in: Mercer, R. (ed) *Farming Practices in British Prehistory.* Edinburgh University Press, pp. 123-162.

Hillman, G. 1984. Interpretation of archaeological plant remains : The application of ethnographic models from Turkey, in: van Zeist, W., and Casparie, W.A. (eds.) *Plants and Ancient Man : Studies in palaeoethnobotany.* Balkema, Rotterdam, pp. 1-41.

Hillman, G., Colledge, S., and Harris, D. R. 1989. Plant-food economy during the Epipalaeolithic period at Tell Abu Hureyra, Syria : dietary, diversity, seasonality, and modes of exploitation, in: Harris, D. R., and Hillman, G. (eds.) *Foraging and farming : the evolution of plant exploitation,* Unwinn and Hyman, London, pp. 240-268.

Hjelmquist, H. 1973. Some economic plants from ancient Cyprus, in: Karageorghis, V. (ed.) *Salamis, 5, Excavations in the Necropolis of Salamis 3,* Nicosie, pp. 231-255.

Hjelmqvist, H. 1977. Some economic plants from the Greek Bronze age, Appendix I, in: Aström P. (ed.) The Cuirass tomb and other finds at Dendra. Part I : the chambre tombs. *Studies in Mediterranean Archaeology* 4 : 123-135.

Heurtley, W. A., and Hutchinson, A. 1926. Report on Excavations at the Toumba and Tables of Vardaróftsa, Macedonia, 1925, 1926. Part I. The Toumba, *Britsh Scholl at Athens* 27 (1925-26): 1-66.

Hobbs, J. J. 1998. Troubling Fields: The Opium Poppy in Egypt. *The Geographical Review* 88 (1) : 64-85.

Hopf, M. 1955. Formveranderungen von Getreide-Körner beim Verkohlen. *Berichte der Deutschen Botanischen Gesellschaft* 68 :191-193.

Hopf, M. 1961. Pflanzenfunde aus Lerna/Argolis. *Der Züchter,* 31 : 239-247.

Hopf, M. 1962a. Nutzpflanzen vom Lernäischen Golf. *Jahrbuch des Römisch-Germanischen Zentralmuseums,* 9 : 1-19.

Hopf, M. 1962b. Bericht über die Untersuchung von Samen und Holzkohlenresten von der Argissa-Magula aus den Präkeramischen bis Mittelbronzenzeitlichen Schichten, in: Milojcic, V., Boessneck, J. and Hopf, M. (eds.) *Die Deutschen Ausgrabungen auf der Argissa-Magula in Thessalien I.* R. Habelt Bonn, pp. 101-119.

REFERENCES

Hopf, M. 1971. Plant remains from the Athenian Agora Neolithic to Byzantine, in: Immerwhar, S.A. (ed.) *The Athenian Agora : The Neolithic and Bronze Ages, vol. XII* ASCSA Princeton, pp. 267-269.

Hopf, M. 1978. Plant remains, in: Amiran, R. (ed) *Early Arad, I. The Chalcolithic settlement and Early Bronze Age city.* Israel Explor. Soc. Jérusalem, pp. 64-82.

Hopf, M. 1983. Jericho plant remains, in: Kenyon, K. M., and Holland, T. A. (eds.). *Excavations at Jericho,* Vol. 5. British School of Archaeology in Jerusalem, London : 576-621.

Hort, A. (ed and trad.) 1916-1926. *Theophrastus Enquiry into Plants and Minor works on odours and weather signs,* The Loeb Classical Library, Hort Harvard University Press, 2 volumes.

Housley, R. A. 1981. *The Palaeoethobotany of Servia.* Msc. Thesis, University of Southampton.

Hubbard, R.N.L.B 1975. Assessing the botanical component of human palaeoeconomies. *Bulletin of the Institute of Archaeology* 12: 197-205

Hubbard, R.N.L.B. 1979. Ancient agriculture and ecology at Servia : Appendix 2, in: Ridley, C., and Wardle, K. A. (eds) Rescue excavation at Servia 1971-1973 : A preliminary report. *The Annual of the British School at Athens,* 74 : 226-228.

Hubbard, R. N. L. B.1980 Development of Agriculture in Europe and the Near East: Evidence from Quantitative Studies. *Economic Botany* 34:51-67

Hubbard, R.N.L.B., and Azm, A. 1990. Quantifying preservation and distortion in carbonised seeds; and investigating the history of friké production. *Journal of Archaeological Science,* 17 : 103-106.

Hurtley, W. A 1939. *Prehistoric Macedonia. An Archaeological Reconnaissance of Greek Macedonia (West of the Struma) in the Neolithic, Bronze and Iron Age.* Cambridge University Press.

Jacquat, C. 1988. *Hauterive-Champréveyres, 1. Les plantes de l'âge du Bronze, Catalogue des fruits et graines.* Archéologie neuchâteloise 7, Ruau, St Blaise.

Jahns, S. 1993. On the Holocene vegetation history of the Argive Plain (Peloponnese southern Greece) *Vegeation. Hististory and Archaeobotany,* 2 :187-203.

Jameson, M. H., Runnels, C., and van Andel, T. H. 1994. *A Greek countryside : the southern Argolid from Prehistory to Present Day.* Stanford University.

Jardé, A. 1925. *Les céréales dans l'Antiquité grecque.* Bulletin de l'Ecole Française d'Archéologie de Rome, 130.

Jarman, H. N, Legge, A. J., and Charles, J. A. 1972. Retrieval of plant remains from archaeological sites by froth flotation, in: Higgs, E. S (ed.) *Papers in Economic Prehistory,* Cambridge University Press, Cambridge, pp. 65-82.

Jean-Blain, C., and Grisvard, M. 1973. *Plantes vénéneuses. Toxicologie.* La Maison Rustique, Paris.

Jessen, K., and Helbaek, H. 1944. Cereals in Great Britain and Ireland in prehistoric and Early historic times. *Biologiske Skrifter,* 3 (2) : 3-68.

Johnson, M. 1999. Chronology of Greece and South-East Europe in the Final Neolithic and early Bronze Age. *Proceedings of the Prehistoric Society,* 65 : 319-36.

Jones, G. 1979. *An analysis of the plant remains of Assiros Toumba.* Unpublished M.Phil. Thesis, University of Cambridge.

Jones, G. 1981. Crop Processing at Assiros Toumba: A Taphonomic Study, *Zeitschrift für Archäologie* 15: 105-111.

Jones, G. 1982. Cereal and Pulse Remains from Protogeometric and Geometric Iolkos, Thessaly. *Anthropologika,* 3 : 75-78.

Jones, G. 1983. *The use of ethnographic and ecological models in the interpretation of archaeological plant remains : case studies from Greece,* (Diss. Univ. of Cambridge).

Jones, G. 1984a. Interpretation of archaeological plant remains: Ethnographic models from Greece, in: van Zeist, W., and Casparie, W. A. (eds.) *Plants and Ancient Man : Studies in palaeoethnobotany.* Balkema, Rotterdam, pp. 43-61.

Jones, G. 1984b. The LMII Plant Remains, in: Popham, M. R. (ed.) The Minoan Unexplored Mansion at Knossos. *The Annual of the British School of Archaeology at Athens, supplément,* 17 : 303-306.

Jones, G. 1987. *The Annual of the British School of Archaeology at Athens* 82 : 115-116

Jones, G. 1991. Numerical analysis in archeobotany in: van Zeist, W., Wasylikowa, K., and Behre, K. E. (eds.) *Progress in Old world palaeoethnobotany.* Rotterdam, Balkema, pp. 63-80.

Jones, G. 1992. Ancient and Modern cultivation of *Lathyrus Ochrus* (L.) DC in the Greek Islands. *The Annual of the British School of Archaeology at Athens,* 87: 211-217.

Jones, G. 1995. Charred grains from Late Bronze age Gla, Boiotia. *The Annual of the British School at Athens,* 90 (centenary volume) : 235-238.

Jones, G., Wardle, K., Halstead, P., and Wardle, D. 1986. Crop storage at Assiros. *Scientific American,* 254 (3) : 96-103.

Jones, G., and Halstead, P. 1993a. An Early Find of Fava from Thebes *The Annual Of the British School At Athens,* 88 : 103-104.

Jones, G., and Halstead, P. 1993b. Charred Plant remains from Neolithic-Bronze age Platia Magula Zarkou, Thessaly. *The Annual Of the British School At Athens,* 88 : 1-3.

Jones, G., Valamoti, S., and Charles, M. 2000. Early crop diversity : a « new » glume wheat from northern Greece. *Vegetation History and Archaeobotany,* 9 : 133-146.

Jones, G. and Valamoti, S. 2005. Lallemantia, an imported or introduced oil plant in Bronze Age northern Greece. *Vegetation History and Archaeobotany* 14: 571-577

88

Jones, H. (ed. and trans.). 1917-32. *The Geography of Strabo*. Vols 1-8.The Loeb Classical Library.

Jones, M. 1991. Sampling in palaeoethnobotany, in: van Zeist, W., Wasylikowa, K., and Behre, K. E. (eds.) *Progress in Old world palaeoethnobotany*. Rotterdam, Balkema, pp. 53-62.

Jones, W.H.S. (ed. and trans.) Pausanias *Description of Greece*, The Loeb Classical Library, Cambridge.

Jorgensen, G. 1977. Acorns as a food source in the Later Stone Age. *Acta Archaeologica* 48: 233-38

Iakovides, Sp. 1989. *Gla*. Athens.

Karali, L., Megaloudi, F., and Marinval, P. 2001. Karpologia: Orismoi kai Texnikes *Technologia* ETBA 10-11 : 55-58

Karg, S. 1991. Knoblauchzehen aus dem mittelalterlichen Laufen BE. *Archäologie der Schweiz,* 14 : 237-260.

Kattamis, C., Kyriazakou, M., and Chaidas, S. 1969. Favism: Clinical and Biochemical Data. *Journal of Medical Genetics* 6: 34-41

King, H. 1995. Food and Blood in Hippocratic Gynaeocology, in: Wilkins, J.,

Harvey, D., and Dobson, M. (eds.) *Food in Antiquity*. Exeter: University of Exeter Press, pp. 12-24.

Kislev, M.E. 1986. Archaeobotanical Findings on the origins of *Lathyrus sativus* and *L. cicera*. in: Kaul, A. K., and Combes, D. (eds.) *Lathyrus and Lathyrism. Proceedings of colloque Lathyrus 1985*. New York, pp. 46-51.

Kislev, M.E. 1988a. *Pinus pinea* in agriculture, culture and cult, in: Küster, H. J. (ed.) *Der prähistorische Mensch und seine Umwelt*. Theiss, Stuttgart, pp. 73-79.

Kislev, M.E. 1988b. Nahal Hemar Cave :dessicated plant remains an interim report. *Atiqot* (Dept. Antiquities et Museums Jerusalem) 38 :76-81.

Kislev, M.E. 1989., Origins of the cultivation of *Lathyrus sativus* and *L. cicera* (Fabaceae). *Economic Botany,* 43 : 262-270.

Kislev, M.E. 1995. Wild olive endocarp at submerged Chalcolithic Kfar Samir, Haifa, Israel. *Journal of The Israel Prehistoric Society,* 26: 134-145.

Knörzer, K. H. 1970. *Novaesium IV. Römerzeitliche Pflanzenfunde aus Neuss*. Limesforschungen, 10. Berlin, Gebr. Mann.

Knörzer, K. H. 1991. Deutschland nördlich der Donau In: van Zeist, W., Wasylikowa, K., and Behre, K. E. (eds.) *Progress in Old world palaeoethnobotany*. Rotterdam, Balkema, pp. 189-205.

Knörzer, K. H., Gerlach, R., Meurers-Balke, J., Kalis, A. J., Tegtmeier, U., Becker, W. D. and Jürgens, A. 1999. *Pflanzenspuren. Archäobotanik im Rheinland : Agrarlandschaft und Nutzpflanzen im Wandel der Zeiten. Mat Bodenkmalpflege Rheinland, 10*. Köln-Bonn.

Körber-Grohne, U. 1987. *Nutzpflanzen in Deutschland. Kulturgeshichte und Biologie*. Stuttgart : Konrad Theiss Verlag.

Körber-Grohne, U. 1991. Identification Methods, in: van Zeist, W., Wasylikowa, K., and Behre, K. E. (eds.)

Progress in Old world palaeoethnobotany. Rotterdam, Balkema, pp. 3-24.

Kowalski, K., Malinowski, T., Wasylikowa, K. 1976. Coprolites from a castrum of Lusatian culture in Komorowo, Poznan District. *Folia Quaternaria,* 48 : 1-13.

Kroll, H. 1979a. Pflanzliche Grossreste vom Siedlungshügel bei Kastanas. *Jahrbuch des Römisch-Germanischen Zentralmuseums Mainz,* 20 : 66-77.

Kroll, H. 1979b. Kulturpflanzen aus Dimini, in: Körber-Grohne, U. (ed.) *Festschrift Maria Hopf, Archaeo-Physika,* 8 : 173-189.

Kroll, H. 1981. Thessalische Kulturpflanzen. *Zeitschrift für Archäologie,* 15 : 97-103.

Kroll, H. 1982. Kulturpflanzen von Tiryns. *Archäologischer Anzeiger* 1982 : 467-485.

Kroll, H. 1983. *Kastanas. Ausgrabungen in einem Siedlungshügel der Bronze- und Eisenzeit Makedoniens 1975-1979. Die Pflanzenfunde.* Prähistorische Archäologie in Südosteuropa 2, Volker Spiess, Berlin. Table 51.

Kroll, H. 1984a. Bronze age and Iron age Agriculture in Kastanas, Macedonia, in: van Zeist, W., and Casparie, W. A. (eds.) *Plants and Ancient Man*, Balkema, Rotterdam, pp: 243-246.

Kroll, H. 1984b. Zum Ackerbau gegen Ende der mykenischen Epoche in der Argolis. *Archäologischer Anzeiger* 1984 : 211-222.

Kroll, H. 1991. Südosteuropa, in: van Zeist, W., Wasylikowa, K., and Behre, K. E. (eds.) *Progress in Old World Palaeoethnobotany* Balkema, Rotterdam, pp. 161-177.

Kroll, H. 1992. Einkorn from Feudvar, Vojvodina, II. What is the difference between emmr-like two-seeded einkorn and emmer? *Review of Palaeobotany and Palynology,* 73 : 181-185.

Kroll, H. 1993. Kulturpflanzen von Kalapodi. *Archäologischer Anzeiger,* 1993 Heft 2: 161-182.

Kroll, H. 1999a. Byzantinischer Roggen von Aghios Mamas, Chalkidike. *Byzantinische Zeitschrift,* 92 : 474-478.

Kroll, H. 1999b. Vor und frühgeschichtliche Weinreben-wild oder angebaut? Eine abschliessende Bemerkung. *Trierer Zeitschrift,* 62 : 151-153.

Kroll, H. 2000. Agriculture and Arboriculture in Mainland Greece. *Pallas, 52 :* 61-68.

Kroll, H. 2003. Rural Plenty : The Result of Hard Work-Rich Middle Bronze age Plant Remains from Aghios Mamas, Chalkidike, in: Wagner, G., Pernicka, E., and Uerpmann, H. P., (eds.). *Troia and the Troad, Scientific Approaches*. Springer Berlin, pp. 293-430.

Koukoules, F. 1952. *Life and Civilisation of Byzantine People*. Papazisi Publications Athens

Kučan, D. 1995. Zur ernährung und dem Gebrauch von Pflanzen im Heraion von Samos im 7. Jahrhundert v. Chr. *Jahrbuch des Deutschen Archäologischen Instituts,* Band 110 : 1-64.

Kučan, D. 1998. Zur Ernährungsgeschichte des Spätmitt und der fruhen Neuzeit in Oldenburg anhand der

REFERENCES

botanischen Untersuchungen der Altstadtgabungen. *Probleme Küsten-Forsch*, 25 : 242-279.

Lamb, W. 1936. *Excavations at Thermi in Lesbos.* Cambridge University press.

Lange, F., and Carty, F. 1975. Salt water application of the Flotation Technique. *Journal of field Archaeology,* 2 : 119-123.

Leclerc, H. 1925. *Les fruits de France.* Masson, Paris.

Lewthwaite, J. 1986. The transition to Food production: a Mediterranean perspective, in: Zvelebil, M. (ed). *Hunters in transition: Mesolithic Societies of Temperate Eurasia and their Transition to farming.* Cambridge, Cambridge University Press, pp. 53-66.

Littré , E. 1839-61. *Les Œuvres complètes d'Hippocrate* 10 vol. Paris (reprinted 1961 : Amsterdam)

Logothetis, V. 1970. *I exelixis tis ampelou kai tis ampelourgias is tin Ellada kata ta archaiologika eurimata tis perioxis (the development of the vine and of viticulture in Greece based on archaeological findings in the area).* Aristoteleion Panepistimion Thessalonikis. Thessaloniki.

Luce, J.-M., Marinval, P., Renault-Miskovsky, J., and Thiebaut, S. forthcoming. *Fouilles de Delphes, Tome II Topographie et architecture, à la frontière du Profane et du sacré.* Ecole Française d'Athènes.

MacDonald, W.A., and Wilkie, N.C., 1992. *Excavations at Nichoria in Southwest Greece, vol. II. The Bronze Age occupation.* Minneapolis :University of Minnesota Press.

Maier, U. 1995. *Moorstratigraphische und paläobotanische Untersuchungen in der jungsteinzeitlichen Moorsiedlung Ödenahlen am Federsee. Forschungen und Berichte zur Vor- und Frühgeschichte in Baden-Württemberg,* 46, Stuttgart.

Malamidou, D., and Papadopoulos, S. 1993. Anaskafiki ereuna ston proistoriko oikismo Limenarion. To Archaiologiko Ergo sti Makedonia kai Thraki *AEMTH,* 7 : 559-572.

Malamidou, D., and Papadopoulos, S. 1997.Proistorikos Oikismos Limenarion : I Proimi Epochi tou Chalkou. To Archaiologiko Ergo sti Makedonia kai Thraki *AEMTH,* 11 : 585-596.

Mangafa, M. 1990. *The plant remains from the Late Neolithic/Early Bronze Age site of Dikili Tash, Macedonia, Greece.* MSc Thesis, University of Sheffield.

Mangafa, M. 1993. Archaiovotaniki meleti tou spilaiou Skoteinis sta tharounia Euboias, in: Sampson Ad. (ed.). *Skotini Tharounia. To spilaio, o oikismos kai to nekrotafeio (Skoteini Tharounia. The cave, the settlement and the cemetery).* Athens, pp. 360-369.

Mangafa, M. 1998. Apothikeusi fitikon proionton se dimosio ktirio tis Isteris Archaiotitas. Archaiovotaniki meleti stin Plateia Dioikitiriou. Parartima. To archaiologiko Ergo sti Makedonia kai Thraki *AEMTH,* 9 (1995) : 209-217.

Mangafa, M. 2000. I ekmetalleusi ton phiton apo ti Mesi Paleolithiki eos ti Neolithiki periodo: apo ti karposillogi sti karpokalliergeia. Archaiovotaniki meleti tou spilaiou Theopetra, in: Kiparissi-

Apostolika, N. (ed.) *Spilaio Theopetra 12 xronia anaskafon aki ereunas 1987-1998. Praktika Diethnous Sinedriou Trikala 6-7 Noemvriou 1998 (Theopetra Cave, 12 years of excavation and research 1987-1998, Proceedings of International Conference, Trikala 6-7 november 1998).* Athens, pp. 135-138.

Mangafa, M., and Kotsakis, K. 1996. A New Method for the Identification of Wild and Cultivated Charred Grape Seeds. *Journal of Archaeological Science,* 23 : 409-418.

Mangafa, M., Koukouli-Chrysnthaki, Ch., Malamidou, D., and Valamoti, S. 2003. Neolithikos oinos: arxaiologikes martiries apo ton proistoriko oikismo Filippon Dikili Tash. *Techne kai Technike sta Ampelia kai tous Oineones tis V. Elladas* Athens, ETBA Publications, pp. 21-35.

Manniche, L. 1999. *An Ancient Egyptian Herbal.* (1ère édition 1989). British Museum Press, Londres.

Manning, S. W. 1995. *The Absolute Chronology of the Aegean Early Bronze Age : archaeology history and radiocarbon.* Monographs in Mediterranean Archaeology 1. Sheffield : Sheffield Academic Press.

Marchant, E.C. (ed. and trans.). Xenophon : *Oeconomicus,* The Loeb Classical Library.

Margariti, E. 1998. *Archaeobotanical remains from Room 24 at Assiros Toumba.* MSc Thesis. University of Sheffield.

Margariti, E. 2002a. Archaiovotanika dedomena apo ton neolithiko oikismo tis Stavroupolis Thessalonikis : mia proti prosseggisi, in: Grammenos, D., and Kotsos, E. (ed.) *Sostikes anaskafes sto Neolithiko oikismo Stavroupolis, Thessalonikis.* Archaiologiko Institouto Boreias Elladas. Thessaloniki, pp. 805-824.

Margariti, E. 2002b. Archaiovotanika kataloipa apo ti geometriki Krania Pierias. Appendix. *Archaia Makedonia.* Thessaloniki. Ministry of Culture.

Margaritis E. and Jones, M. K.(in press). 'Beyond cereals: crop-processing and *Vitis vinifera* L. Ethnography, experiment and charred grape remains from Hellenistic Greece.' *Journal of Archaeological Science.*

Marinval, P. 1986. Découvertes et utilisations de *Lathyrus sativus* et *Lathyrus cicera* en France du Mésolithique (9000 B.P.) jusqu'au Moyen Age (1300 A.D.), in: Kaul, A. K., and Combes, D. (eds.) *Lathyrus and Lathyrism. Third World Medical Research Foundation .* New York, pp. 37-45.

Marinval, P. 1988. *Cueillette, agriculture et alimentation végétale de l'épipaléolithique jusqu'au 2e Âge du Fer en France méridionale. Apports palethnographiques de la carpologie.* (Diss. Univ. Ecole des Hautes en Etudes Sociales, Paris).

Marinval, P. 1999. Les graines et les fruits. La carpologie, in: Ferdière, A. (ed.) *La botanique.* Collection Archéologiques. Errance, Paris, pp. 105-137.

Marinval, P. 2000. Archéologie des Cucurbitacées de l'Ancien Monde : du Néolithique à l'époque romaine. *Espèces de courges. Cultures et usages des cucurbutacées.* Les Alpes de Lumière/Equinoxe/Musées et Patrimoine de Cavaillon, pp. 60-65.

Marinval, P. 2001. Recension des analyses carpologiques en France du Paléolithique à l'époque moderne. Première partie : (1638-1998), in: Marinval, P. (ed.) *Histoires d'homme, Histoires de plantes. Mémoire de Plantes* 1, Toulouse, pp. 223-253.

Mason, S.L.R. 1992. *Acorns in Human Subsistence.* (Diss. University College London).

Mason, S.L.R. 1995. Acornutopia? Determining the role of acorns in past human subsistence, in Wilkins, J., Harvey, D. and Dobson, M. (eds.) *Food in Antiquity.* Exeter: University of Exeter Press, pp. 12-24.

Matterne, V. 1993. *Etudes des macrorestes et du paysage d'un Tell de Macédoine Orientale au Néolithique récent : Dikili Tash.* Mémoire de D.E.A., Université de Paris.

McLaren, F. S., and Hubbard, R. N. L. B. 1990. The archaeobotanical remains, in: Tringham, R., and Krstic, D. (eds) *Selevac, A Neolithic Village in Yugoslavia,* Los Angeles, Institute of Archaeology, University of California, pp. 247-254.

Meeks, D. 1993. Oléiculture et viticulture dans l'Egypte pharaonique, in: Amouretti, M.-C., and Brun, J.-P. (eds.) La production du vin et de l'huile en Méditerranée *Bulletin de Correspondance Hellénique, suppl.* 26 : 3-38.

Megaloudi, F. 2004. *Economie végétale et alimentation en Grèce du Néolithique à l'époque Hellénistique : les apports de la Carpologie,* (Diss. Univ. Ecole des Hautes Etudes en Sciences Sociales, Paris).

Megaloudi, F., 2004. Funeral plant offerings from historical sites: a preliminary study, in: Smejda, L., and Turek, J. (eds) S*patial analysis of funerary areas.* University of West Bohemia, Plzen, pp. 109-114.

Megaloudi, F. 2005. Wild and Cultivated Vegetables, Herbs and Spices in Antiquity (900-400 BC). *Environmental Archaeology* 10.1: 71-80

Megaloudi, F. 2005b. Agriculture in mainland Greece at the Protogeometric period, *Eulimene* 5 (2004), 151-160

Megaloudi, F. 2005c. Burnt sacrificial offerings at Hellenistic Times: An archaobotanical case study from Messene, Peloponnese, Greece. *Vegetation History and Archaeobotany* 14: 329-340

Megaloudi, F., and Marinval, P. 2002. Données préliminaires sur l'économie végétale du site de Ftelia, Cyclades (Grèce) au Néolithique récent, in: Sampson, Ad. (ed.). *The Neolithic settlement at Ftelia, Mykonos* University of Aegean, Rhodes, pp. 191-200.

Megaloudi, F., Marinval, P., Labadie, D. and Sampson, A. 2003. L'alimentation Néolithique à Mykonos. *Archéologia,* 396 : 58-65.

Megaloudi, F. (in press) The Sarakenos Cave: Archaeobotanical analysis from the Late Neolithic Levels, in: Sampson, Ad. *The Neolithic and Bronze*

Age Occupation of Sarakenos Cave in Boeotia, Greece.

Megaloudi F. (in press) Archaiovotanika kataloipa apo ti thesi Limenaria Thasou, in : Papadopoulos, S., and Malamidou, D. (eds.) *Deka xronia anaskafikis erevnas ston proistoriko oikismo Limenarion Thassou,* 11-7-2003, Thassos, YPPO-IH EPKA, Thessaloniki.

Miller, N. F. 1991. The Near East, in: van Zeist, W., Wasylikowa, K., and Behre, K. E. (eds.) *Progress in Old World Palaeoethnobotany.* Balkema Rotterdam, pp. 133-160.

Miller, W. (ed. and trans.) Xenophon : *Cyropaedia* The Loeb Classical Library, Cambridge.

Moody, J. 1987. *The environmental and cultural Prehistory of the Khania Region of West Crete : Neolithic through Late Minoan III.* (Diss. Univ. of Minnesota).

Moody, J., Rackham, O., and Rapp, G. Jr. 1996. Environmental Archaeology of Prehistoric NW Crete. *Journal of Field Archaeology,* 23 :273-295.

Moore, P.D., Webb, J. A., and Collinson, M. E. 1991. *Pollen Analysis.* Blackwell Scientific Publications, Oxford.

Moule, C. 1982. *Plantes sarclées et diverses. Phytotechnie spéciale.* La Maison Rustique, Paris.

Murray, M.A. 2001. Archaeobotanical report, in: Peltenburg, E., Bolger, D., Ceoft, P., Goring, E., Irving, B., Lunt, D. A., Manning, S. W., Murray, M. A., McCartney, C., Ridout-Sharpe, J. S., Thomas, G., Watt, M. E., and Elliott-Xenophontos, C. (eds.) *Excavations at Kissonerga-Mosphilia,1979-1992.* http://www.arcl.ed.ac.uk/arch/publications/cyprus/kis sonerga.

Mylonas, G. 1929. *Excavations at Olynthus part I, the Neolithic settlement.* Baltimore.

Mylonas, G. 1959. *Aghios Kosmas.* Princeton University Press.

Nesbitt, M., and Samuel, D. 1996. Archaeobotany in Turkey : a review of current research. *Orient-Express,* 3 : 91-96.

Netolitsky, F. 1934. Pflanzliche Nahrungsmittel und Hölzer aus dem prähistorischen Kreta und Kephallonia. *Buletinul Facultatu de Stunte din Cernauti,* 8 : 172-178.

Pals, J. P., and Voorrips, A. 1979. Seeds, fruits and charcoal from two Prehistoric Sites in Northern Italy. *Archaeo-Physica,* 8 : 217-235.

Papa, M., and Besios, M. 1999. The Makriyalos project. Rescue excavations at the Neolithic site of Makriyalos, Pieria. Northern Greece, in: Halstead, P. (ed.) *Neolithic society in Greece.* Sheffield University Press, pp. 108-120.

Papadopoulos, S.and Malamidou, D. 2002. Oi Proimes phaseis katoikisis tou Neolithikou Oikismou ton Limenarion. To archaiologiko Ergo sti Makedonia kai Thraki *AEMTH,* 14 (2000) : 25-32.

Papadopoulos, S., Aristodemou, G., Kougioumtzoglou, D., and Megaloudi, F., 2003. I teliki Neolithiki kai i Proimi Epoxi tou Xalkou sti Thaso : I Anaskafiki

Ereuna stis theseis Aghios Ioannis Loukas kai Skala Sotiros. To archaiologiko Ergo sti Makedonia kai Thraki *AEMTH*, 15 (2001) : 55-65.

Pearsall, D. 1989. *Palaeoethnobotany. A handbook of procedures*. Academic Press, San Diego.

Pelt, J.-M. 1993. *Des légumes*. Fayard, Paris.

Pérez Jorda, G. 2000. La conservacion y la transformacion de los productos agricolas en el mundo ibérico. *Saguntum Extra* 3 (III reunion sobre economia en el Mon ibéric) 47-68.

Perlès, C. 2002. *The Early Neolithic in Greece*. Cambridge World Archaeology.

Petrucci-Bavaud, M., and Vesceli, M. 1999. Ein Essen für die Toten. Fleisch, Brot, Früchte und andere Nahrungsmittel in römischen Brandbestattungen. *Archäologisch Schweiz*, 22 (1) : 31-34.

Phitos, D., Strid, A., Snogerup, S., and Greuter, W. (eds.) 1997. *Flora Hellenica : volume 1: Gymnospermae to Caryophyllaceae*. 1 col. Frontispiece. XXXVI, 512p.

Phitos, D., Strid, A., Snogerup, S., and Tan, K (eds.) 2002. *Flora Hellenica : volume 2 : Ceratophyllaceace to Platanaceae*. 1 col. Frontispiece. XVI, 668p.

Piperno, D.R. 1988. *Phytolith analysis. An Archaeological and Geological Perspective*. Academic Press.

Polunin, O. 1969. *Flowers of Europe : a field guide*. Oxford University Press, Oxford.

Polunin, O. 1980. *Flowers of Greece and the Balkans*, Oxford University Press, Oxford.

Polunin, O., and Huxley, A. 1974. *Flowers of the Mediterranean*. Chatto and Windus, London.

Popham, M.R. (ed.) 1984. The Minoan Unexplored Mansion at Knossos. *The Annual of the British School of Archaeology at Athens supplément*, 17. Athens.

Postgate, J.N. 1987. Some vegetables in the Assyrian sources/ Notes on fruit in the cuneiform sources. *Bulletin on Sumerian agriculture*, 3 : 115-144.

Pritchett, W. K. 1953. The Attic Stelai I. *Hesperia*, 22 : 225-299.

Racham, H. (ed. and trans.). *Aristotle: Politics*. The Loeb Classical Library, Cambridge.

Racham, O. 1972. Appendix III: Charcoal and plaster impressions, in Warren, P. (ed) *Myrtos: an Early Bronze settlement in Crete*, Thames and Hudson, pp. 299-304.

Racham, O. 1983. Observations on the historical ecology of Boeotia. *British School at Athens Annual Report*, 78 : 291-351.

Rapp, G. J. R., and Mulholland, S. C. (eds.) 1992. *Phytolith systematics. Emerging Issues*. Advances in Archaeological and Museum Science, 1, Plenum Press.

Renault-Miskovsky, J. and Petzold, M., 1989. *Spores et Pollen*. La Duraulie, Paris.

Renfrew, C., Gimbutas, M., and Elster, E.E. (eds.) 1986. *Excavations at Sitagroi. A prehistoric village in Northeast Greece*, 1. Los Angeles : Institute of Archaeology.

Renfrew, J.M. 1966. A report of recent finds of carbonized cereal grains and seeds from Prehistoric Thessaly. *Thessalika*, 5 (E) : 21-36.

Renfrew, J.M. 1968. The Cereal Remains. Appendix 10, in: Evans, J. D., and Renfrew, C. (ed.). *Excavations at Saliagos near Antiparos*. Thames and Hudson, London.

Renfrew, J.M. 1969. *Palaeobotany and the Neolithic Period in Greece and Bulgaria*, (Diss. Univ. of Cambridge).

Renfrew, J.M. 1971. Recent finds of *Vitis* from Neolithic contexts in south east Europe. *Acta Museorum Agricultura*, 4 : 123-135.

Renfrew, J.M. 1972. The Plant Remains, in: Warren, P. (ed.). *Myrtos : an early Bronze Age settlement in Crete*. Thames and Hudson, Oxford, pp. 315-317.

Renfrew, J.M. 1973a. *Palaeoethnobotany : the prehistoric Food Plants of the Near East and Europe*. New York, Columbia University Press.

Renfrew, J.M. 1973b. Agriculture, in: Theocharis D. *Neolithic Greece*, National Bank of Greece, Athens, pp. 147-164.

Renfrew, J.M. 1977. Seeds from Area K, in: Coleman, J. E. (ed.). *Keos 1. Kephala*. Princeton Nex Jersey, American School of Classical Studies, pp. 127-128.

Renfrew, J.M. 1979. The first farmers in southeast Europe. *Archaeo-Physica* 8 (Festschrift Maria Hopf), 243-265

Renfrew, J.M. 1987. Fruits from Ancient Iraq : the paleoethnobotanical evidence. *Bulletin Sumerian Agriculture*, 3 : 157-161.

Renfrew, J.M. 1989. Carbonized grains and seeds, in: Gimbutas, M., Winn, S., and Shimabuku, D. (eds.). *Achileion : A Neolithic Settlement in Thessaly, Greece 6400-5600 B.C.* Los Angeles, California, pp. 307-310.

Renfrew, J.M. 1995. Palaeoethnobotanical Finds of Vitis from Greece, in: Mc Govern, P. E., Fleming, S. J., and Katz S. H. (eds) *The origins and Ancient History of Wine*, Luxembourg, Gordon and Breach publishers, pp 255-267.

Renfrew, J.M. 1997. Plant Husbandry at Prehistoric Dimitra. Appendix 14, in: Grammenos, D. *Neolithiki Makedonia*, Ipourgeio Politismou Dimosieumata tou Arxaiologikou Deltiou Ar. 56. Athens, pp. 220-225.

Renfrew, J.M. 2003. Grains, seeds and fruits from prehistoric Sitagroi, in: Elster, E. S., and Renfrew, C. (ed) *Prehistoric Sitagroi: Excavations in Northeast Greece, 1968-1970, vol.2: The Final Report*, 1-28. Los Angeles, Cotsen Institute of Archaeology

Rindos, D. 1984. *The origins of Agriculture: An Evolutionary Perspective*. Academic Press, Orlando

Rivera, D., Inocencio, C., Obon, C., Carreno, E., Reales, A., and Al Caraz, F. 2002. Archaeobotany of capers (*Capparis*) (Capparaceae). *Vegetation History and Archaeobotany*, 11 : 295-313.

Rumney, G. 1968. *Climatology and the world's Climates*. The Macmillian Company, New York.

Runnels, C., and Hansen, J. 1986. The olive in the Prehistoric Aegean : The evidence for domestication in the Early Bronze age. *Oxford Journal of Archaeology*, 5 (3) : 299-307.

Runnels, C., and van Andel, Tj. 1988. Trade and the origins of agriculture in the Eastern Mediterranean. *Journal of Mediterranean Archaeology*, 1 (1) : 83-109.

Sallares, R. 1991. *The Ecology of the Ancient Greek World*, Ithica, Cornell University Press

Sarpaki, A. 1987a. *The Palaeoethnobotany of the West House, Akrotiri, Thera : a Case Study.* (Diss. Univ. of Sheffield, UK).

Sarpaki, A. 1987b. Palaioethnobotanoligikes paratiriseis apo to Spelaio Aghios Georgios stis Kalithies Rodou, in: Sampson Ad. (ed.). *I Neolithiki Periodos sat Dodekanisa*, Ipourgeio Politismou Dimosieumata Arxaiologikou Deltiou Ar. 35. Athens, pp. 153-155.

Sarpaki, A. 1992 The Palaeoethnobotanical approach. The Mediterranean triad or is it a quartet? In: Wells B. (ed.). *Agriculture in Ancient Greece* Skrifter Utgivna av Svenska Institutet I Athen, 4, XLII, Stockholm, pp. 61-76.

Sarpaki, A. 1995. Toumba Balomenou, Chaeronia : plant remains from the Early and Middle Neolithic levels, in: Kroll, H., and Pasternak, R. (eds). *Res Archaeobotanica*. 9th Symposium IWGP, Kiel, pp. 281-300.

Sarpaki, A. 1999. Method of data retrieval; The archaeobotanical study of Tzambakas House, Rethymnon, Crete, in: Tzedakis, Y., and Martlew, H. (eds) *Minoans and Mycenaeans. Flavours of their time.* Athens, pp 40-41.

Sarpaki, A., and Jones, G. 1990. Ancient and modern cultivation of *Lathyrus clymenum* L. in the Greek Isalnds. *The annual of the British School at Athens*, 85 : 363-368.

Schiemann, E. 1953. *Vitis* in Neolithicum der Mark Brandenberg. *Der Züchter* 23: 318-326.

Schliemann, H. 1886. *Tiryns. Der prähistorische Palast der Könige von Tiryns. Ergebnisse der neuesten Ausgrabungen.* Leipzig.

Schoch, W.H., Pawlick, B., and Schweingruber, F. H. 1988. *Botanische Makrorestes.* P. Haupt, Bern.

Schweinfurth, G. 1896. *Die letzten botanischen Entdeckungen in den Gräben Ägyptens.* Engler's Jahrb. 18.

Shay, J., and Shay, T. 1978. Modern Vegetation and fossil plant remains, in: Rapp, G. Jr, and Aschenbrenner, S. E. (eds.). *Excavations at Nichoria in Southwest Greece, vol. 1, Site, environs and techniques.* University of Minnesota Press, Minneapolis, pp. 41-59.

Shay, J., Shay, T., Kapinga, M. R. M. 1998. Appendix 4. The Bronze Age plant and insect remains and modern vegetation, in: Wahlberg, G. *Excavations on the Acropolis of Midea. Results of the Greek-Swedish Excavations. Vol 1.1. The excavations on the Lower Terraces 1985-1991*, Skr Svenska Inst Athen 4° 49 1.1. Stockholm, pp 299-357

Sheehan, M. C. 1979. *The Postglacial vegetational history of the Argolid Peninsula, Greece,* (Diss.

Univ. of Indiana).

Sheehan, M. C., and Whitehead, D. R. 1981. The late Post-Glacial vegetational history of the Argolid Peninsula, Greece. *National Geographic Society Resources Report*, 13 : 693-708.

Shelmerdine, C. V. 1985. *The Perfume Industry of Mycenaean Pylos.* Göteborg.

Sherratt, S. (ed.) 2000. *The Wall Paintings of Thera. Proceedings of the First International Symposium*, 30 August-4 September 1997, 2. Athens.

Smith, RL, 1992. *Elements of Ecology*, 3rd ed. HarperCollins Publisher, New York

Stanley, P.V. 1982. KN Uc160 and Mycenaean wines. *American Journal of Archaeology* vol. 86: 577-8.

Stemler, A.B.L. 1980. Origins of plant domestication in the Sahara and the Nile Valley, in: Williams, M.A.J., and Faure, H. (dir.). *The Sahara and the Nile*, Balkema, Rotterdam, pp. 503-526.

Stol, M. 1987. The Cucurbitaceae in the cuneiform texts, in: Postgate, J. N., and Powel, M. A. (dir.). *Bulletin on Sumerian Agriculture*, 3 : 81-92.

Strid, A. (dir.) 1986. *Mountain Flora of Greece. Volume 1.* University Press, Cambridge.

Strid, A. 1996. Flora Hellenica Bibliography : A critical syrvey of floristic, taxonomic and phytogeographical literature relevant to the vascular plants of Greece, 1753-1994. *Fragmenta Floristica Geobotanica Supplementum* 4.

Strid, A., and Tan, K. 1991. *Mountain Flora of Greece. Volume 2.* University Press, Edinburgh.

Strid, A., and Tan, K. 1992. Flora Hellenica and the threatened plants of Greece. *Opera Bot.* 11 : 356-367.

Sfikas, G. 1978. *Fleurs sauvages de la Grèce.* Athènes Efstathiadis Group.

Tanaka, T. 1976. *Cyclopedia of Edible plants of the world.* Keisaku Pub. Co. Tokyo.

Televantou, Ch. 1998. O archaios oikismos tis Ipsilis stin Andro : stoicheia apo tis os tora anaskafes. *Andriaka Chronika 29 : Andros kai Chalkidiki, Praktika Simposiou Andros 23 augoustou 1997.* Kaireios Vivliothiki, Andros : 31-47.

Terral, J. F. 1997. *La domestication de l'olivier (Olea Europaea) en Méditerranée*

nord-occidentale: approche morphométrique et implications paléoclimatiques, (Diss. Univ.of Montpellier II, France).

Terral, J. F., Alonso. N., Buxo, R., Chatti, N., Fabre, L., Fiorentino, G., Marinval, P., Jorda, G. P., Pradat, B., Rovira, N., Alibert, P. 2004. Historical biogeography of olive domestication (Olea europaea L.) as revealed by geometrical morphometry applied to biological and archaeological material. *Journal of Biogeography* 31: 63-77

Toussaint-Samat, M. 1987. *Histoire naturelle et morale de la nourriture.* Bordas, Paris.

Treuil, R. 1983. *Le Néolithique et le Bronze ancien Egéens. Les problèmes stratigraphiques et chronologiques, les techniques, les hommes.* Ecole Française d'Athènes, diffusion de Boccard, Paris.

Treuil, R. (ed.) 1992. Dikili Tash. Village Préhistorique de Macédoine Orientale I, Fouilles de Jean Deshayes (1961-1975), volume 1. *Bulletin de Correspondance Hellénique, Suppl. 24.* École Française d'Athènes.

Tromaras, L. 1988. *Apicius The cooking of Romans.* University Studio Press, Thessaloniki

Tsountas, C. 1908. *Ai Proistorikai Akropoleis Diminion kai Sesklon.* Bibliotheke tis en Athinais Archaiologikis Etaireias, Athens.

Turner, J., and Greig, J.R.A. 1975. Some Holocene Pollen diagrams from Greece. *Revue of Palaeobotany and Palynolology* 20 : 171-204.

Tzedakis, Y., and Martlew H (eds) 1999. *Minoans and Mycenaeans. Flavours of their time.* National Archaeological Museum, Athens.

Valamoti, S. 1992 Apanthracomena fitika kataloipa apo tin proistoriki Thermi. Mia prokatarktiki meleti. *Makedonika,* 27 : 443-455.

Valamoti, S. 1995. Georgika proionta apo to neolithiko oikismo Giannitsa B : prokatarktiki prossegisi meso ton archaiobotanikon dedomenon. To archaiologiko ergo sti Makedonia kai Thrak*i AEMTH,* 6 (1992) : 177-184.

Valamoti, S. 1997. Archaiovotanika kataloipa apo ton oikismo tou Archondikou : anaskafiki periodos Septembriou 1993. To Archaiologiko Ergo sti Mekedonia kai Thraki *AEMTH,* 7 : 155-158.

Valamoti, S. 2001. *Archaeobotanical Investigation of Late Neolithic and Early Bronze Age agriculture and plant exploitation in northern Greece.* (Diss. Univ. of Sheffield, UK).

Valamoti, S. 2002. Food remains from Bronze age Archondiko and Mesimeriani Toumba in Northern Greece ? *Vegetation History and Archaeobotany,* 11 : 17-22.

Valamoti, S. 2004. *Plants and People in Late Neolithic and Early Bronze Age Northern Greece. An archaeobotanical investigation.* BAR International Series 1258.

van Andel, T.H., and Runnels, C. 1987. *Beyond the Acropolis : a rural Greek Past.* Stanford University Press.

van Andel, T. H., and Runnels. C. 1988. An Essay on the 'Emergence of Civilization' in the Aegean World *Antiquity* 62: 234-247.

van Andel, T.H. and Runnels, C.N. 1995. The earliest farmers in Europe: Soil preferences and demic diffusion pathways; *Antiquity* 69: 481-500.

van der Veen, M. 1984. Sampling for seeds, in: van Zeist, W., and Casparie, W.A. (dir.). *Plants and Ancient Man, Studies in Palaeoethnobotany,* Proceedings of the 6th symposium of the I.W.G.P., Groningen, 30 may – 3 june, 1983, Balkema, Rotterdam, pp. 193-199.

van der Veen, M. 1985. Carbonized seeds, sample size and one site sampling, in: Fieller, N.R.J., Gilbertson, D. D., and Ralph, N.G.A. (dir.). *Palaeoenvironmental Investigations,* British Archaeological Reports, International Series 258, Oxford, pp. 165-174.

van der Veen, M., and Fieller, N.R.J. 1982. Sampling seeds. *Journal of Archaeological Science,* 9 : 287-298.

van Zeist, W. 1972. Palaeobotanical résults of the 1970 season at Cayönü, Turkey. *Helinium* 12 (1) : 3-19.

van Zeist, W. 1978. Chared plant remains from tell Gomolava. *Rad. Vojvodanskich Mezeja* 23-24, 5-18

van Zeist, W. 1980. Aperçu de la diffusion des végétaux cultivés dans la région méditerranéenne, in: *La mise en place, l'évaluation et la caractérisation de la flore et des végétations, circum méditerranéennes,.* Coll. Fondation L. Emberger, Naturalia Monspeliensa, pp. 129-145.

van Zeist, W. 1981. Plant remains from cape Andreas-Kastros (Cyprus), in : Le Brun, A. (ed) *Un site neolithique pre-ceramique en Chypre: cap Andreas-Kastros,* (Recherches sur les grandes civilizations, memoire 5) Paris, Editions A.D.P.F.

van Zeist. W. 1983. Some aspects of early Neolithic plant husbandry in the Near East *Anatolica,* 15 : 49-67.

van Zeist, W., and Bottema, S. 1971. Plant husbandry in Early Neolithic Nea Nikomeideia, Greece. *Acta Botanica Neerlandica,* 20 : 524-538.

van Zeist, W., and Bottema, S. 1983. Palaeobotanical studies of Carthage. A comparison of Microscopic and macroscopic Plant Remains. *CEDAC, Carthage* 5 : 18-24.

van Zeist, W., and Vynchier, J. 1984. Palaeobotanical investigations of Tell ed-Dèr, in: de Meyer, L. (ed.). Tell ed-Dèr IV, *Progress reports (Second Series),* Uitgeverij P., Leuven, pp. 119-143.

van Zeist, W. and Bakker-Heeres, J.A.H. 1985. Archeaological studies in the Levant 1. Neolithic sites in the Damascus basin : Aswad, Ghoraifé, Ramad. *Palaeohistoria,* 24 : 165-256.

van Zeist, W. and de Roller, G. J. 1993. Plant remains from Maadi, a Predynastic site in Lower Egypt. *Vegetaion History and Archaeobotany,* 2 :1-14.

van Zeist, W., Cappers, R.T.J., Ouderkerken, M.G., Palfenier-Vegter, R.M., de Roller, G.J. and Vrede, F. 2000. *Cultivated and wild plants in Late and post-medieval Groningen. A study of archaeological plant remains.* Groningen.

Vaughan, S.J., and Coulson, W.D.E. 1999. *Palaeodiet in The Aegean.* Oxbow Books : American School of Classical Studies ar Athens

Vargas, A., Touloumis, K., Anagnostou, I., Valamoti, S. and Christidou, R. 1995. Anaskafes stin proistoriki Toumba tou Arkadikou Dramas (excavations at the prehistoric dwelling mound of Arkadikos, Drama). To archaeologiko ergo sti Makedonia kai Thraki *AEMTH,* 6 : 577-585.

Vencl, S. 1985. Zaludi jako potravino. K poznçni vyznamu sberu pro vyzivu v praveka (Acorns as food. Assessing the significance of food gathering for prehistoric dietary habits) *Archeologicke Rozhledy* 37: 516-65

Vermeeren, C. and Kuijper, W. 1996. Pollen from coprolites and recent droppings: useful for reconstructing vegetations and determining the season of consumption ? *Analecta Praehistorica Leidensia,* 26: 213-220.

Vickery, K. 1936. *Food in Early Greece.* Illinois Studies in the Social Sciences, University of Illinois Press, vol. 20, no 3, Urbana.

Vince, J.H. (ed. and trans.) Demosthenes : III *Against Androtion,* Loeb Classical Library.

Wace, A.J.B. and Thompson, H. (1912). *Prehistoric Thessaly.* Cambridge University Press.

Wagner, G. 1988.Comparability among recovery techniques, in: Hastorf, C. and Popper, V. (eds.). *Current Paleoethnobotany,* University Press of Chicago, Chicago, pp. 17-35.

Wahlberg, G. 1998. *Excavations on the Acropolis of Midea. Results of the Greek-Swedish Excavations. Vol 1.1. The excavations on the Lower Terraces 1985-1991,* Skr Svenska Inst Athen 4° 49 1.1. Stockholm

Wardle, K.A. 1989. Excavations at Assiros Toumba, a preliminary report. *Annual of British School at Athens,* 84 : 447-463.

Warren, P. 1972. *Myrtos : an early Bronze Age settlement in Crete.* Thames and Hudson, Oxford.

Wasylikowa K., Carciumaru M., Hajnalova E., Hartyanyi B.P., Pashkevich G.A. and Yanushevich Z.V. (1991). East-Central Europe. *In :* van Zeist W., Wasylikova K. and Behre K.H. (dir.). *Progress in Old World Palaeoethnobotany.* Balkema, Rottterdam : 207-239.

Wasylikowa K. and van der Veen M. 2004 An archaeobotanical contribution to the history of watermelon *Citrullus lanatus* (Thunb.) Matsum. & Nakai (syn. *C. vulgaris* Schrad.) *Vegetation History and Archaeobotany* 13: 213-217.

Watrous, L.V. 1987. The Role of the Near East in the Rise of the Cretan Palaces, in: Hagg, R., and Marinatos, N. (eds.) *The Function of the Minoan Palaces.* Proceedings of the 4th International Symposium at the Swedish Institute in Athens, 10-16 June, 1984. Stockholm, pp. 65-70.

Watrous, L.V. 1994. Review of Aegean prehistory III: Crete from the earliest prehistory through the protopalatial period. *American Journal of Archaeology* 98, 695-753.

Wellmann M. (ed and trans Dioscorides : *De Materia Medica,* ed. Max Berlin.

Wijmstra T.A. 1969. Palynology of the first 30 metres of a 120 m deep section in Northern Greece. *Acta Botanica. Neerlandica,* 18 : 511-527.

Wilkins, J., Harvey, D., and Dobson, M. 1996. *Food in Antiquity.* University of Exeter Press.

Willerding, U. 1973. Bronzezeitliche Pflanzenreste aus Iria und Synoro," *Tiryns VI* : 221-240.

Wilson D.G. 1984. The carbonization of weeds seeds and their representation in macro-fossil assemblages. In van Zeist W. and Casparie W.A. (dir.). *Plants and Ancient Man : Studies in palaeoethnobotany.* Balkema, Rotterdam: 201-206

Xhuvel L. and Schultze-Motel J. 1995. Neolithic cultivated plants from Albania. *Vegetation History and Archaeobotany,* 4 : 245-248.

Zervos C. 1957. *L'art des Cyclades.* Les Cahiers d'Art, Paris.

Zohary D. and Spiegel-Roy P. 1975. Beginnings of fruit growing in the Old World. *Science,* 187 : 319-327.

Zohary D. and Hopf M. 2000. *Domestication of Plants in the Old World.* Clareton Press, Oxford.

www.ingramcontent.com/pod-product-compliance
Lightning Source LLC
Chambersburg PA
CBHW061009030426
42334CB00033B/3418